# New
# Playwriting
# Strategies

# New Playwriting Strategies

*A Language-Based Approach to Playwriting*

PAUL C. CASTAGNO

*A Theatre Arts Book*

**ROUTLEDGE**

NEW YORK    LONDON

A THEATRE ARTS BOOK

Published in 2001 by
Routledge
29 West 35th Street
New York, NY 10001

Published in Great Britain by
Routledge
11 New Fetter Lane
London EC4P 4EE

Routledge is an imprint of the Taylor & Francis Group.

Excerpts of *American Notes*, *Dark Ride*, *Limbo Tales*, *My Uncle Sam*, and *Poor Folk's
Pleasure* from *Dark Ride and Other Plays* by Len Jenkin (Los Angeles: Sun & Moon
Press, 1993). Copyright ©Len Jenkin. Reprinted by permission of the publisher.

Printed on acid-free, 250–year life paper.
Manufactured in the United States of America.

10   9   8   7   6   5   4   3   2   1

Library of Congress Cataloging-in-Publication Data

Castagno, Paul C., 1950–
        New playwriting strategies : a language-based approach to playwriting / Paul
C. Castagno.
        p. cm.
        Includes bibliographical references and index.
        ISBN 0–87830–135–6 – ISBN 0–87830–136–4 (pbk.)
        1. Playwriting. I. Title.

PN1661.C364      2001
808.2—dc21           2001019246

*For my wife, Molly, and my sons, Andrew, Peter, and Christopher*

# Contents

Preface      ix

1   New Playwriting Strategies: Overview and Terms      1

**PART I   STRATEGIES OF LANGUAGE AND CHARACTER**      15

2   On Multivocality and Speech Genres      17

3   Polyvocality and the Hybrid Play      35

4   The Theatricality of Character      52

5   Len Jenkin's Dramaturgy of Character:
From Stage Figures to Archetypes      72

6   Eric Overmyer: Some Principles of
Character Transformation      80

7   Mac Wellman: Language-Based Character      87

**PART II   STRATEGIES OF STRUCTURE AND FORM**      93

8   The Dialogic Beat      95

9   Scenes, Acts, and Revisions      120

10   Foundations of Contemporary Monologue      137

11   Dialogic Monologue: Structure and Antistructure      148

Works Consulted      175

Index      179

# Preface

My introduction to the new playwrights came at the January 1990 Key West Literary Seminar: New Directions in American Theater. Inaugurating the final decade of the last century, the conference featured major figures and approaches in American playwriting. Polarizing the contemporary mainstream was the ebullient Wendy Wasserstein, countered by the reserved Lanford Wilson. Straddling the middle ground between the mainstream and cutting edge were the stylistic luminaries: John Guare, Christopher Durang, and Maria Irene Fornes. The new playwrights featured Mac Wellman, along with notables Eric Overmyer, Len Jenkin, and Connie Congdon. Prior to the conference I had read several plays from (and feature articles about) this latter group, who seemed onto something new and exciting. This conference offered me the perfect opportunity to hear these playwrights speak and interact within the broader context of contemporary American playwriting.

At stake was the future direction of American playwriting—or so the organizers of the conference would have had us believe. Would London-based musicals and mainstream comedies continue to prevail on the commercial Broadway stage? Was the traditional play format endangered by the proliferation and success of director-based "auteur" projects? Were minorities' and women's voices being heard? Would language playwriting finally become a force in the regional theaters? And what did these playwrights think about being "developed to death"? Establishing the historical context marked by the fall of communism, Joseph Melillo's keynote address trumpeted the moment as a call to American playwrights to embrace a more globalized view in making their plays. Curiously, over ten years later, we find many of the same issues and themes the stuff of conference panels and discussions.

Each New Directions panel was intended to focus the participants around a given topic. However, it was the interpersonal dynamic between playwrights that became far more striking as self-serving posturing countered blasé complacency and ideological convictions vied with aesthetic principles. Force of personality seemed to drive the discussions more than the "headier" topics suggested by the planners. The interactions were visceral and, at times, contentious. Defining what constitutes a play or the present state of American playwriting had become deeply personalized.

Amid the occasionally rancorous exchanges, I became struck by an energized, articulate group of playwrights who had been collectively categorized in the 1980s as the "language playwrights" (see chapter 1). Across the board, they seemed committed to forwarding a new aesthetic rather than promoting a thematic agenda—quite unusual in the "politically correct" climate circa 1990. While pragmatically cynical of their chances to move beyond the margins of mainstream theater, they were passionately determined to have their voices heard. If they lacked the crossover celebrity of the engagingly flippant Durang, or the grandiloquent Guare, they commanded respect as accomplished, award-winning playwrights. Led by the outspoken Wellman, they were consciously aware of their moment in the development of American playwriting. As they took the aesthetic "high ground" in panel after panel, I began to sense the seismic shift that was taking place in American playwriting.

Widely known within New York's playwriting circles, the language playwrights have neither been read nor produced much in academe. (The notable exception, of course, is Overmyer's *On The Verge*, widely produced in the late 1980s and early 1990s.) As a result, scant research has been done that brings their playwriting innovations to light. Yet it was obvious in recruiting graduate candidates or in planning workshops that this material interested the best students. During the seminar's socializing in a hall dedicated to the eponymous Key West resident, Tennessee Williams, I discussed with Wellman, Jenkin, and Overmyer the potential of developing some new work at the University of Alabama. The playwrights seemed eager to visit Tuscaloosa, perhaps as much for its historical and cultural resonance as to explore their new work with graduate students.

After the seminar, I set out to explore their plays in detail, hoping to establish some shared tendencies in structure and characterization. Meanwhile, the leading language playwrights visited the University of Alabama for workshops, readings, and master classes—providing graduate students contact with the most creative playwrights in America. The playwrights' residences at the University of Alabama solidified and clarified many of my theoretical findings—serving, in a sense, as a living archive. The results have led to numerous conference panels, grants, and several publications in notable journals; inspired two of my own plays; and ultimately culminated in this book.

If the Key West New Directions in American Theater seminar succeeded in shifting and galvanizing my interests toward language playwriting, did it achieve its larger mission of defining the course playwriting would take to the beginning of a new millennium and beyond? Recent publications such as Bonnie Marranca's *Ecologies of Theater*, have certified the increasing intersection of global methodologies in the theater. Certainly, the playwriting output of the past eleven years suggests that new aesthetic directions have become more commonplace. The influence of the language playwrights has been profound on numerous theater artists and in developing new audiences for the theater. For example, in 1999, Mac Wellman was honored by a yearlong festival across New York City dedicated to producing all his plays. Yet until now there has been no attempt to synthesize the innovations of the new playwrights into a pragmatic approach for playwrights.

The goal of *New Playwriting Strategies: A Language-Based Approach to Playwriting* is to clarify and codify these practices into a coherent, working aesthetic for playwrights. Herein I demonstrate in significant detail a challenge to the prevailing orthodoxy in playwriting. In fact, I heartily feel that we have only tapped the surface as to what great playwriting can be. In this light, I hope you are inspired by *New Playwriting Strategies* and find it useful in your development as a playwright.

ACKNOWLEDGMENTS

I would like to thank the Research Grants Committee at the University of Alabama for providing the seed money and follow-up support beginning with my sabbatical in 1996, when I began formulating the book. I also offer sincere appreciation to Theatre Department Chair, Ed Williams, and former Dean Yarbrough of the College of Arts and Sciences. I want to thank professional colleagues Mark Bly, David Crespy, Chris Jones, Jeffrey Jones, Matthew Maguire, Ruth Margraff, Jerry Rojo, Michael Wright, and members of the ATHE and LMDA for their contributions and encouragement of this project.

Moreover, I offer my appreciation to the talented and inspiring new playwrights who have visited UA during my tenure as director of the New Playwrights' Program, including Len Jenkin, Mac Wellman, Eric Overmyer, Neena Beber, Heather McCutcheon, Matthew Maguire, Ruth Margraff, and Jeffrey Jones. I also extend my heartfelt appreciation to the M.F.A. playwriting students at UA, who have served diligently over the years as a trial group for the exercises included in the book. By the publication date, I will have assumed the Director of Theater position at Ohio University. I wish to thank the faculty of the School of Theater, and Dean Raymond Tymas-Jones for their confidence in me and this work. I would like to thank my brother Tony for his encouraging words at the right times. Finally, I thank my beloved sons, Andrew, Peter, and Christopher, who fill my life with joy and wonder. Most of all, I am forever grateful for the help from my cherished wife, Molly, for her editorial wisdom and for inspiring me during the process with grace, humor, and love.

# 1

# New Playwriting Strategies: Overview and Terms

*New Playwriting Strategies* explores playwriting from an innovative, forward-looking perspective. It presents a fundamentally different theoretical and practical approach to character, language, and dramatic form. The book challenges the underlying premises and assumptions that currently determine what constitutes a play. But the real goal is to provide you with the necessary tools to challenge *your* status quo as a playwright, so that you can write plays with an expanding range of new strategies and techniques.

As you are probably well aware, orthodoxy rules in the teaching and development of plays and playwrights. Many playwriting texts, including those written within the past ten years, rehash the core tenets of Aristotle's *Poetics* (ca. 325 B.C.) with long-standing "common-sense" dictums like conflict, the central protagonist, and character-specific dialogue. A purview of this literature leads to the undeniable conclusion that playwriting texts are resistant to change and innovation. There is no doubt that it is time to change the paradigm. In fact, the best playwrights in the past ten years already have.

In the face of "common-sense" traditional approaches to playwriting, we find increasing experimentation in the writing of plays not just at the margins, but in the mainstream. Many of the Pulitzer Prize–winning plays of the 1990s, including Margaret Edson's *Wit*, Paula Vogel's *How I Learned to Drive*, Edward Albee's *Three Tall Women*, and Craig Lucas's *Prelude to a Kiss* used innovative forms and techniques to tell their stories. Now more than ever there is a widening gulf between the writing of contemporary plays and what is prescribed as correct playwriting. Certainly, the best playwriting students want to learn and incorporate the latest, most challenging techniques. Those collaborators involved with new play development, including producers, directors, literary managers, dramaturgs, and actors desire a point of entry into the new playwriting—the language of orthodoxy simply does not apply. It is time to talk about how plays are made and shaped in a different way.

*New Playwriting Strategies* stems from the basic premise that playwriting is language based. As such, language remains the dominant force in the shaping of characters, action, and theme. The playwright orchestrates the voices in the text, entering into a kind of dialogue with characters and language.

The playwright is open to language in its widest sense, whether coded in a specific genre, found in another text, or produced by the linguistic impulses that unleash slang, unusual syntax, foreignisms, discourses, and so on. While "writing through" the other (often multiple) voices, the playwright remains the creative or orchestrating force behind the text. The term *dialogism* describes how the interactive relation between voices in the playtext shapes the play as an act of discovery.

A new approach to playwriting requires a distinctive set of terms and working tools, most of which are defined in this chapter. The following chapters establish a theoretical foundation that explores a new way of thinking about playwriting. Comparative charts demonstrate basic distinctions from traditional or orthodox approaches. Along the way, I provide numerous practical examples and exercises for the playwright. The point of view is from the perspective of the playwright—I am primarily interested in what useful strategy or technique can be gleaned from a given play. Therefore, the book does not probe thematic questions or underlying ideologies of the plays or playwrights. The result is a pragmatic study of new playwriting that challenges you to expand your imagination and technique.

## FROM THEORY TO PRACTICE

While playwrights generally shy away from theory, it is necessary in this case to establish some fundamental principles about the new playwriting. In *Literary Theory: A Very Short Introduction,* Jonathan Culler describes theory as a "critique of common sense, of concepts taken as natural" (1997, 15). *New Playwriting Strategies* questions many assumptions or "givens" about playwriting while offering alternative premises. Further, Culler states that theory is analytical and speculative. This book analyzes a number of plays by a group of playwrights, demonstrating how these works can spark the playwright's imagination and sense of invention. Herein we speculate on what a play might or can be. Finally, Culler tells us, theory is drawn from other disciplines, where removed from its original context it offers special insights and applications. Along these lines, I utilize the concept of dialogism as the inspiration and organizing principle for this book.

The Russian literary critic Mikhail Bakhtin first coined the term *dialogism.* He used it as a means to reevaluate certain nineteenth-century Russian novels that could not be categorized into traditional genres. These hybrid novels juxtaposed sophisticated literary techniques with storytelling elements drawn from folk culture, while other texts featured an array of linguistic styles, dialects, neologisms, and slang. Bakhtin used the term *polyvocal* to describe the divergent source materials that made up the text. (The term *multivocality* is used when multiple speech styles are bulked within a single character.)

Bakhtin assessed that the polyvocal text was an interactive system in which each element was *in dialogue* or *dialogized* with the other elements within the novel. Each part reacted with or against other parts in the text to create a dynamic sense of meaning and interest, which could not be distilled into a simple statement or unified arc. Plural, often contradictory, voices gave the dialogic text freer reign than traditional monologic formats. Rather than one narrator or point-of-view, multiple narrators vied with each other to tell the story. While the hybrid text resisted capture and classification, dialogism had offered a means of describing its inner workings and mechanisms.

By appropriating a definition of the dialogic novel, and substituting the word *play* for *novel*, we can establish a working definition of the dialogic play. The dialogic play is "fundamentally polyvocal (multi-voiced) or dialogic rather than monologic (single-voiced). The essence of the [play] is its staging of different voices or discourses and, thus, of the clash of social perspectives and points of view" (Culler, 1997, 89; bracketed text added). Formally, dialogism represents the play's capacity to interact within itself, as if the various components were in dialogue with each other.

## LANGUAGE PLAYWRITING

To be credible, a new theory and method need models that "work," or help to demonstrate certain points. To a great extent, the models used in the book are from the plays of an inspiring group of writers known as the "language playwrights" or "new playwrights." The language playwrights have emerged over the past twenty years to stake out a significant territory in American theater. Since the 1970s they have been produced (and published) in and out of New York, and have been a major influence on the practice and pedagogy of playwriting. While their influence has been extraordinary within the field, they have been largely ignored for production in mainstream theater, and for the most part have escaped further critical inquiry.

Some of the award-winning leading figures are Mac Wellman, Len Jenkin, Constance Congdon, Eric Overmyer, Suzan-Lori Parks, Jeffrey Jones, Paula Vogel, and Matthew Maguire. Other significant playwrights, like Richard Nelson, Tony Kushner, and Craig Lucas, explored this territory earlier in their careers but have since crossed over into other areas with greater commercial success. Furthermore, a number of these playwrights head (or teach in) top programs in playwriting at the university level: Jenkin at New York University; Wellman and Vogel at Brown University; Overmyer, Jones, and Parks at Yale University; and Maguire at Fordham University at Lincoln Center. This double-edged sword of teaching young writers and creative playwriting is already impacting future generations of playwrights.

## THE DIALOGIC CLASH

While these playwrights each have a distinctive style, their methods of writing plays are fundamentally dialogic. Two examples of the dialogic approach demonstrate how this process works: Len Jenkin's *Kitty Hawk* represented a breakthrough in terms of defining what constitutes a play, and opened the door for a surge in new playwriting, while Eric Overmyer's *On the Verge* was the most widely produced of the new playwrights' works.

OBIE Award–winning playwright Len Jenkin first gained notice from Joseph Papp (of New York's Public Theater) and others through plays that were essentially dialogic in approach. One of his earliest works, *Kitty Hawk*, began simply by introducing the Wright brothers, inventors of the first airplane. As Jenkin proceeded to work on the play, he decided as an experiment to add various brother acts throughout American history, including such notables as the Smith brothers (cough drops) and James brothers (outlaws). The resultant play was unique in its formulation: dialogic in the juxtaposition and interaction between brother acts, each engaging different historical periods and levels of discourse in American culture.

Jenkin's background in comparative literature, in particular his interest in Russian literature, may explain his ease in handling multiple narrators and storytellers within the play. Jenkin's creative process is intuitive; he dialogizes the script by asking, What if this other brother act enters? What interactive dynamic can be energized? The relativity and number of acts is discovered in the making of the script; plot occurs as a kind of frisson or friction between character groups. There was no book that guided him to make plays this way; by ignoring the language of normative "how-to" playwrights, Jenkin developed his uniquely dialogic playwriting style. When I interviewed Jenkin several years ago, he stated that in revising his plays he still works dialogically: moving segments or blocks of text, attempting to discover an arrangement that works best for the play.

To date, the most widely produced work of the new playwrights has been Eric Overmyer's *On the Verge: The Geography of Learning*. Across America, university and regional theaters produced this "palpable hit" in the late 1980s and early 1990s. The play's complex vision was disguised by accessible, attractive features: three major roles for women, and a strong sense of language and period. The acting and design style required of the three women "trekkers" suggested the Victorian romantic adventure genre. Easily identified, this genre provided familiar moorings to a contemporary audience that was witnessing a revival in interest of nineteenth-century subject matter, particularly in the film industry (for example, films based on the Brontë novels). Even conservative audience members felt comfortable with the independence of these late-nineteenth-century women explorers, their slightly feminist wrinkle, and the play's literary challenges and references. Overmyer, presumably, was repackaging an old form popular at the turn of the century, the time of expansionism and colonialism, when daring independent women smoked cigarettes and struck out on their own.

Suddenly, the characters were thrown into a kind of time warp. Overmyer had subverted the familiar context, and with it the audience's comfort zone. By intermission, the expectations of the audience were totally dismantled. Overmyer's terra incognita undermined expectations, breaking the conventions established at the beginning of the play. Overmyer had reinvented the "rules of the game," as this play was no longer about familiar genres. Audiences participated in the characters' journey or were frustrated by the move. Some spectators felt misled, even violated, by the shifting expectations.

Overmyer's play established a model of the *dialogic clash*, which pitted its characters' historically based Victorian phraseology against a rapidly changing, twentieth-century landscape, thus causing it to lose coherence as the characters were hurled forward through a rapidly changing, twentieth-century culture. This shift created a continuing *recontexting* of language through which new objects and experiences were mediated. A simple eggbeater, for example, became imbued with talismanic powers. This clash became the stuff of the play, superseding character development or traditional conflict. Content was factored on a moment-to-moment basis, as language and meaning altered continually through the shifting historical context. By the play's end, the audience had experienced a new form that privileged the journey of language, as much, or more so, than the voyage of the characters.

As playwrights, we can glean something more profound: the play itself is a system of language. Traditionally, the playwright strives for coherence at all costs. Coherence is the by-product of recognizable conventions insofar as it comes about from rules that set up probabilities and expectations. In *On the Verge*, Overmyer establishes coherence, and then bursts the bubble. Dialogue does more than bring the characters into interaction; it becomes the free radical that "osmoses the future." Characters blurt newly discovered utterances, surprising themselves and the audience with each new value and meaning. It is "through language" (*dia* meaning "through," *logos* meaning "language"), that we experience Overmyer's play.

## VIRTUOSITY AND THE NEW PLAYWRITING

A distinction can be made between the new playwriting and more traditional methods: the striving for virtuosity and stunning effects versus the notion of the script as a vehicle for actors and production. Realism favors the more or less unseen hand of the artist/playwright since the goal is to simulate or represent reality. Unfettered by these concerns the new playwright is able to create an antiworld of his own, and thus allotted a great deal more flexibility. Theater seems to downplay the virtuosic today, although the heritage of greatness and the marvelous is part of our legacy as theater artists. The language playwrights are exploring the power of stage language, reigniting the appeal of virtuosic writing for the theater.

## WHY FOCUS ON NEW PLAYWRITING?

Because new playwriting celebrates the playwright as a virtuoso of language, it represents the optimum model for a playwriting study. Because of its interest in space and time functions, new playwriting offers marvelous solutions to creating mise-en-scène or for overcoming aggravating problems such as frequent blackouts and ponderous scene shifts. New playwriting promotes the aesthetic nature of play construction over political or thematic content. To this extent, new writing is devoid of an overt political agenda or particular cause. It is about the exploration of writing strategies and formal devices, so there is a great deal to study and learn. While many of the plays are thematically rich, they speak "on their own terms," rarely serving as mouthpieces for the political views of the playwrights. As a playwright you can gain specific insights into your craft without feeling cornered into an ideological camp. It is up to you to supply the particular content and thematic focus. Along the way we will examine how various performance and theater artists are utilizing similar techniques in developing performances.

Unlike some other contemporary theatrical forms, new playwriting has not totally abandoned narrative. Many of these plays maintain story lines or plots, albeit in nontraditional formulations. To this extent, the plays and methods are more accessible than abstract, suggesting to the playwright new tools and methods of storytelling.

## LANGUAGE AS STRUCTURE

New playwrights do not attempt to mirror or represent the visible world; rather, they create a world parallel to it, a world with its own ontology and conventions. This inimitable world enters into a dialogic relation with the "real" world. New playwriting, as does dialogism, "exploits the nature of language as a modeling system for the nature of existence" (Holquist 1990, 33). In this sense, language not only serves to shape the play's universe and fabricate character, but also provides the primary building blocks of the play itself. In the polyvocal play, structure is a product of the relational pattern between building blocks while style is determined by the nature of sequence and transition. The process of determining the best pattern is a major component of revision.

## WIDER APPLICATIONS

Many of the terms that follow can be applied to a variety of theatrical phenomena beyond language playwriting. Performance art is often based on a system of juxtaposition and layering of polyvocal elements. The current trend toward "hybrid" performances suggests many instances of dialogic formulation. For example, Cirque du Soleil juxtaposes a variety of cultural and theatrical forms to redefine our notion of what a circus can be. In the 1940s and 1950s the playwright Bertolt Brecht experimented with hybrid forms in a manner that was essentially dialogic. The energy and conflict in Anna Deavere Smith's *Fires in the Mirror* derived from a clash of discourses and cultures. The applications of dialogism are wider than the niche "new playwriting" would suggest. Director-auteur constructions such as Robert Wilson's visual and aural landscapes or Elizabeth LeComte's work with the Wooster Group are formulated "hybrids," which in many instances operate dialogically.

## DEFINING TERMS

Familiarize yourself now with the terms that are used throughout this book. To progress more quickly, you will benefit by setting aside several afternoons or evenings to acquaint yourself with the plays referred to in each chapter. You're more apt to "get at it" and feel confident because you will have established a frame of reference. Most of the selected plays are published and readily accessible through any university library, or may be purchased through the publishers, at the Drama Book Shop in New York, or over the Internet. A final word on the plays: read with the eyes of a craftsperson—give a close reading! Pay particular attention to the use of language, how sequences and transitions are made, narrative and dramatic devices, and the "raw materials" or sources used by the playwright.

If you like, you can proceed directly to the appropriate section in the book for a more detailed explanation and for examples and exercises. Cross-references to other terms in this list are indicated by SMALL CAPITALS.

**Absent "other."** An offstage character addressed in monologue through indication, symbol, or by substitution. See chapter 10.

**Back channels.** In the TURNS-oriented approach, *back channel* refers to a section of dialogue that is recapitulated later in a sequence, after it has been dropped as a topic in the dialogue. The successful use of back channels allows the playwright to thread a narrative while maintaining a TURNS approach.

**Beat.** The smallest identifiable unit of action, language, or thought that the playwright works with. Can be isolated from other units and is the building block of the script. See chapter 8.

**Beat segment.** Multiple BEATS are grouped together around a given action or topic. A beat segment can vary in length from several beats to a dozen or more. A significant structural component in the development and, later, revision of the playscript. See chapter 8.

**Captioning.** A narrative or rhetorical device in which a speaker announces a shift in scene or locale, or provides brief commentary to a stage event. Captioning is a variation of FRAMING. See chapter 11.

**Carnivalesque** has to do with strange combinations, the overturning of expected norms, and the grotesque. Usually featured are abrupt shifts from high to low diction, whether slang, specific speech regionalisms, colloquialisms or profanities. Carnivalesque characters conflate bestial and human traits or exhibit other oddities:

1. Santouche in Mac Wellman's *Harm's Way* alternates elevated language with vulgar speech and profanity. Speech is carnivalesque

rather than character specific. It masks and unmasks, is impulsive and full of surprises.

2. Dennis Wu in Eric Overmyer's *In Perpetuity throughout the Universe* moves between Chinese and American English, often to create articulatory effects, or commentary. Foreignisms take on a poeticizing aspect that features the phonic over semantic.

3. The carnivalesque Crab Boy in *Poor Folk's Pleasure* is part crab indicating a conflation between human and bestial realms.

For more on the carnivalesque see chapter 2.

**Character clash.** The juxtaposition of characters from opposing historical eras, genres, languages to create polyvocality and difference in the play. See chapter 3. An early example is Adrienne Kennedy's *The Owl Answers*, which juxtaposes characters from various historical eras; another is Jenkin's *Kitty Hawk*, as discussed above.

**Character specific.** In traditional play development, *character specific* refers to the principle that each character should speak a consistent way or within a certain range, dependent on education, cultural background, occupation, and the like. See chapter 2.

**Chops.** The confidence and facility of technique. The playwright's "sound." On a level of force and confidence beyond what is being said, chops give stamina to the play. See chapter 9.

**Commedia dell'arte.** A late Renaissance theatrical form that emerged in Italy and was based on specific, predetermined character types denoted by costume, mask, movement patterns, dialects, and behaviors. The harlequin, for example, always wore a patchwork or diamond-shaped costume and a black mask, and was governed by opposite behavioral traits: cunning/stupid; lazy/agile and quick; thief/confidant. See chapter 4.

**Contexting** defines how a term or word can shift meaning in a play's text depending upon its function in a specific context. In DIALOGISM, a word is never isolated nor a meaning fixed; instead, words are "in dialogue" with other words in constantly changing circumstances. Contexting is derived from Bakhtin's technical term *heteroglossia*. See chapter 3. As examples:

1. Wellman's Girl Hun in *Whirligig* establishes new meanings for 1960s lingo by conflating it with contemporary 1980s vernacular.

2. The alien characters in Constance Congdon's *Tales of the Lost Formicans* are plummeted into a world in which the relation between word and function provides the basis for the humor. The audience delights in the imaginative means given to everyday objects, now imbued with talismanic powers.

**Contour.** Each BEAT SEGMENT suggests a certain definable shape, or contour: jagged, sinuous, flat, rounded, straight-ahead, angular, S-shaped, or elliptical, for example. A stylistic consideration, since it provides the "signature" of the playwright. See chapter 8.

**Deictic language** is language that provides orientation: adverbs such as *here*, *there*, and *now* indicate immediate spatial or temporal conditions; pronouns, particularly second person (*you*, *yours*, etc.), create presence "in the moment." Deictic language connects characters to each other or to a given environment.

**Dematrixing.** The device of breaking or fracturing the mold of a specific character through a variety of means. Often, the results will FOREGROUND the actor over the character. See chapter 11.

**Dialogism.** The play is "fundamentally polyphonic or dialogic rather than monologic (single voiced). The essence of the play is its staging of different voices or discourses and, thus, of the clash of social perspectives and points of view" (Culler 1997, 89). *Internal dialogism* refers to the play's capacity to interact within itself, as if the various components were in dialogue with each other.

**Dialogic clash** occurs when language levels, speech genres, or discourses collide in the play's script. See chapter 3.

**Difference.** Opposed to unity, difference seeks to establish arbitrary or intentional breaks in convention or expectation, utilizing techniques of juxtaposition or conflation. For example, an eighteenth-century figure enters into a play set in the present. Another current practice is to set an apparent period for a play, then violate it with present-day references or commentary. See chapters 3 and 4.

**Disponbilité.** A concept term coined by the French surrealists that suggests an openness or spontaneity in the act of creation.

**The dominant.** A literary device that provides the structural underpinning of the play. See chapter 11.

**Equivocal character.** The capacity to switch or transform from one character into another and back again. See chapter 6.

**Euclidean character.** Wellman's derogatory term describes the traditional approach to characterization, whereby every "character trait must reveal an inner truth about the character, and each trait must be perfectly consonant with every other trait." See chapter 4.

**Foregrounding.** Giving special emphasis to make a word, device, or character stand out from surrounding factors or circumstances. Foregrounding is achieved through interruption, repetition, intonation, or reversal of expectation.

**Formalism.** The study of language and language devices as primarily aesthetic concerns. Language is considered as it functions autonomously from meaning or content. The Russian formalists, who emerged in the early part of the twentieth century, influenced developments in futurism and semiotics.

**Found texts.** Existing works that can be used or appropriated as source materials for new works. See chapter 3.

**Framing.** A metadramatic technique utilized to change a spatial or temporal setting. In practice, framing is related to a narrator who "sets the stage" for a theatrical or dramatic event. Shifts levels of "reality" in a play and draws attention to the structure. Other elements such as sound, setting, or lighting can serve as frames.

**Free radical.** In a TURNS-ORIENTED approach, the free play or words or phrases affects rapid shifts in dialogue and monologue. When language is the free radical the play "becomes a discovery," as Overmyer posits. The free radical SPINS a line of dialogue or monologue in a different or divergent direction. See chapter 8.

**French scene.** A structural unit defined by a character's entrance or exit. See chapter 9.

**Grafting.** Recycling FOUND TEXTS into new work. Lifting "strips of dialogue" from their original sources and utilizing these strips as character dialogue. See chapter 3.

**Hybridization** is the mixing or clashing of different genres, cultural or historical period styles, and techniques. For example, the farcical mixes with the serious, the high-toned with the vulgar, the sophisticated literary with traditional folk tales; Eastern performance traditions exist side by side with Western approaches.

1. Overmyer's *In Perpetuity throughout the Universe* juxtaposes Eastern mysticism and characters against the marginalia and lingo on the New York publishing scene.
2. Jenkin's *Poor Folk's Pleasure*: in this ensemble play a mélange of characters performs various roles. The play mixes futurist performance, children's songs, a game show, carnival sideshow, and scripted and scenarioed sketches with a linguistic range from gibberish to Finnish.
3. In *Dark Ride,* Jenkin conflates the journey form with a carnival sideshow that displays the body of John Wilkes Booth. The effect recalls the traveling snake-oil shows of the nineteenth century.

For more on hybridization see chapter 3.

**Interruption.** Used to break continuity, impede the easy access of form and content. A character changes into another character, interrupting the previous character's "through line." Interruption causes the audience to refocus attention, to work at "getting it," in a sense. Related to the formalist device of impeded form. See chapter 6.

**Journey play.** A common structural format in new playwriting, the journey play involves the passage of space and time and usually includes a traveler figure that moves the action about. Often based on a quest or search. See chapters 3 and 11.

**Markers.** Signals for the audience that suggest various phenomena: a change in direction or character; anticipation of forthcoming events; a key name or identifying characteristic. Markers are important structural components of a dramatic work. See chapter 8.

**Metadrama.** A self-referential literary element or device that exposes the machinery of the play. Some examples include a play within a play, an interpolated story, or a prologue delivered by an emcee. Story forms like fables and parables call attention to form. Homage, through references to past plays, literary works, or playwrights, offers another example of a metadramatic device as does intertextuality—a play's relation to past or similar plays, or specific dramatic conventions.

**Metatheater** acknowledges the existence of the audience—through direct address, asides, song, eavesdropping, and so forth. Metatheater exposes the artifice of the representational world. It foils the so-called willing suspension of disbelief. Any element that calls attention to the theatrical event may be considered metatheatrical. The traditional metatheatrical devices are augmented in the new playwriting to include sound techniques such as voice-overs, miked narrators, and other effects. The performer who "drops the mask" and acknowledges self as actor during performance qualifies as metatheatrical.

**Monologism.** Monologic approaches tend to be more planned, or static; the play "knows where it's going." Thus, traditional approaches to writing dialogue are usually more monologic than dialogic. See chapters 10 and 11.

**Monologic/dialogic continuum.** Table 1.1 demonstrates the difference between monologic and dialogic playwriting and how new playwriting differs in varying degrees from conventional approaches. While set in opposition these terms operate in a continuum of more or less; some or all elements on the list may apply in a given context.

**TABLE 1.1  Monologic versus Dialogic Plays**

| MONOLOGIC | DIALOGIC |
| --- | --- |
| unity | difference |
| linearity | juxtaposition |
| consistent genre | hybrid (multiple sources, genres) |
| tracking | turns |
| integral character | split or bifurcated characters |
| created materials | found, borrowed materials |
| drama | metadrama |
| language reflects culture | language is a counterpoint to culture |

**Multivocal character.** The multivocal figure combines multiple speech strategies in a single character. This character can change level or approach to language "on a dime." See chapter 2.

**Negative space.** The space between speeches or dialogue; includes the use of ellipses, pauses, silences, and other breaks of dialogue or monologue to create tension and interest. See chapter 8.

**Nouning.** Wellman's technique involving the linear stacking of nouns or phrases, which are read sequentially, usually in a monologue format.

Wellman describes the cumulative effect as "radioactive," insofar as word collisions create a kind of fission. See chapter 11.

**Ostranenie.** A term from Russian formalism, a "making strange," the dislocation in agreement, function, or context, such as that between word and object. Related to Brecht's concept of alienation. As examples:

1. In Overmyer's *On the Verge*, eggbeaters found by the characters, who are unaware of their traditional function, are transformed into pistols.

2. In Congdon's *Tales of the Lost Formicans*, a hole in the backrest of a chair is seen by aliens as "the ever present eye of God." (I:1)

**Point.** The culminating moment of emphasis or action in the scene. Should reveal something that is of crucial significance in the script. See chapter 9.

**Polyvocality.** Multiple language strategies and sources coexist in the play. Characters and narratives within the script may contain diverse interests or objectives, expressed in different speech forms. Polyvocality resists the notion of a single or dominant point-of-view in a narrative, thereby supplanting the single or privileged authorial voice. See chapter 3. As examples:

1. Multiple narrators in Jenkin's *My Uncle Sam* foil any sense of linear narrative or central character.

2. The shifting narrators in Jenkin's *Dark Ride* undercut any sense of TRACKING the narrative.

**Riffing.** Repetitions, embellishments, or variations derived from a word or phrase of dialogue. See chapter 8.

**Role-Playing.** The character takes on a specific performative function, either by assuming a different character or front specific to a profession. Fronts are typical behaviors associated with a given profession to manage an impression. See chapter 2.

**Scenario** is a BEAT-BY-BEAT narrative description of what happens in the play. It represents a sketch outline of the play.

**Speech acts.** Words or phrases that anticipate immediate or deferred action. Speech acts can take a number of forms; some examples include threats, promises, vows, or commands. See chapter 8.

**Spinning.** In a turns-oriented approach, dialogue feeds off itself, developing an oblique momentum that quickens the scene; this vertiginous effect is called *spinning*. See chapter 11.

**Stage figures.** Unlike a standard character, a stage figure is given identifiable form by the playwright and actors through gesture, movement, posture, and costume; these forms are recognized and given specific traits and characteristics by the audience. Once formulated, the image of the character speaks for itself. See chapter 4.

**Story forms, genres.** The formalist device of reinventing old forms such as parables, fables, or detective novels can create a dialogic and metatheatrical tension between content and form. New subject matter is "framed" through recognizable or antique story forms. The adherence to the story form is somehow made strange, oblique, or parodic. See chapter 3. As examples:

1. Several critics considered Wellman's *Harm's Way* to be a perverse parable based on the Jim Jones massacre at Guyana.
2. Len Jenkin's *Kid Twist* represents a bowdlerized version of the gangster legend.
3. Overmyer's *Dark Rapture* echoes the style of the hard-boiled detective yarns of Dashiel Hammett.

**Telegraphing** occurs when a thematic "message" or other information is stated or divulged gratuitously by the playwright. Telegraphing serves the convenience of the playwright. See chapter 11.

**Tracking.** Plot-oriented approach structured toward intensification, with complications building to a climax. Adjusting the dialogue to a previously constructed scenario rather than a language-oriented approach.

**Turns** simulate the give-and-take of dialogue and may include digressions, hesitations, BACK CHANNELS, even blind alleys or dramaturgical non sequiturs. Spontaneous and exciting for the writer, the turns approach keeps action in the present moment. Characters respond to the flow of language and situation. The downside is that it may lead to more significant revision than the tracking method. Table 1.2 indicates the different outcomes between the tracking and turning approach.

**TABLE 1.2   The Tracking Approach versus the Turns Approach**

| TRACKING APPROACH: DIALOGUE DETERMINED BY PLOT | TURNS APPROACH: DIALOGUE AS FREE RADICAL |
| --- | --- |
| monologic play | dialogic play |
| character-specific dialogue | multivocal characterization |
| genre (comedy, farce, tragedy) | hybrid (mixed genres) |
| theater | metatheater |
| definite historical period | conflated or contrasting periods |
| world of the play | clash of worlds |
| actor becomes character | actor performs character |
| one character per actor | two or more characters per actor |
| character's internal motivation | device of language as motivation |
| one narrator privileged | multiple narrators |
| protagonist-driven | no central character necessary; may be ensemble |

**Writing "off the line."** Characters speak obliquely; meaning is carried subtextually.

**Writing "on the line."** Characters state directly what they mean.

## EXAMPLES AND EXERCISES

Most of the preceding terms are defined more thoroughly in the following chapters. The terms are supplemented with examples and exercises that encourage practice in a specific technique. Generally, exercises follow the narrative discussion or analysis of a given example. To reemphasize: your understanding of each example will be enhanced if you read the entire play. Read the plays primarily for technique and strategy. Even if you do not like the play, you should be able to glean pertinent data from it. The exercises that follow the examples have been classroom or workshop tested by undergraduate and graduate playwriting students. They are designed to increase your playwriting skill and dramaturgical understanding. Jargon is kept to a minimum, although certain "concept" words are necessary to accurately describe and categorize techniques.

## WHAT IT MEANS TO WRITE DIALOGICALLY

For the language playwrights, there is never a case of reducing the character to an idea; rather, there is the energizing of the capacity of language to give the character freer reign in exploiting the linguistic possibilities present in the dramatic moment. The result is the creation of formidable character identities shaped and sculpted by language rather than predetermined by psychological profile. To write dialogically, the playwright must let the characters speak their turn—each character shares the spotlight striving to be "first among equals."

From the playwright's standpoint, the creation of the dialogic play can be construed analogically as a way of governance through sharing. Some have sensed its political corollary in pure nontotalitarian Marxism, which argues that "sharing is not only an ethical or economic mandate, but a condition built into the structure of human perception, and thus a condition inherent in the very fact of being human" (Holquist 1990, 34). The character as independent self determines the direction of the play; put another way, the character imbued as self can assume "authorial" function, whereas the traditional character serves the function of the author. *New Playwriting Strategies* mandates that the "other" is always a factor in the creation of the play, that, at times, the author may be considered an orchestrator or arranger as much as an originator.

The system that follows should be seen not as rigid dogma but as both a *point of entry* into new playwriting and a *point of departure* for your explorations in playwriting. It is my hope as a playwright, coach, and developer that you will encounter the observations and examples to challenge your current writing practices. I wish you success!

# PART I

Strategies
of Language
and
Character

# 2

# On Multivocality and Speech Genres

A core characteristic of the new playwriting is its emphasis on the *multivocal* character and the *polyvocal* text. The principle of multivocality refers to a single character's speech strategies throughout the play's script. Polyvocality expands this scope to include the orchestration and juxtaposition of all voices present in the play. Generally, the polyvocal text combines or draws from various language-based materials, although some sources may be image or sound oriented. The next chapter explores polyvocality in the creation of the hybrid play. Because multivocality bulks speech strategies within one performer, the term is associated with the development of character in new playwriting.

The multivocal character is primarily constructed from language and written to speak with unlimited linguistic potential and range, from street slang to high-toned discourse, and across languages, dialects, and speech genres. As a product of language, the character assumes a carnivalesque capacity for conflation and juxtaposition—in other words, differing speech styles and strategies coexist in a variety of combinations. The term *carnivalesque* also suggests some overturning of traditional norms governing dialogue and characterization. It is as though the language eclipses or transcends characterization as the playwright pursues some residual essence or defining moment. The writing of the play becomes an encounter with language; the playwright challenges character (and actor) throughout a kind of indeterminate journey. Ultimately in new playwriting, character emerges as a function of language.

In traditional dramaturgy, language is a subordinate ingredient—one factor among many in the creation of the character. A character exercise earmarked for beginning playwrights makes this fact readily apparent: the creation of the saturated biography. The "saturated bio" explores all elements of the major character's "back story," the fictional history of the character before the beginning of the play. The playwright concocts cultural, educational, and geographic data that combine to influence a character's patterns of speech, word choice, and linguistic bent. This fictional world that the author (sometimes in workshops with the actor) creates establishes a specific psychological profile emphasizing a subtextual approach to characterization. This subtextual probing precedes the exploration of the real text. Inevitably, the actor will know a character's superobjective before fully engaging what the playwright has written. Tangential factors outside of the play become increasingly important; actors may balk at readings, or in rehearsal, taking the position that "my character would never say this."

The goal in traditional character development is to achieve *character-specific* language for each character. Character-specific dialogue has become a canonized term for play developers, surrounding the formation of character like a hawk, swooping down to eliminate digressions or anomalies in an attempt to neaten the character's arc or progression across the play. *Character-specific* as a descriptor suggests that the writer has found a "voice" or sounds specific to each character in a play—one that simulates real life and promotes the exploration of subtext. The problem with character-specific dialogue is that in real life people change mode, style, and level of speech to fit each situation. Most of us change speech strategies and corresponding gestural indicators to fit a context or circumstance. Nonetheless, character-specific dialogue ensures a degree of consistency in characterization and as such still reigns as a benchmark of playwriting craft.

On the other hand, the new playwright approaches multivocal speech strategies as a restaurant customer approaches a smorgasbord: with variation and multiple combinations in mind. For the playwright, variation may be shaped by a circumstantial shift in the play, or self-directed, arbitrary, and impulsive. This impulsive aspect can offer the playwright a wide menu for developing the nuances of a character's voice. It may establish a more or less carnivalesque turn (like Jell-O on the roast beef at the smorgasbord), overturning self-censorial restrictors in the establishment of dialogue. It unlocks the character from the limitations of a speech that is class or ethnically determined. In Mac Wellman's *Harm's Way*, the character named By Way of Being Hidden oscillates between a pompous, distancing, high-toned level of speech and a brutal, "in your face" approach. The gangster figures in Eric Overmyer's *Dark Rapture* speak with an intellectual fervor that is at first shocking as it transcends their more normative, cliché, tough-guy talk. The multivocal approach offers the playwright the option to conflate or juxtapose formal patterns or rhetorical strategies. The formal patterns may vary from single syllabic repetitions to the polysyllabic to simple articulatory sounds, as indicated by examples from Suzan-Lori Parks's *Imperceptible Mutabilities in the Third Kingdom*; as Douglas Messerli notes, the character Kin-Seer's " 'Gaw gaw gaw gaw eeee,' . . . is representative of the monosyllabic utterance to the [character Us-Seer's] purely articulatory . . . 'FFFFFFFFF' " (Messerli 1998, 877). This nonsemantic use of language recalls the futurists' penchant for transrational language, with its strictly auditory appeal.

The rhetorical style may vary instantly from the massively monologic to the transparent one-liner: Messerli notes that the character Ray's four-page *crise de couer* in Wellman's *The Hyacinth Macaw* is capped by Dora's laconic rejoinder, "As we burn so are we quenched" (Messerli 1998, 1098). Often in new playwriting there is fluctuation from the conversational to literary styles, as exhibited in the writer's speech in Len Jenkin's *Limbo Tales*:

> WRITER: [ . . . ] Am I awake? I've dreamed poems before, but this is extraordinary. I remember every word of it. It may even be good. Good? Genius! Stately pleasure dome! Caves of ice! This one will hit the anthologies for sure! . . . Uh . . . or . . . What if I forget it? What am I thinking? I'm a writer. I'll write it down. (*Sound of typing. . . .*) Sunless sea! Nicely turned . . . decree, sea . . . This is fabulous—I don't even have to think! . . . Mazy motion . . . ah! . . . A miracle of rare device? I love it, and there's more.
>
> (Jenkin 1993, *Limbo Tales*, 43)

In this passage, Jenkin is exploring two common features of multivocality: the juxtaposition of language styles and a patently dialogic approach to monologue (see chapter 11). Moreover, there is a playful self-satisfaction in the character's unfolding discovery of language at the moment of its creation. While Jenkin's multivocal strategies are often used to effect structural aspects of his dramaturgy, in many cases, they simply provide grace notes or a sense of delight in word choices and combinations. The playwright is refreshed by a discovery, and this uncovering triggers more pursuits. The journey through language becomes a curious search for essences and wonder.

## A MULTIVOCAL MENU

An effective way to achieve multivocal characterization is to shift the core vocal strategy, to alter the code. These shifts can be gradual or extreme depending on the effect desired. This multivocal menu will provide you with a range of possibilities as you begin a new play or plan a revision of an existing work:

1. Alter the level code: high-toned to standard to primitive; colloquial to slang.

2. Alter the mode/code of speech: rhetorical, political, technical, jargon laden, literary, poetic, and practical.

3. Alter the language or dialect code: character has second language or uses multilingual foreignisms, broken English, regional dialects— some of which may be understood by other characters. Foreign words may carry articulatory interest.

4. Alter the syntactical code: deviate from traditional sentence structure, tense agreement; unique word arrangements in the script (see nouning, chapter 11).

5. Alter semantic code: words, speech genres, and so on shift meanings throughout the play. Neologisms and obscure words replace mundane

descriptors. Proper names become signposts, adding specificity to the speech.

COMMENT: Jumps within and across speech codes are most evident in new playwriting. These leaps create color or "radiance" of speech and affect a kind of "aura" about the language. These qualities inspire confidence and interest in the playwright's craft. While some leaps may seem extreme, it is important to consider that the multivocal character is an inevitable outgrowth of our multicultural, global environment.

## EXERCISE:
### Shifting levels of speech

1. Write a scene in which two characters utilize a particular level of speech. For example: Character A grunts, is inarticulate, or speaks in profanities. Character B delights in jargonized, highly elevated speech.

    a. Give them an action: each one is trying to describe the same event, a physical object, or person using a speech strategy from the multivocal menu.

2. Bracket areas of the scene where you will insert multivocal speech.

    a. This should vary from the character's primary mode of speaking.

3. Allow A to speak in fluid English with an enlarged vocabulary and sense of polish. Let the speech carry the same intention as in the initial draft, but note the difference in effect and interest. Find a different vocal range for B. For example, B might shift to lower level slang, profanities, etc.

4. Note how intention seemingly follows the shift in vocal mode, as the characters react to the shift. Try to have each character "top" the other.

5. Which language strategy dominates, in other words, which character wins the argument; or, do they reach an impasse; is the "action" resolved.

COMMENT: Experiment with multivocality, testing the limits of what characters can say, and how other characters respond. Allow a character's language to trigger reactions in the other character. Note the specific shifts in language during the scene. "Topping," in which one speaker attempts to outdo the other, will stretch the playwright's linguistic abilities.

### OVERMYER'S MULTIVOCAL DRAMATURGY: A SENSE OF THE BAROQUE

Another way of understanding how multivocality works is to compare it to the baroque style. The baroque is a recipe for opposition and tension as opposed to harmony and balance. The baroque intertwines, juxtaposes, is serpentine, or swings between polarities of high and low, comic and serious. There is a sense of sweep, mass, grandeur, and an exploration of the passions. In art, consider the florid, sensual paintings of Peter Paul Rubens, or the tension between light and dark areas in Michelangelo da

Caravaggio, or, in sculpture, the serpentine movement that belies the mass of Giovanni Bernini's figures. In dramatic literature, the baroque describes the late-sixteenth-century Spanish Golden Age plays that explore the polarities of love versus duty; comic versus serious, and religious versus sensual. Baroque is always associated with the emergence of opera, which is grandiose in scale and features virtuoso singing and special effects. Baroque operas and plays contain heightened, overreaching characters. Their dramaturgies feature: (1) abrupt shifts or contrasts from scene to scene; (2) double or multiple plotting; (3) the contrast between the serious and the comic; and (4) a sense of the ornamental or florid. Through its oppositional nature, the baroque approach simulates a dialogic strategy in which carefully constructed tensions are held in taut balance.

A self-described baroque sensibility is evident in Eric Overmyer's plays: through his heightened characters' aria-like speeches with their sudden twists and turns—as in Babcock's opening monologue in *Dark Rapture*, or in Hungry Mother's vocal tirades of dialogic circumlocution in *Native Speech*, which exhibits mass and dimension. Note the sharp turns of phrase and topic in the hyped-up disk jockey Hungry Mother's aria, late in the play:

> And now this hour's top short stories . . . Dengue Fever raging out of control across Sub-Sahara Africa . . . absolutely terminal, no, I repeat, no antidote . . . Green Monkey Virus spreads from Germany to Georgia! If you gush black blood you've got it! And you're a goner! Isn't that something?! . . . And . . . the Pope is engaged! We'll be back later in the week with more on the Forty-Second Street sniper. These are this hour's top tales, brought to you by Ominous Acronyms— Ominous Acronyms, dedicated to raising the ante no matter the pot. And now a spiritual word of advice from the pastor of the First . . . Chinese Baptist . . . Church of the Deaf! ("chinee") Leveland Bluce Ree here. Lememble! Don't wait for the hearse to take you to church! (*Cheery*) Thank you Leveland Bluce. Next hour, my impression of a JAP. And I don't mean Japanese. Don't miss it. But first— . . .
>
> (Overmyer 1993, *Native Speech*, 39)

Overmyer's oppositional push and pulls within this speech reflect the baroque dynamic of creating form through dynamic tension. Rather than emphasizing the internal psychology of the character, Overmyer's multivocal shifts demand an external, hyperbolic acting approach that favors verbal and gestural exaggerations. For example, Hungry Mother's mimicked Chinese dialect reflects not only its articulatory aspect, but also, the derisive edge in the intonation of the accent. Overmyer requires the actor playing *Hungry Mother* to make pinpoint shifts, challenging the actor to differentiate topics through intonation, rhythmical emphasis, or changes in rate. These juxtaposed *turns* are indicative of the extreme dialogism inherent within and across the speech strategies.

We can now examine multivocal strategies at closer range, dissecting individual components that make up the language-based approach to playwriting.

## SPEECH GENRES

In his later writings, Mikhail Bakhtin stressed the importance of speech genres as a means to understand how certain utterances emanate style and meaning and provide a sense of intonation. By definition, a speech genre is coded language that is suggestive of a certain group, occupation, literary genre, cultural bias, and so on. As such, speech genres may include discourses, dialects, idioms, and slang; in everyday usage they typically function as a kind of linguistic shorthand. For this reason, speech genres offer a valuable language option to playwrights who seek to establish context quickly and avoid lengthy expository dialogue. In *Poor Folk's Pleasure* Len Jenkin establishes a sense of place and circumstance through the repetitive patterns and staccato rhythms typical of the game show host:

> GIRL: We have a winner, we have a winner! Number 18. Seven tickets, any prize, bottom row. Known from the rock-bound coast of Maine to the sun-kissed shores of California, it's Fascination. Time for another game of Fascination, Time for another game of Fascination! (*rings bell*) Roll 'em up! Roll 'em up! And the first ball is out.
>
> (Jenkin 1993, *Poor Folk's Pleasure*, 9, 286)

Because the speech genre of the game show host immediately establishes a sense of context, the playwright is open to explore nuances in texture, rhythms, and coloration. The structure of *Poor Folk's Pleasure* juxtaposes numerous speech genres (e.g., salesman, newsman, carnival barker, etc.) across the play to create a collage-like polyvocality.

Speech genres operate dialogically, functioning specifically within the play while referring back to the cultural site of linguistic origin. David Mamet utilizes specific speech genres to establish power struggles but also rituals of male bonding in *Glengarry Glen Ross* (salesman talk); and *Speed the Plow* (Hollywood movie lingo). As a strategy, the playwright can alter, or appropriate, the context of the speech genre to effect thematic resonance. Harold Pinter, for example, utilized the idiomatic "odd man out," taken from sports parlance, to describe the triadic dynamic underscoring the characters in his play *Old Times*. Once the genre is established it can be manipulated or "played with" as material in the text. This dialogic tension creates meaning and interest. For example, Hungry Mother's arias are based on the speech rhythms of a typical disc jockey whose patter is broken up with weather reports and on-mike advertisements. Throughout the play, Overmyer subverts or "makes strange" the standard hourly weather report by substituting Hungry Mother's "street drug reports." He parodically names the station's paid advertiser "Ominous Acronyms." For Overmyer, the deejay's linguistic bent provides the format and point of departure for this virtuosic defamiliarization.

In new playwriting, the use of speech genres is a core language strategy: witness Mac Wellman's interest in intergalactic vocabulary in *Whirligig* and *Albanian Softshoe*; Jenkin's proclivities toward the 1940s slang of detective novels and film noir in *Kid Twist* and *My Uncle Sam*; Overmyer's use of foreignisms and dialects throughout *In Perpetuity throughout the Universe*; Suzan-Lori Parks's parody of black dialect in *The Death of the Last Black Man in the Whole Entire World*. Establishing several speech genres across a play will effect polyvocal tension. For example, in Jenkin's *Gogol*, Pontius Pilate's arcane biblical phraseology clashes against the epigrammatic tendencies that identify the quack, Dr. Mesmer, with utterances like, "My motto is service" or "cop and blow."

## EXERCISE:
### Speech Genres

The objective in this exercise is to become acquainted with the use of speech genres.

1. Tape an announcer of a sporting event, game show, auction, or carnival.

2. Transcribe the key phrases, repetitions, transitions points, attempting to grasp the rhythms and intonational subtleties of the speaker.

3. Write a monologue using the transcription as a point of departure.

4. Recontextualize the genre along the lines of Overmyer's Hungry Mother's "take" on the traditional disc jockey.

COMMENT: This exercise runs the gamut, requiring the playwright to use technical means (taping, transcription) to achieve imaginative ends. The execution of step 4 will offer the potential for wonder and interest by refitting the genre into a new context. Intonation, which determines how words and phrases are voiced by the actor, is embedded or coded within the speech genre. Intonation suggests the way of saying a phrase or speech style, whether from the carnival huckster, the gangster tough guy, or the sly femme fatale. In *Dark Rapture* Overmyer offers a Marlene Deitrich–like approach to stating sexual desire through the femme fatale Julia. Julia's breathy call for sex is "Pull my focus, cowboy."

## DIALECTS AND FOREIGNISMS

How far can the playwright go with dialects and ethnic stereotyping without being offensive? New playwriting has largely refuted the move to politically correct orthodoxy, which it decries as a form of self-censoring. For example, Jenkin parodies the Charlie Chan type in several plays that feature a Chinese laundryman ("no tickee, no shirtee"); similarly, opium den denizens are found in Jenkin's *My Uncle Sam* and Overmyer's *The Heliotrope Bouquet*. Wellman's seminal article, "Theatre of Good Intentions," derides the politically correct model as voiding the theater of energy and risk. Indeed, the problem of properly identifying with the correct sociopolitical agenda has been a difficulty for the African-American playwright Suzan-Lori Parks. Her play *The Death of the Last Black Man in the Whole Entire World* (Mahone 1994, 239–80) conflates black American dialect with the conventional speech genre of the "stage Negro," a character type derived from minstrelsy. The character Queen Then Pharaoh Hatshepsut offers an example in the first scene:

> Before Columbus thuh worl usta be roun they put uh /d/ on thuh end of roun makin roun. Thusly they set in motion thuh end. Without that /d/ we coulda gone on spinnin forever. Thuh /d/ thing ended things ended.

> (Mahone 1994, *The Death of the Last<br>Black Man in the Entire World,* 251)

Parks's strategy of dialect, linguistic event, and typification of character diminish the importance of the content-related issues concerning Christopher Columbus and the shape of the world. Through the speech, a phonetic, actually phonemic variable /d/, has significant repercussions suggesting that the inclusion of /d/ changed the course of history. Parks's focus on the phoneme /d/ further draws associations to the colonization of the New World, and by implication, its connection to slavery. At the same time, the /d/ draws our attention to the language-oriented nature of the play—here bracketed in its smallest phonemic sense. For new playwrights interest extends beyond words to what can be verbalized or vocalized—it can be about syllables, sonic utterances, or phonemic variables. The bracketed /d/ dialogizes between its formal capacity as a sound unit and its ideological ramifications.

Parks's typified character names establish a risky ideological context: Black Man with Watermelon; Black Woman with Fried Drumstick; Lots of Grease and Lots of Pork; and so on. Parks shapes their language into formal linguistic patterns using stereotyped inflections and accents. The result is a form of parodic metaspeech (speech that calls attention to itself). Parks's concern with creating a unique language for her plays, and for being absorbed in the formal or plastic quality of language, has led to criticism from members of the African-American community who define the need of the African-American theater to be consciousness-raising, thereby advancing social, cultural, and economic awareness.

The use of foreign utterances can certainly provide tension between formalist and sociocultural aspects of language. In Overmyer's play *In Perpetuity throughout the Universe*, the Chinese American character Dennis Wu recounts a joke in Chinese:

DENNIS: New gee ng gee do Cock Robin mei yup ying yip gai gee chin hoy geo mut murn? Kurn jal hey geu jo Penis Rabinowitz! (*Laughs uproariously, Then tells the joke in English:*) What was Cock Robin's name before he changed it to go into show business? Penis Rabinowitz. (*Stone-faced. Shrugs.*)

(Overmyer 1993, *In Perpetuity*, scene 23, 211.)

Overmyer provides a multilingual example of dialogism, in which the real humor is disclosed through the articulatory aspect of the sound of the words rather than their meaning, which for American audiences would be unknowable. Dennis's deadpan shrug seems to acknowledge the tired mundanity of this old vaudeville joke, contrasting with his expressive response to the ersatz foreign version.

Combining dialects or foreignisms with other speech strategies will enhance the aural texturing of the playwrights' work. The performance/art/theatrical works of Guillermo Gomez-Peña, what he describes as installation pieces, are replete with multivocal language strategies. In his award-winning book *New World Border*, Peña introduces the dialect/language he speaks (the most common dialect now spoken in America). He describes it as Spanglish, a hybrid of English and Spanish.

## EXERCISES:
### Multiple Languages or Dialects

A. Write a two-character scene that involves the beginnings of a committed relationship. One of the characters speaks a foreign language or relies on dialect; use dialect or ethnic expressions.

    1. Have the other character react to these speech patterns, to either provide a source of insight or conflict with the "other."

    2. The characters work through obstacles of alienation, frustration, desire, and so on. Resolve scene as they either come together or pull apart.

B. Place several diverse characters in a situation or event where they cannot clearly understand each other, yet are thrown together: in a lifeboat, a room in a burning building, or a hostage takeover—the setting exerts pressure on the individuals.

    1. Use language to create or motivate comic outcomes based on the situation. Allow language interactions to reflect cultural differences in customs or conventions, for example.

Here are three exercises to work into a play you are redrafting, or a new play you are conceiving:

    1. Utilize a strong dialect or ethnic "take" on English, as a springboard for an apparently weaker character.

    2. Give all the characters in your play a different dialect, language, or regionalism, attempting to use the speech as a comic handicap. In other words, there are misunderstandings, strange pronunciations, and ethnic idioms that must be interpreted and played off of by other characters.

3. Review several movies from the thirties and forties that feature the speech of recent immigrants; attempt to transcribe phrases and key words. Integrate these into the dialogue of a character you are currently working on.

## FROM DISCOURSE TO SLANG

In Mac Wellman's *Three Americanisms*, three characters without names (see chapter 7) are juxtaposed in a clash or collage of discourses and slang rearranged through Wellman's idiosyncratic syntax. Discourse, unlike normal dramatic or conversational language, is distinguished by coded words, "buzz-phrases," often with a reliance on technical terms or argot. Underlining the strategy of a discourse is an essential ideology and historicity. To this extent, discourse is time bound. Examples of discourses include the Marxist, academic, feminist, theory-based, technology-based, scientific, fascist, medical, religious Right, traditional liberal, American oratorical, environmental, and so on. Discourse gives a character an ideological front or façade that may be activated strategically to empower, intimidate, moralize, or to aid and inform. In new playwriting, however, discourse tends to be more ruminative than argumentative, more marginalized than mainstream. It moves along by association and incremental repetitions rather than by progressive trails of logic. In this sense it is more dialogic than dialectic since new playwrights rarely advance politically committed positions. Its dialogic and ruminative bent tends to personalize the rendering of language; thus, a character emerges rather than a thematic cipher—telegraphing the playwright's message. Often, the character will reflect upon or work over the discourse being said. This passage from Jenkin's *Limbo Tales* illustrates that move from the anthropology professor Driver's taped pedagogical discourse to his commentary on his lecture for Anthropology 201:

> Once the Mayans constructed their grand pyramid at Uxmal, on top of it was stationed a man chosen by lot, called the Illum Kinnal, the Time Watcher. His job is to protect the sequence of orderly time, to keep it running smoothly from past to future. He does this by guarding it with his eyes. If his attention weakens for one moment, there is a subtle break in the time line. Past. Present and future mix. Work in the fields stops. People have visions, headaches, momentary hallucinations. The priests notice, and the Illum Kinnal is killed, his heart offered to the gods, and he's replaced by another time watcher. . . .
>
> DRIVER: I don't think I'll mention it to Anthropology 201, but the truth is that the Mayans were nuts.
>
> (Jenkins 1993, *Limbo Tales*, 21)

Invariably lively and entertaining, new playwrights often use historicized discourse to instruct, combining what the nineteenth century called "lay

*American Notes,* is typical:

> This is amazing country. Sea to shining . . . I'll tell you what it is. It's
> fertile. I was on my way out the door one day, little buddy of mine,
> about to take my mayoral constitutional, had a handful of pumpkin
> seeds to munch on the road. I turn around to wave goodbye to the
> wife and kids, and one seed fell outta my hand. Before I could turn
> back around that seed had taken root in the earth sprouted up and
> spread so high and wide that I was dangerously surrounded by enor-
> mous serpentine vines, caught in their green clutches. The volunteer
> fire department had to break out the axes and cut me loose . . .
>
> (Jenkin 1993, *American Notes,* 242)

Along these lines is the discourse that stems from a troubled consciousness: note the beginning speech of the Translator in Jenkin's *Dark Ride,*
who strives to find the meaning of an ancient text. His various interpreta-
tions provide the basic story line for the play. Interest in the character is
created as he works over the possibilities in front of the audience.
Depending upon its application, discourse usually provides the character
with special knowledge about a person, object, place, event, worldview,
and so forth. The Translator figure has special knowledge about interpreting nuances of arcane manuscripts.

## EXERCISE:
### Scene Revision/Special Knowledge

This revision exercise gives a character in a scene special knowledge about
something; this knowledge can be emphasized by raising or lowering the level
of diction. Len Jenkin factors in special knowledge to "professionals" that show
up in his plays: the tattoist, the mesmerist, the game show host, or the others who "have the goods on someone else."

1. Select a scene from something you have written that contains two or three
   characters of a specific social class.

2. Allow one character a heightened level of knowledge about another character. The disclosure of this knowledge should surprise others in the scene.
   The information revealed is crucial to the action of the scene. It may be a
   particular secret, something hidden that is revealed.

3. Utilize coded words, special jargon, foreignisms, and so on. To varying
   degrees, this framing of discourse establishes an ironic or self-parodying
   take on what is being said.

Capability Brown's ruminations on gardening in Jenkin's *My Uncle Sam*
demonstrate his special knowledge within the framework of eighteenth-
century historicized discourse:

The apple, poppies, pumpkins, and all melons come to fruit. HAVE FOLLOWING: IN THE EARTH: mounds, grotto crypts. ON THE EARTH: groves, labyrinths, fountains. IN THE AIR: aviaries, containing the ostrich, peacocks, swans, and cranes. Buzzy bees. A slew of automata among the rocks. Include my patented mechanism for the production of artificial echoes.

(Jenkin 1993, *My Uncle Sam*, 181)

Lifting directly from Capability Brown's eighteenth-century journals on designing the English garden, Jenkin reframes Brown's discourse within a contemporary play. The "estranged" context and linguistic eccentricities (e.g. "Buzzy bees") create particular interest in this theatrical character. Rather than being built from a psychological model, the character emerges from a particularized discourse and sense of place. In new playwriting, the projection of discourse never seems arid or pretentious because the actor can sense an underlying earnestness, sincerity, or buoyancy in writing that is eminently playable.

## EXERCISE:
### Developing Discourse

Character as discourse: Revise a scene you have written by introducing a character who serves as a narrator/commentator on the action. Multivocal characters might change the levels of discourse across the play or in a given speech. When several discourses are present in a play, they create an internal dialogism.

1. Make this narrator figure an expert—such as a doctor, psychologist, witch doctor, professor, biologist—of some arcane knowledge; the more extreme and marginal the better. Imbue the character with a particular discourse. Use coded phrases, vocabulary, and syntactical choices.

2. Write a monologue in which the character attempts to describe a discovery just made. This may involve an object, an experiment, a body, and so on.

COMMENT: Dramatic interest need not be tied to rising action, structures of causality, and strong protagonists. Within the dialogic scheme, more options appear for the playwright willing to experiment, opening the notion of what defines a play. In the above monologue, the character, through description is really attempting to gain control of the object. Nevertheless, the recontextualized discourse offers both juxtaposition and comic potential in action.

## SLANG AS SPEECH GENRE

Slang is the flip side of formal discourse: operating as coded language, its usage is initially restricted to those "in the know." Identifiable through its subversive and often profane words and phrases, slang is a species of speech genre, and is introduced along the societal margins before it is accepted into mainstream usage. As it assimilates into general parlance, slang takes on broader applications and meanings depending on context. Eventually, slang dates itself, and is mediated out of contemporary speech. This state of flux makes its usage solvent for playwrights because historicized "lingo" is immediately identifiable to audiences, creating a specific sense of genre and period. Onstage slang becomes "framed" or foregrounded. Transplanted from its particular sociohistorical context, it is reframed in a theatrical context.

Moreover, slang operates dialogically, resonating between current and contemporaneous contexts. While the word *buzz* in the 1970s may have referred to the reaction to an illegal substance, now it more often connotes a level of interest or reaction by a particular group. Sometimes, gestures operate similarly to slang. For example, an actor making the peace sign (a *V* with his fingers) will be read differently by a Vietnam veteran, a war protester, or a twenty-year-old who has no personal associations with its historical origin. Other gestures provide shorthand corollaries to their more or less profane utterances.

Slang is usually made up of neologisms, or it may be recycled from a different context or era. The language may range from impolite to profane, but should be colorful. In contemporary usage, discourse often combines with slang to create juxtapositions in sound and meaning. Slang encapsulates a specific action or take in a short phrase, with language full of "pizzazz." To no small degree, the popularity of new writing can be attributed to this linguistic "aura," a by-product of the writing style and the sound of the spoken language.

## EXERCISE:
### Slang at the Utimate Party

1. In the class or workshop playwriting students should take a specific period and group to study with the goal of capturing slang, colloquial expressions, regionalisms, or foreignisms that define historicized or ethnicized Americana. Consider the widest range, from pioneer, beatnik, or early immigrant to current New Yorker. Other eras rich in colloquialisms or slang were the swing era, the Roaring Twenties, the Old West, or the be-bop, surfer, hippie, yuppie, preppie, generation X, grunge, or valley girl eras. Consider using language-based dialects such as Cajun, Creole, Chicano (Spanglish), British, Irish, and Latino; also consider idioms from "the mob," the service (army, navy, etc.), the jailbird, or sports-related figures, and so on. (Overmyer frequently uses Spanish or Chinese speakers in his plays; he utilized Chinese effectively in *In Perpetuity throughout the Universe*. Wellman juxtaposes street language with various colloquial formats.)

2. Compile as many expressions, words, phrases, and gestures as possible, setting a time limit of about one month so that ample research can be conducted. Movies, books, and other contemporary references are appropriate.

3. Make a four- or five-columned list that might define the way a character speaks. The lists should be from opposing groups you have compiled. For

example, one might be service-related, another generation X, another beat-nik, and so on.

4. Construct a multicharacter scene that demonstrates the most incredible and extreme party you can imagine. Make certain that each figure you construct interacts at least once with each other figure. Vary the lingo according to character. Attempt to create a polyglot of speech. Don't be tame, really explore and explode the boundaries to the limit.

5. Allow the collision of lingo to somehow lead to a catastrophic event and pivotal moment.

COMMENT: The exercise above is a variation on the "Ultimate Party" exercise that award-winning playwright Matthew Maguire conducted in my University of Alabama playwriting workshop. It challenges you to stretch your imagination and linguistic capacities. You will develop your ear and open your awareness to the richness of the American language. There are several questions to address: Why and how does language determine our perception of character? How does speech precede and predict events? In what ways does the context of the "ultimate party" allow for a release of the self-censor?

## MULTIVOCAL PROFANITY

American playwriting in the 1960s and 1970s probably contained more profanity than we find in current plays. The early plays of David Mamet and David Rabe had the power to shock audiences with profanity, but in the contemporary theater profanity has lost its capacity to surprise, shock, or advance fresh and daring subject matter. If certain audience members find its excessive use offensive and the majority is inured to its effect, then there is little payoff for the playwright. Nevertheless, profanity can be an effective means of characterizing an individual, particularly if contrasted with other linguistic styles in the play. A well-known example is Tony Kushner's rendition of Roy Cohn in *Angels in America*. Profanity works as character-specific speech in portraying the hardball style of Cohn. Unfortunately, young playwrights are prone to using profanity indiscriminately. In fledgling attempts to ape Mamet's macho, misogynistic style, they fail to match his nuances of rhythm and intonation.

Profanity can establish a level of multivocality when uttered impulsively by a character at an unexpected moment. In some cases, the "f word" is resplendent in its dialogic mutability. Note the various connotations of *fuck* in this selection from Jeffrey Jones's *Seventy Scenes of Halloween*:

JEFF: All right! I fucked her! Is that what you want to hear? Is it? You want to know, goddamn it, you're going to know: Three times I fucked her! One right after the other (which we never do). And the third time in the morning! And I can get hard right now just think-ing about it. And yes—I feel guilty—okay? And, yes—I know it's fuck-ing everything up—okay? And I'm not saying it's right or it's wrong except it's something I've wanted all my life and now I have the chance for it and I am not going to spend the rest of my life wishing I hadn't let it slip away! Does this mean anything to you or are you too fucked up with your own self-pity? I mean, look at you—look at you! Nine years! Nine fucking years, Joan, and none of it matters, does it? (The Twenty-Second Scene, 84–85)

(Wellman 1985, *Seventy Scenes of Halloween*, 84–85)

The poignancy of this cruel revelation notwithstanding, Jones is certainly "playing" with the meanings as he progressively alters the connotations of the word *fuck*. Each meaning is contextually derived, its semantic range from denotation (intercourse); to emphasizing the ongoing futility in their marriage ("fucking years"); to a descriptor of his wife's mental state ("fucked up"); and the state of their marriage, how Jeff, the character's actions are "fucking everything up." Jones's strategic use of *fuck* makes a powerful statement that would not be as forceful or edgy otherwise. Moreover, he allows the actor significant latitude in terms of intonation, a factor the playwright should consider when profanities are sprinkled throughout the text.

The above example demonstrates how profanity/slang ranges from cursing and confrontation to more casual assessments ("fucking everything up"). In general conversation, the expression *Fuckin' A* signifies a benign form of agreement ("you got that right") or plaintive sigh, depending upon intonation. The speaking style—irreverent, flip, and uninhibited—may seem more spontaneous and endearing than threatening to audiences. The profane aspect is downplayed in most speaking contexts. In Mikhail Bakhtin's scheme, profanity is defined as a form of grotesque speech offering strange juxtapositions or conflations that are colorfully scatological (e.g., "shithead" or "buttface"). These conflations have been staples of low comedy and farce since the Greek old comedy, but they may never exhaust their potential for new and more provocative configurations.

## EXERCISE:
### Playing Profanities

This is a good exercise for working through or getting out the desire to see profanity in print. Indeed, for many young playwrights in the workshop writing out this desire might serve as a rite of passage. Again, it's not a question of being censorial; rather, it's about the need to interest and surprise through the use of language. Sometimes profanity is the best or only way to get it done. For this exercise, use the example from Jeffrey Jones's play as a point of departure.

1. Write a moderate-length monologue in which a character either serves up, or receives bad news. Another character is addressed who may be present or absent.

2. Use one profane term four to six times, in various configurations. Consider the variety of meanings and intonations so that they are continually shifting.

3. Strive for some novel juxtapositions or conflations.

4. The character should make a transition from the beginning to the end of the speech; for example, from anger to resignation, indignation to humiliation, or ignorance to understanding.

5. Members of the workshop should read their monologues aloud, vocally indicating the changes in intonation.

## EXTREME RHETORICAL LEVELS

Language playwrights utilize rhetorical tropes and figures in their plays. Hyperbole, distortions, and diminutions stretch the boundaries or limits of language. They are most effective in determining a dominant language style for certain characters or types. The character Senator Armitage appears only once to deliver a monologue in Wellman's *Bad Infinity*, but his exaggerated, rhetorical style defines his pompous, overblown nature. Jenkin's oddball professors, like the "defrocked" scientist in *American Notes*, consistently try to persuade characters through exempla (examples). This persuasive tactic backfires when it reveals the twisted logic of the character's mind. Occasionally, Wellman explores a political matter, albeit in an estranged theatricalized way. The following speech of Sam's, near the conclusion of *The Professional Frenchman*, follows the banal comments of the characters regarding a professional football game that Sam and Jacques have been watching and gambling on. Sam speaks:

> Take my advice Mevrouw. Never gamble
> Gamble against professionals.
> They are merciless.
> > (*They laugh. Pause. Sam speaks in a strange demoniac, deep voice*)
> You have to beat them
> Into submission. Once you get a man down
> In America, blessèd America,
> You have to fucking pound
> Him into the clay, you have
> To finish him off. Destroy Him. Pulverize him. Be-Cause
> if you show a man any mercy,
> Any kindness. If you leave him with any
> Small part of his self-respect He'll never forgive you, he'll
> Make you bloody well pay
> For every fucking thing you Ever did. For him.
> Never give a man a second chance. When you get the
> > opportunity
> To eat a human being

Swallow him whole
Or grind him to
Pulp, but never NEVER
Leave the tiniest bit
Of living humanity left
Or you'll be sorry for it.
      You can bet your ass
Reagan won't. Reagan—Reagan the first . . .

                (Wellman 1985, *The Professional Frenchman*)

Wellman's rhetorical strategy is typically made ironic by the Grand
Guignol excesses of portrayal (demoniac, low voice). While formatted as
monologue the rhetoric is dialogic: Wellman draws upon the genre of
"coach speak," the annihilation rhetoric of the football coach, the dog-eat-
dog ethos that is this character's competitive, capitalistic mantra.
Ideologically, through this rhetorical tirade, Wellman captures an essential element of the Reagan years with a mocking, searing jest.

Language playwrights maximize the rhetorical proclivities and predis-
positions of their characters. To begin, I urge you to explore the comic
potential of the rhetorical. For example, you don't want a character to be
pedantic and dull, as might be the case in reality. Pomposity, or the long-
winded, can be handled in a humorous or ironic way if: (1) the character
delights in her wordsmithing; (2) other characters dissect the speech in a
satirical mode; (3) bizarre or peculiar linguistic relationships are posited
and made palpable.

In Jenkin's *Dark Ride*, Mrs. Lammle's rhetorical flights on the "world of
coincidence" not only offer bizarre stories and a humorous characterization but also indicate that the worlds of this play are dialogically interre-
lated through coincidence. Mrs. Lammle's omniscience establishes a
rhetorical or quasi-rhetorical stance, since the special knowledge of the
omniscient character requires a degree of pontificating.

The playwright won't "hold the boards" with long speeches or philo-
sophical debate unless these are somehow coded into the play. Wellman's
example above, for instance, demonstrates an extreme take on character—
it is theatrically coded. Moreover, Mrs. Lammle's waxing about coincidences is reflected in the action of the play.

## FACETING

Conceptualizing the multivocal character is similar to preparing a finely
cut gem. The exploration in the early drafts is analogous to the jeweler's
preparation of the roughly hewn gem—now to be realized in all of its
refined facets: shaped, honed, and buffed to a fine finish. For the multivocal character, the facets of language create a network of dialogic relations that are held together in exquisite tension.

Multivocal faceting is evident in Wellman's one-person play, *Terminal Hip*. The re-formation of representational speech is accomplished through syntactical aberrations that try the seemingly familiar:

> "Your shoes are worth fifteen dollars a day, and buddy
> we'll pay you hard cash money for them shoes
> you got because we believe in giving hard cash money to people
> such as yourself who as gots shoes on they feets sure you bet.
>
> (Wellman 1994, *Terminal Hip*, 264)

While the first three lines establish or ground a kind of character-specific speech mode, Wellman quickly refacets his intention in the final line with his disorienting syntactical choices.

Rather than reflect or imitate "conversation," Wellman arranges phrases and speech fragments to confront the context of representational meanings in language, both echoing various speech rhythms and styles, while corrupting standard syntactical strategies. *Terminal Hip* explodes audiences' expectations of how language operates within the world of the play, as it celebrates the playwright's unique reformulation of contemporary language. In this sense, Wellman is the formalist, exercising the right of language to move beyond its representational capacity, to unleash the power of language as the modernist painters released painting from its need to represent objects. Faceting promotes a kind of formal arrangement of speech strategies, and can be put to best use in the revision of the multivocal character.

## SPEECH STRATEGIES AND THE IMAGINATION

As this chapter demonstrates, the multivocal approach offers numerous strategic options to the playwright. Tactically, as a matter of craft, they can be combined, conflated, or juxtaposed. Nevertheless, it is up to the playwright's imagination to transform the patchwork into a satisfying quilt, one that holds interest and elicits wonder. So while you dutifully pour over these elements of craft and construction never be afraid to let the imagination trigger your foray into language. Open all your senses to the possibilities—anticipate the wonder that is coming, as the character Tim does in Jenkin's *American Notes*:

> TIM: You are a man who can smell true love when it's coming down the street, you can smell it coming to you cross the rivers and seas, its odor mixing with the salt spray and the quick perfume of the flying fish. . . .
>
> (Jenkin 1993, *American Notes*, 234)

# 3

## Polyvocality and the Hybrid Play

The dialogic play is by definition polyvocal. Polyvocality suggests that a variety of language strategies, voices, and source materials may be used by the playwright to construct the play's text. Variable language strategies might include changing the level of language or speech style through slang, discourse, or speech genre; or playing with syntax. Unlike a single "playwright's voice," a hallowed term in play development circles, the new playwright may orchestrate a polyphony of voices across an array of characters. For example, one character may speak with a dialect, while another utilizes foreign terms. Some voices are taken from transcriptions, others from arcane, popular, or historical sources. The myriad sources include film and literary genres that may "frame" our perception of the written play. Or, the source might be an arbitrary word from a dictionary inserted into the dialogue to provoke the playwright and the play in a different direction.

The new playwright is continually responding to the "other" in the shaping of the script. Quite simply, the playwright synthesizes, alters, and rechannels the component voices and sources, establishing, as the play is written, the nature of the juxtapositions, clashes, and conflations. In order to accomplish this effectively, the new playwright must become a master strategist as well as an imaginative creator. A knowledge of various strategies will in fact enhance creativity by providing the playwright with more choices and reference points. Optimally, the playwright's voice will be stretched and exercised in different directions, thus expanding the range of possibilities in the writing of the play. Ultimately, the goal is virtuosity, but to begin, it is important to achieve competency in the basic principles involved. In this chapter, we will probe characteristics of polyvocality and how they can be implemented into the making of the play.

Polyvocality mandates that different, diverse, and often clashing elements converge in the making of the playtext. The outcome of the polyvocal approach can be described as the hybrid play.

### DEFINING THE HYBRID PLAY

What is the hybrid play? The hybrid play is a literary and theatrical crossbreed, a blending of genres and disparate sources both textual and performative. In many cases, the sources are unrelated and may appear given to arbitrary selection. The hybrid play may take on myriad forms and combinations: from literary pastiche to collage-like performance pieces. In fact, the collage is an apt corollary from the world of art, since collage transforms diverse found materials into a new, aesthetic whole. The collage artist gives over to the potential of the raw material, while exploiting them for his creative ends. The transformation in the function of the materials gives the collage its sense of wonder; new playwriting, which has been described as the "theater of wonders," shares this magical capacity with art.

The history of the hybrid play features the putative master, William Shakespeare. Generally, Shakespeare's plays are constructed hybrids; materials are drawn from diverse sources, genres, and historical accounts. Story lines or entire plays (e.g., *King John*) are reformulated to fit the author's scheme. Shakespeare was not beyond synthesizing well-known or commonplace materials in shaping his plays. *Cymbeline* embeds a popular story from a Giovanni Boccaccio novella with elements adapted from a commedia dell'arte pastoral scenario.

Shakespeare adapted characters and traits from other idioms: the advising father Polonius, from *Hamlet*, is a descendant of Pantalone from the commedia dell'arte—a literary and performative source. Many of his royal characters are drawn from Elizabethan historical accounts documented in the *Holinshed Chronicles*. Early plays reflect the wit and badinage of early modern speech genres, and Shakespeare's background in Latin. Historically, the measure of artistic genius in the late Renaissance was based on the success of the invention (*inventio*) the author applied to found materials, and the arrangement of parts (*dispositio*), rather than the creation of a work solely from the imagination or observation of real life. Then, the author would focus on the execution of language (*elocutio*), which included figures of speech, metaphors, and the degree of wit and example. So while sources were lifted, the author impressed the audience with skills in language and characterization. This process is really quite similar to the making of the contemporary hybrid play.

Along the way, the hybrid has been difficult for some periods and authorities to accept. Theatrical hybrids, such as the opera, pantomime, and vaudeville, have been extremely popular and successful with audiences. However, these forms have met with staunch resistance from authorities. French seventeenth-century academies declaimed the contamination of dramatic genres in an attempt to codify tragedy and regulate comedy. English politicians in 1737 licensed out of existence a number of the successful companies performing pantomimes (harliquinades) and ballad operas. Until recently, scholars and academics have relegated the theatrical hybrid to inferior status or have simply ignored it as a subject of study. Preference is given to dramatic literature that can be categorized in terms of genre. Published anthologies privilege those dramas that fit into categories: realism, neoclassicism, classical tragedy, restoration comedies of manners, and so on. A towering figure such as Shakespeare gains entry, but only through the sheer force of his talent. The fact that his work is derivative is rarely considered in depth.

The twentieth century brought the advent of the living newspaper plays, and of course, Bertholt Brecht's epic theater. The hybrid structure that allows for multimedia could be used to serve political ends. Brecht recycled cabaret songs, elements from the folk theater, and story forms like the parable. His *Caucasian Chalk Circle*, for example, includes an opening section reminiscent of the proletarian "socialist realism" plays common in East Germany at the time. To answer a problem that arises, a Capo uses the Simon and Grusha folktale to make a didactic point. This inner story is presented as a kind of absurd parable with the entry of the corrupt Azdak, the benchmark of arbitrary justice. Brecht's move from socialist realism to folktale represents a clash of literary genres. No effort is made to synthesize the two, although both "texts" inform each other. Brecht's socialist prologue in *Caucasian Chalk Circle* framed the traditional folktale—that is, the journey of Simon and Grusha—toward a didactic outcome.

In 1978, I attended a performance of Spalding Gray's seminal *Rumstich Road*. I was struck by the juxtaposition of Gray's own character with the voice of his mother as it was heard through the theater's sound system. Gray recycled tapes his mother had made with her psychiatrist prior to her suicide, and integrated them into the performance text. As found objects the tapes were recontextualized within a performance mode. Gray's one-person, autobiographical hybrid was a seamless pastiche of found and created materials. Here the playwright serves as compiler, adapter, and arranger—more accurate a descriptor than playwright as creator. Anna Deavere Smith, Eric Bogosian, Karen Finley, Peggy Shaw, and Guillermo Gomez-Peña (among others) have continued this form of theatrical polyvocality: for example, both Smith and Gomez-Peña juxtapose racial and cultural voices; Shaw and Finley express the multiple and contradictory voices of gender. These playwrights/performers serve as the conduit or filter for multiple voices and media, which they recycle and integrate into aesthetic form. At the borders or boundaries between "voices" meaning is determined. Similarly, the ensemble Wooster Group recycles and juxtaposes textual and found materials to create truly dialogic performance texts. In the hybrid form, narrative is often diminished in favor of aural landscapes and exciting spectacle. Some of the most popular theatrical work in the past ten years has been the product of theatrical hybridization: examples are Cirque du Soleil, the musical revue *Stomp*, and Blue Man Group.

## NEW PLAYWRITING AND THE HYBRID

A widely held belief among theatergoers is that great playwrights possess signature, distinctive voices that are immediately identifiable. Although new playwrights work away from the mainstream, their virtuosic use of language sets them apart in a crowded field. Indeed, they could be considered benchmarks of the individuated style. Their harshest critics laud their use of language, if not their unique dramaturgy. However, underlying the identifiable "sound" of each playwright are shared characteristics that can be explored and recapitulated.

New playwrights, whether by plan or intuition, embed diverse source materials, styles, formats, and approaches into their plays. The combinations may be integrated into the text, or stand side by side, as juxtapositions in the hybrid structure. Len Jenkin's plays reflect these hybrid options: in *Kid Twist*, the mafioso, gangster idiom is integrated into sketches involving American icons like Babe Ruth and the Joker, from Batman comics, as well as the signature event of the Nazi dirigible the *Hindenburg*'s burning; *Limbo Tales* is really two separate acts linked only by a narrating character, the Master of Ceremonies, who also provides an "intermezzo" bridge between the separate acts. The two acts of *Limbo Tales* stand in juxtaposition but are neither thematically nor dramatically similar. In his recent play *Like I Say*, Jenkin provides a trackable, sequential through line that is interpolated with puppet shows and intermezzo breaks. The intermezzi and puppetry are throwbacks to the Renaissance practice of offering variety entertainment during the act breaks. *Poor Folks Pleasure* is a hybrid in its overall formation; a structure that is mirrored in a number of scenes. Scene 4 interpolates a scene from the movie *Spartacus* into the ongoing action to create a kind of surrealistic effect:

> SALESMAN: I believe I'm in a hotel. I'm sure of it. I've been in them before. Not exactly like this one. Similar. I have no conception of why my employers imagined I should be able to sell here. The planet's dead. I think I'll watch some local television. Uh oh. No television in my room. I'll go down to the TV viewing lounge in the hotel basement.
>
> *He moves to another area where a MAN watches television.*
>
> The TV is already on. Kirk Douglas in Spartacus. A man is watching . . . I think it's the same man who welcomed me at the desk. . . . Hmmm . . .
>
> *A portion of Spartacus is performed, live: noble Romans with British accents, Kirk, slaves etc. The MAN watching turns off the TV.*
>
> Now he's not looking at the TV any more, but at a picture that hangs on the wall nearby. It's of a young girl. [To MAN] Excuse me, I'd like to pester you with some sales talk if I may.
>
> MAN: Look at her. Carefully. Tell me what you see.
>
> SALESMAN: She looks very pretty . . . and a little sad, Perhaps she lost her . . .
>
> MAN: She was a murderess . . .
>
> (Jenkin 1993, 274–275)

Later in the scene the "live" version of Spartacus returns. Hybrid elements are "made strange" as they are removed from their original contexts. Jenkin's scene clashes theater and film worlds, but also performance styles and genres. Rather than run a tape of the movie, which would not read theatrically, Jenkin "exploits" the theatricality of the *Spartacus* segment with its theatrically historicized costumes and Kirk Douglas impersonator. Jenkin derives humor and whimsy from the juxtapositions of real-time action and virtual time parody; contemporary dress versus "historical" costume; and dramatic versus performative values. As in many of Jenkin's plays, language dialogizes between spatial realities, and across narrative, dramatic, and theatrical elements to create a kind of restless dramaturgy. The *Spartacus* segment, as a "send-up" of the film, primarily serves as a comic marker, although many of the male baby boomers in the audience have special attachment to the film as a cultural icon. The embedding of American cultural icons in his plays is a standard of Jenkin's dramaturgy.

In creating the hybrid play, the playwright serves as conceptualizer/adapter as much as author of materials. While remaining authorial, the playwright may not be the sole generator of textual materials. In the early going, the actual writing process may serve as one of several components, including selection, arrangement, and formulation. It is important for the playwright to recognize this change in function from the sole creative source to the imaginative responder of plural elements. At this stage, *scorer of the performance text* is probably a more appropriate term than *author of the dramatic text*. For example, the first act of Jenkin's *Limbo Tales* involves a live-voiced narrator, material from a cassette tape, and various intrusions from a car radio. These multiple audio sources all take place "on the road," and are demonstrated by the major character's car moving across or up and down a miniature-scale road map. The map follows the various travels of the Professor, as he narrates during his commute to work or to his girlfriend's house. Jenkin formats the right half of each script page with the real-time voice of the professor and the recorded voiceovers; on the left side of the page he scores the road action. The format demonstrates the dialogic interaction between elements. The second act is also scored (and scenically diagrammed) with two speaker cabinets, A and C, placed to either side of the central character, each speaker representing the goings-on in adjacent hotel rooms as amplified voice-overs. Overall, *Limbo Tales* is an aural hybrid combining natural, taped, miked, and telephoned voices.

## HYBRID SOURCES

As instructors of graduate-level playwriting students, Mac Wellman and Len Jenkin require their students to build plays from "stuff." In a workshop given at the University of Alabama, Jenkin assigned students a basic checklist of items that would provide the genesis of a new work: a picture/work of art; a piece of music (to inspire, not underscore, the work);

several tangible items that a character could hold or use; a caption; and a short piece of writing. Some of these items could be utilized in the play, while others served as creative spurs or points of departure. Wellman prods his students to observe beyond their own interests, to "see what's in the newspaper," noting bizarre or interesting events that might prod the imagination. Wellman's fascination with the phenomenon of fur balls in *Sincerity Forever* and other plays stems from an article that demonstrated their potential to shut down a major city's sewage system. Wellman took delight in the serious ramifications of something as benign and innocuous as a fur ball. Moreover, he notes the strong associational and visual values emanating from the term.

Wellman patches various words, phrases, and interesting words into his plays with openness to the direction in which they will take the play. He will also work a word or strategy in more than one play until he exhausts its potential. Wellman's process is both ecological and dialogic: he is not only a great recycler of language, but thrives on the clash or frisson brought on by the juxtapositions of varied elements. Rather than strive for unity, Wellman creates dramaturgical interest through difference and surprise, energizing the gaps between disparate, yet contiguous elements.

In new playwriting, sometimes the frisson between scenes can energize an entire play. The assassination scene at the Armenian-American car dealer's lot in Eric Overmyer's *Dark Rapture* is in its political force and violence unrelated to anything else in the play. Embedded within the structure of the first act and drawn from a real-life account, the scene frames the violence and menace that informs the rest of the play. Dramaturgically anomalous, it places the most intense scene in the play away from the major character, Babcock. Moreover, it raises a thematic, political question that remains unresolved throughout the rest of the play. Interestingly, audiences have found this scene to be the play's most compelling. Its ineluctable, gratuitous force is magnetic, functioning to draw the audience into the thematic implications of the text.

## EXERCISE:
### Conceptualizing the Hybrid Play

The following examples offer some strategies for beginning the hybrid play. The list is open-ended and intended to prompt your imagination to further exploration.

1) Clip quotes from a celebrity or political figure. Use several sources as your guide, enough to create an overall profile of the character.

    a. Establish a well-known historical figure that has some resonance with your main character.

    b. Consider two periods of history in the play: perhaps the present and the period of your historical figure. (Stoppard's *Arcadia*; Jenkin's *My*

*Uncle Sam*; Brenton's *Romans in Britain* offer good models). Scenes may conflate, exist side by side, or be sequential.

   c. Specific objects or props that can be used across historical periods.

   d. Designate some music that somehow informs the piece.

   e. Find a piece of writing that "says" something about the material (for example, quoted material, famous sayings, wise aphorisms, etc.).

COMMENT: Found materials offer convenient sources for the hybrid play. A corollary in the world of art is the assemblage. The Wooster Group uses this method of assemblage to revisit and reexamine historicized texts, behaviors, and performance idioms. The playwright can integrate hybrid structure in various ways. For example, the play may juxtapose characters from film or literary genres against more normative types. Or, several historical periods may be juxtaposed in successive scenes, then converge into one story line. The hybrid is a good vehicle for satire or parody because the form values inherent in a given genre may themselves comment on the material or subject at hand. The appropriation of well-known fairy-tale characters such as the three little pigs or the big bad wolf has obvious implication when positioned against a political troika or fundamentalist preacher, for example.

## JEFFREY JONES AND GRAFTING CONTEXT

Probably the most self-consciously hybrid plays of the new playwriting are written by Jeffrey Jones. His play *Der Inka von Peru* is representative of his "contexting" approach. As a dramaturgical strategy, contexting explores how meaning in language is determined. Mikhail Bakhtin used the term *heteroglossia* to describe how meaning is factored only in the moment of utterance; it is reliant on circumstances, intonation, and past histories. In other words, meaning is mediated through shifting contexts. Five years ago "surfing" referred to the aquatic sport; the term had a specific, context-bound meaning. Now, of course, the word "surfing" has been mediated by its mainstream connotation with the Internet, and its original aquatic referent has been moved to the background. The word *wired* may even have contradictory meanings depending upon context. The variance in connotations, whether from a historical or contemporary perspective, gives words dialogic bounce.

To create this exemplar of contexting, with regard to *Der Inka von Peru*, Jones became a contemporary palimpsest, scraping, lifting, and recycling what had already been spoken. In the play Jones combines soap opera dialogue, quotes uttered by celebrities in popular magazines like *People*, and historical accounts detailing Francesco Pizarro's conquering of the Inca in Peru. Jones grafted sections of found text as a given character's dialogue. These grafted entries offer counterpoint to the author-created dialogue of the other characters; in some cases, the grafted dialogue is the exclusive language spoken by the character. The clash of language sources—banal TV dialogue, celebrity "strips," historicized "lingo" relating to Pizarro, and Jones's self-generated choices—

provides the interest and "meaning" of the play, although meaning itself is indeterminate. Traditional dramaturgical phenomena such as the through line or unity are superseded by the polyvocal clash that propels this hybrid.

While the lifted passages bear no relation to their original context, they are still ensconced within the larger cultural milieu. Dialogism occurs in several ways:

1. Jones establishes an internal dialogism in the script, in which two languages systems operate codependently. Neither is privileged, yet both interact and inform each other. The texturing activates a surface frisson. New playwriting acknowledges that the surface and external form is the site of meaning.

2. Jones allows the "other" to enter into a dialogue with his own creative process of producing language. In traditional playwriting, the playwright feels he has "ownership" of all written materials. New playwriting opens the playwright to how language can be generated in the creation of the script.

3. The "strips of language" operate inside and outside of the play; they are intermittently within and outside the frame of the play. This linguistic phenomenon allows Jones more flexibility in dialogizing between the "found strip" and the actors' interpretation of and response to it.

The beat poet William Burroughs had worked with a similar process in constructing his poems. Burroughs would cut out words from various written sources, then rearrange them in random fashion; this collage effect abstracted the arrangement of words on the page. With Jones, more conscious planning is used to fabricate the script, although the grafting process remains similar.

## BUILDING THE JOURNAL/SCRAPBOOK FROM PASTICHE TO HOMAGE

Some playwrights keep journals, sourcebooks, or scrapbooks, but many of them have a difficult time maintaining the discipline over time. Of the new playwrights, Mac Wellman keeps a journal or scrapbook, not in the soul-searching way but as a compilation of useful materials that can be practically applied. Many of his strange references (his interest in fur balls, or funny words, like *wiggly*), have arisen from the scrapbook. Len Jenkin, on the other hand, finds the discipline of keeping a journal taxing or tedious, and too diverting from the limited time he can spend on his playwriting.

To be effective, the journal should be utilized as the commedia dell'arte actor used the *zibaldoni*—a sourcebook collection of found or created materials that provides fodder for creative and imaginative expression. Consider play building as pastiche, allowing a wide array of sources to enter your journal, and later, your work. This "resourcing" or recycling of found materials into your play is a dialogic strategy, when the "other" is mediated by your own creative and imaginative talents.

You can focus your journal to increase the polyvocal level in your plays. Include foreign literary and conversational references; foreign idioms with interesting sounds; maxims and quotes; peculiarities in regional syntax; wise sayings and rubrics from religions and primitives; "technospeak" from various professions; strange etymologies; proper names of businesses, people, towns, and so on. Graft appropriately into your plays. At other times, the journal will provide the inspiration to begin a play, or answer the riddle to the revision in a play you have shelved. As you build the journal, you are consciously developing your "ear" for language. Moreover, just as the zibaldoni gave strength and endurance to the commedia actor, it provides you, the playwright, with the resources to complete more ambitious projects.

The following exercises should be undertaken at the beginning of the term. The journal should be integrated as much as possible into the student work, or it will become a tiresome appendage.

## EXERCISE:
### Billboarding

The billboarding exercise is an effective way to begin building a journal.

1) Note the billboard and advertising signs between your home and a destination that you frequent regularly, as in a daily commute. Usually, billboards are contracted monthly, so changes occur, particularly around seasonal events. In the journal, jot down slogans, terms, and proper names, dating the entries.

2) You should observe several repeating motifs: the scraping off of the old, the plastering over with the new, the relation between them; when the old begins showing through torn or faded sections.

3) Note how each sign suggests a different thought or action, imposes an outside force on your reality, or suggests you change your life in some way. Note specific phrases.

4) Pay particular attention to *proper* names and key phrases that crystallize a certain phenomenon, or characterize a profession, for example.

5) In the workshop have each participant contribute several slogans, then mix them up and draw them out of a hat, randomly.

6) Brainstorm collectively about play ideas, using other shared slogans and materials, from the participants' lists.

7) Now write a scene or monologue. Utilize phrases, proper names, and conflations to stimulate, augment, or direct a character's internal journey or realization, about some change in her life.

COMMENT: Allow this exercise to run over several months. After all students have compiled a list of items in the journal you will be ready. Proper names, mottoes, and product tag lines lend specificity to time and place as they resonate within a cultural milieu. In the Bible-Belt South, the landscape is laced with "voice-of-god" conflations, directing you to save your soul as you enjoy your Dreamland barbecue. When staggered sequentially, the billboard device can serve as a marker for space and time passages. Read Jenkin's *Limbo Tales* (part 1) and *Dark Ride*, or Wellman's *Whirligig* for further probing of this technique.

This technique is useful in a monologue to establish the dialogic relation between *figure* and *ground*. The *figure* is the character, the *ground* the contextual landscape provided by the passing imagery of the billboards. The spatial/temporal signification is totally created by language. The figure is contextually situated and mediated within the shifting landscape.

### GRAFTING DIALOGUE (FROM FRONT TO FAÇADE)

A related exercise might require accessing quotable material from various sources. Comments from celebrity or political figures are available in magazine interviews, other print media, and on-line sources. You might graft the language of celebrities and politicians because, to a great extent, their language is already "framed," or calculated by publicists toward a particular public reception. The celebrity is "fronting" a certain persona for public consumption: a rapper will front a gangster persona; but even when a "bad" image seems authentic (e.g., that of Tonya Harding or Mike Tyson) the press is framing out particular elements that don't fit the public image. In creating the hybrid play, this *framed* language is then *reframed* within the new context of the play. This doubling strategy foregrounds the language itself, and leads to its further exteriorization and sense of façade.

*Fronts*, a term coined by sociologist-linguist Erving Goffman, describe how the self performs in public, particularly in work or social situations. Language is a major component in presenting a front, as are fashion, grooming, and behavior. The end result is what Goffman termed "impression management," the degree to which the individual controls the signal he is sending. Those signals that are controlled are "given," while others (often more important) are "given off." For example, at the funeral of U.S. commerce secretary Ron Brown, former President Bill Clinton appeared tearful and grieving; a few minutes later, assuming he was off-camera, Clinton was laughing and seemingly carefree as he came down the steps from the church. (A large portion of the public grew cynical of Clinton's "fronted" sincerity as a result of his "given-off" behavior.) Nevertheless, the "fronted" sincerity and grieving were successful frames—managing public impressions of the erstwhile president.

### ROLE-PLAYING

An examination of fronts and impression management will sharpen the playwright's awareness of the relationship between language and behavior. The playwright can then manipulate performative levels throughout the play to achieve variety and surprise. In the hybrid play, some characters will *be* their front; others will offer variance, or be constructed from other strategies. When the front persists as the dominant mode of behavior, it can more accurately be described as a *role*. Role-playing requires a performative, externalized approach to characterization. Linguistically, role-playing relies upon the coded speech strategies discussed in the previous chapter. Role-playing has varied applications in the new playwriting. Len Jenkin describes his conception for *Poor Folk's Pleasure* as a "theater piece for five to seven performers. These performers take on a variety of roles" (Jenkin 1996, San Francisco). In *Poor Folk's Pleasure*, the concept begins with the actor *as* performer, rather than the notion of a character who performs several roles. Its ensemble orientation bulks roles to fit the strengths and interests of the performers involved.

Another example of role-playing occurs when a character assumes a different front depending upon the circumstances in the play. The character may assume a part in an acted-out sequence in the play (a play within the play) or perform a given role as the script demands. Jenkin's *Pilgrims of the Night* is an example of the latter. Playwrights can utilize role-playing and its essential theatricality to explore options that are performative rather than psychological. This fuller palette can be particularly effective in comedy, where characters are forced to perform unlikely or awkward roles. In the new playwriting, role-playing is usually a facet of the multivocal character. For example, the charlatan Crowsfoot, in Wellman's *Harm's Way*, drops in and out of his role as a carnival pitchman. The tension between the character's and the role's level of language creates a significant level of interest, as it layers several voices and performance approaches for the actor.

Playwrights should begin by exploring fronts or façades in terms of speech and behavior. As you become more confident in delineating these levels, you can integrate role-playing as a strategy. The difference between a *front* and a *role* is one of degree. A front may occur over one or several beats, while a role persists as a dominant strategy across beat segments or entire scenes. These explorations will increase your dialogic, multivocal instincts as they afford you new techniques. As you begin to sense the layering possibilities you can experiment with scenes within scenes, or the play within a play.

## EXERCISE:
### Fronts and Façade

Incorporate media clippings into the building of a character. There are some issues this process raises:

1) Language as front or façade versus language that drops the front.

2) The playwright as collector of language. In a manner similar to visual artists who keep examples of other artists' fragments (a hand, a tree, a piece of fruit, and so on).

Fronts and façades can be differentiated by intention. A front represents playing the role well: dressing appropriately for a profession, or behavior apropos to accepted protocols. On the other hand, the façade is a misrepresentation of self, usually intending to deceive for some gain, or to further one's interest. This exercise works best when one character is dominant, the other subordinate, or where a character gains status through an effective front or façade.

1) Character A uses language and certain front behaviors to create an impression for Character B. Language is used to intimidate, manipulate, make a sale, and so on.

2) Graft strips of language from your journal that work appropriately.

3) Character B attempts to crack the façade or front of B.

4) Character A goes to extreme lengths to maintain front. Graft in quotes from your journal that are effective.

5) Conclude scene with a clear idea of who wins and loses.

## FABLE AND STORY FORMS

Story forms such as the fable, parable, fairy tale, folk tale, tall tale, or legend foreground plot devices that are familiar to audiences. A fable or parable can be condensed structurally, either in part or in whole, then adapted to whatever setting the playwright desires. The recognizable structure informs the material and affects the audience's perception in some way. A dialogic interaction is engaged between the original and the adaptation. This self-reflexive quality is metadramatic, whether the story form is used partially (e.g., the play within a play) or wholly, providing the structural format for the entire play. As a metadramatic tool, story forms can enhance the polyvocal potential of the play's script. As such, they offer the playwright a range of options in manufacturing the hybrid play. Len Jenkin's *Country Doctor* is derived from a story by Franz Kafka that the original author had adapted from a common folktale. The former adaptation is used as a play within a play, whereas the latter (Kafka by way of a folktale) provides the basic format and storyline of Jenkin's play. Eric Overmyer has assiduously adapted and transported Henrik Ibsen's *Peer Gynt*, based on a Norwegian folktale, to the Pacific Northwest. His recent play, commissioned by the Seattle Repertory Theatre, is titled *Alki*.

The young playwright gains technique by studying and then adhering to a given structural format. Poring over story forms, which tend to be brief, enables the playwright to quicken and facilitate his sense of plot, since most short forms feature a taut story line without extraneous materials. Contemporizing the story line will bring about a dialogic tension between the original and the updated version. The treatment of the materials can range from parodic to straightforward.

47

CHAPTER 3 POLYVOCALITY AND THE HYBRID PLAY

## CONDENSING STRUCTURE: THE QUEST ("JOURNEY PLAY")

Certain story forms are repeated enough so that their structures suggest a model or paradigm. One such model will be applied in the following exercise. The quest has its origins in Greek myths, medieval romances, and the Spanish picaresque novel. The quest provides a strong structural basis that includes a central character with an unwavering desire to achieve a goal; a journey that includes an increasingly foreboding series of obstacles or tests that need to be overcome; a definite and desirable destination that is earmarked at the beginning of the quest; a love interest who may be the "destination," serve as "guide," or create the sense of romantic longing (the girl or boy back home); a guide, or omniscient character who unlocks secrets along the way; and characters who provide comic or anecdotal relief. Once the quest is achieved, harmony and balance are restored.

Examples of embedded quest structures in new playwriting include, among others: Jenkin's *My Uncle Sam* and *Dark Ride* (discussed at length later in this book). The motif of traveling to seek fortune or to change one's lot is at the heart of the American psyche and is personified in numerous character types from the historic Yankee and pioneer types to the con men and salesman that frequent Jenkin's plays.

## EXERCISE:
### The Ten-to-Fifteen-Minute Play (The Quest)

The objective will be to write a ten-to-fifteen-minute play utilizing a specific structural format. The configuration of the quest follows three overall stages. The tripartite structure closely mirrors the rites of passage sequence established by the cultural anthropologist Arnold van Gennep.

1) *Separation:* Some separation from family, homeland, or familiar moorings is required.
   a. The separation can be relatively brief in duration.
   b. The main character senses some dilemma that must be addressed. This requires a journey of some sort. Typically, the character is a "fish out of water."
   c. Consider a polyvocal landscape with varied ecologies (see below).
2) *Transition:* This is the longest of the three stages, and the most dramatic: a goal is sought, obstacles are dealt with, and so on. It is marked by uncertainty, negativity, the strange or bizarre, the character's addressing not only the goal but the self as character.
   a. Consider omniscient characters, guides, and fellow travelers. Each has

a specific front or façade. Use your scrapbook to define characters in language.

  b. There is an increasing level of obstacles and frustrations for the major character. Develop adversaries from literary or visual sources. Consider icons.

  c. Alter the dimension of time at some point in this phase.

3) *Reintegration:* The goal of the quest is achieved, a new status for the character results, and there is a celebration, and restoration of (or establishment of a new sense of) balance and equilibrium.

This exercise is suited to the short play format. The playwright will gain skill in condensing and distilling essential story elements. Then, there is the advantage of reading aloud as many of the new plays as possible within the time constraints of the workshop. If possible, playwrights should strive to condense this exercise into a ten-minute-play format (an increasingly popular format for play contests). In the ten-minute format, the tests or obstacles appear quickly and are dealt with in as few beats as possible. The quest can be successfully compressed if the playwright first sketches out the desired end, goal, or destination. In the ten-minute play, I advise writing the ending first, and allowing maximum flexibility along the way. Most ten-minute plays suffer from the lack of a satisfying conclusion or in fact are simply scenes that do not resolve effectively. The strict parameters of this format can be realized by firming up the end at the beginning. Since the final phase in this tripartite structure is reintegration, the nature of the ending is more easily resolved.

Along the journey, explore the nature of the major character through the series of obstacles that confront her; vary the obstacles. Strive for a unique theatrical landscape, and consider alterations in time as crucial. Adhere to the tripartite structure, marking the major moves from separation to transition to reintegration.

COMMENT: Many playwrights have difficulty resolving their plays. *Writing the end* is a pragmatic strategy and can free the playwright from worrying about closure. I remind the playwright that the end can always be adjusted; think of the end as a flexible target that can be moved or removed. Writing the end several times will prove to be a useful focusing strategy. The end should encapsulate the overall thematic statement of the play.

## HYBRID VARIATIONS: SPACE, TIME, AND DIALOGIC CLASH

The hybrid allows significant latitude in establishing spatial/temporal parameters. No longer locked into the fixed rules determined by period and convention, the new playwright is flexible to juxtapose, deconstruct, or reassemble space and time. As we saw in chapter 1, Eric Overmyer's *On the Verge* subverts the conventional guidelines for a fin-de-siècle period play. Paula Vogel's *How I Learned to Drive* fragments the sense of a linear time narrative by moving back and forth from "present" to "past." The clashes among language, action, and context in these plays energizes a dynamic that propels them forward in a way that disorients the viewer. The character, as agent of language and action, is compelled to display each moment in all of its complexity—with texture, transparency, and wonder.

Playwrights can open themselves to this new dramaturgy by shifting the spatial/temporal context of the characters. When language alters space and time, established moorings are loosened, as conventions are interrupted or displaced. The characters are decentered (as is the audience) in a vertiginous environment. This decentering forces the character to make sense of an ever-changing theatrical landscape. The changing environmental factors create an interactive spatial/temporal field that is a dynamic contrast to conventional dramaturgy. It's a different way of "taking your characters to the wall"—the core of good playwriting, according to Romulus Linney. Linney implores student playwrights to make their characters struggle, to confront dangerous, fantastic, or outrageous circumstances.

## CONCEPTUALIZING THE SPATIAL/TEMPORAL HYBRID

Spatial and temporal options are often overlooked in the conceptualization of the play. Allow the imagination to explore the possibilities. For example, what does a shifting spatial/historical context suggest about language? The idea is that contexting allows environmental or historical circumstances to weigh heavily on the action. Some British playwrights have exploited this ground successfully: Howard Brenton's *Romans in Britain* juxtaposes the Roman Empire's occupation of the British Isles with the British occupation of Ireland. Tom Stoppard's *Arcadia* utilizes an early-nineteenth-century country manor to juxtapose scenes set in the period with those featuring present-day occupants of the house.

Expanding the spatial/temporal fields also engages the question of scale. Wellman has experimented with juxtaposing our world with other worlds in several plays. Constance Congdon conflated alien/human characters in *Tales of the Lost Formicans*. The use of multiple landscapes, of bridging cultures and worlds, opts for a larger concept of scale. Bonnie Marranca's *Ecologies of Theater* posits that the future of theater lies in its ability to incorporate this multilandscaped, globalized presence of cultures and theatrical systems on stage. Robert Wilson's "theater of images" has realized this view to an extent, and his hybrid model, which focuses on the mise-en-scène rather than the script, has its corollary in the new playwriting. Wilson's polyvocal theatrical vocabulary blends American, European, and Oriental stage traditions, a performative strategy utilized in Overmyer's *In Perpetuity throughout the Universe*. Overmyer integrates elements of the Peking Opera into his dramaturgy. Wilson agonizes over his storyboard sequences, while Len Jenkin reshuffles blocks of text in his revision process. Whereas Wilson emphasizes gesture and movement, the new playwrights place a stronger formal emphasis on language. Both experiment with formal qualities of juxtaposition, repetition, and patterning.

There is an underlying trust of theatricality that supersedes traditional dramatic procedures. Seen in this light of the external, the plastic, and the theatrical, the new playwright is more like an auteur/director than a traditional dramatist. Here are the shared aesthetic principles at work:

1. The juxtaposition of opposites.
2. The fragmentation, dissolving, or deconstruction of linear time.
3. The recontextualizing of historical systems.
4. The dynamics of scale.

Wilson has been successful at realizing his experiments on a grand scale. Generally, the avant-garde has been relegated to the lofts and small theaters, and this fate has dogged the language playwrights as well. Perhaps Wilson's large-scale productions (consider *Einstein on the Beach, Ka Mountain, CIVIL WarS, The Forest*) offer a more ambitious paradigm to the language playwright in search of the larger venue and audience. Marranca states it rather eloquently in discussing the virtues of Wilson's *The Forest* when she writes, "The biodiversity of Wilson's theater lyricizes both space and time. All species—flora, fauna, human—enliven narrative in this advance stage of theatrical evolution. He frames their adaptability and process of hybridization in scenes that visualize the insistent nature/culture theme as a structural feature of the work. If Wilson loves the city, he needs woods. What is a theatrical landscape but a species of desire?" (Marranca *The Forest*, 38).

## EXERCISE:
### Spatial/Temporal Juxtaposition

The work of Robert Wilson opens up the potential to create plays on a grander scale—through globalized theatrical and dramaturgical forms. Wilson's polyvocal principles and strategies can be adapted by the playwright in the conceptualization of the play. After brainstorming about an entire piece, write several scenes. It may be helpful to work with images or thumbnail sketches. You can even consider elements of language and narrative as large component blocks.

1) Consider some broad cultural/historical event (à la Wilson).
   a. What figures from other eras can be juxtaposed?
2) Articulate a diverse sense of landscapes: city, country, forest, oceans, and so on.
   a. Consider how the shifting landscape alters context of character and language.
3) Establish a narrative center for the piece.
   a. For example, look at the way Laurie Anderson and other performance artists have reinterpreted *Moby Dick*. The text is a point of departure.

4) Embrace a variety of languages, dialects, or speech genres in your consideration of character.

    a. The character may have a performative basis: Noh drama, commedia dell'arte, circus performing, and so on.

5) Consider in this conceptualizing stage the possibilities for clash, contrast, and interaction among the various elements.

6) Rough out a pattern of progression that relies on serial juxtaposition, direct opposition, simultaneity, and/or repetitions.

    a. Consider single-, dual-, or multifocus scenes.

7) Write three or four scenes altering the sequence in order to explore the various configurative possibilities.

The consideration of the spatial/temporal dynamic opens the playwright to thematic concerns that can bring politics into the mix. It is a potential strategy for the committed playwright, who wants to address ideological concerns on a large scale. Guillermo Gomez-Peña's *New World Border,* for example, exploits the hybridization of languages, landscapes, and icons that are at the essence of the Mexican-American experience. Peña's language, in fact, becomes the conflated hybrid of Spanish and English that is known as "Spanglish."

## HYBRID FUTURES

The hybrid has become the accepted format for the performance artists, who present multiart productions in which textuality exists simultaneously with other elements. Traditional playwriting has been resistant to the hybrid, at least in terms of pedagogy if not practice. New playwriting, with its conflation of the performative and the polyvocal, offers the playwright excellent models of hybridization. Ironically, as the hybrid becomes more and more the norm in contemporary theater, it may eventually become classified as a genre with its own subcategories and headings.

# 4

## The Theatricality of Character

### ESTABLISHING NEW APPROACHES TO CHARACTER

A nonpsychological, external basis for character distinguishes the new dramaturgy from conventional approaches. Traditionally, American playwrights have conceived characters based on realistic, psychologically oriented models. There are two primary reasons:

1. Since actors are trained in method-based or Stanislavskian approaches suited to the realistic style, playwrights have responded pragmatically by writing plays for this idiom, thus privileging the internal over the external style.

2. Television and film continue to have a pervasive influence on dramatic styles and approaches.

Prevailing conditions necessitate communicating ideas effectively and quickly, and as a result, the shorthand code of the actors' studio has been established as the dominant language in American theater. Playwrights and play developers have adopted the terms of the actor: *through line, arc, subtext, fleshing-out, intention, obstacle,* and *conflict* are as solvent for the actor as they are for the playwright. Because the central character-driven play still reigns as the model (if not in reality), the often heard "Whose play is it?" is a familiar criticism of new work. Fleshing out a character works for the playwright whose characterization is too thin, but also for the actor who must manufacture "back story" to create more resonance in the "moment." A playwright sharpens a character's intention by eliminating digressions in the script, while the actor focuses on clearer choices in behavior. This shared shorthand is effective in the development of a traditional character, whether for stage or screen. However, an entrenched code is resistant to change and innovation. Moreover, because creating theater involves multiple collaborators, change comes slowly. To a significant extent, theater jargon, or "play speak," has stymied further growth and exploration in playwriting approaches.

Problems emerge when traditional terms are applied to new approaches. Because the old terms do not quite fit, we assume something is wrong with the play. Thus, in play development or rehearsal there is a dilution of the new into old familiar bottles. "Talk back" sessions after a reading almost always bear this out, particularly when the discussion turns to matters of character. When the playwright achieves the stature and publication history of Mac Wellman, Len Jenkin, or Eric Overmyer, he may have directors who "know what they're getting into," but what about other collaborators, from designers to business managers and, of course, the ultimate collaborator, the critic? New playwriting is at a disadvantage because there is no shared language that exists for discussing multivocal, carnivalesque, or equivocal characters. To assess the character Girl in Mac Wellman's *Whirligig* based on the traditionalist Sam Smiley's six crucial qualities of character—volition, stature, interrelation, attractiveness, credibility, and clarity (Smiley 1971, 92)—is impossible and irrelevant. In his revolt against established norms, Wellman's characters actually work against the notions of an integral character with "core" essentials. Does the playwright simply sprinkle in a bit of interrelation or volition? How organic is that? In striving for clarity of character, many playwrights will overboil expository material and suffer rigor mortis in the process. The playwright who is exploring Smiley's text needs to know that his dramaturgical aesthetic is based on the representational or classical premise that character must be considered as an integral whole. With such widespread entrenchment of terms and constructs, it is important to construct a new idiom that will accurately or persuasively represent a different premise of character.

An extensive checklist can numb the mind as readily as focus it. Moreover, not many playwrights are disposed to revising characterizations according to checklists. Experienced playwrights know that revising, or "building-in," character traits alters other factors and relationships in a play.

## BEYOND THE PROTAGONIST-CENTERED PLAY

The protagonist tradition solves a basic problem of playwrights. Unlike some literary forms, such as the novel, a play happens before a live audience. With a single character at the center of the play, the playwright provides the audience with a clear identity to root for or against, and a journey that can be easily followed. The action of the play is more tautly compressed if a clear structural network of relations is established from the top character down. On the other hand, the playwright who establishes several characters at the core of the play continually faces the problem of focus. Multiple protagonists may blur the central action of the play. A strong central figure focuses a play, as the instrumental soloist focuses a concerto. We may admire the supporting players, but only insofar as they support and enhance the efforts of the soloist/protagonist. A limited scope facilitates a unified vision. Quite simply, by linking the central action to the agency of one major character, the playwright achieves a measure of coherence.

Most playwriting instructors and manuals recommend a strong protagonist at the center of the play, which answers the frequently raised question of play developers, "Whose play is it?" Yet it is not the appropriate question to ask about Mac Wellman's *Three Americanisms* that presents three characters constructed as variable discourses rather than psychologically rounded individuals. Further, the canon of Len Jenkin, with the possible exceptions of his adaptations of *Candide* and *Country Doctor*, resists the strictly protagonist-centered play. Even *Kid Twist*, named after the central character, contains divergent twists that veer the play in several directions. The dialogic move to polyvocality works against the unilateral focus of the protagonist-centered play.

Nevertheless, there are several protagonist-based plays that combine elements of the new playwriting with the unifying principle of the single character. Eric Overmyer's *Dark Rapture* places the feckless, middle-aged male character Babcock at the center of the action. Overmyer's adaptation of Ibsen's *Peer Gynt*, entitled *Alki*, sets the protagonist in the Pacific Northwest. Len Jenkin's *Country Doctor*, adapted from Kafka's novel, situates the Doctor as the center of focus. In the anthology *Anti-Naturalism* (Gould 1989) Richard Nelson's *Bal* and Craig Lucas's *Reckless* posit a central character's journey as the major action. These plays use the protagonist as a unifying device while experimenting with some of the exercises and concepts brought forth in this text. Thus, the problem is not the central character model, but rather the tyranny of this format that is considered the standard, particularly in the assessment of new work.

## MOVING FROM THE ARISTOTELIAN MODEL

Although Aristotle was writing about tragic form, his *Poetics* still remains the putative criteria for most dramatic forms. Aristotle's focus on the dramatic rather than the theatrical privileged the literary dimension. He relegated spectacle to the lowest rung on the hierarchical ladder, below plot, character, thought, diction or language, and music. Historically, for dramatic works to break into the canon literary values needed to be emphasized while theatricality was diminished in importance. Moreover, the advent of psychology and psychoanalysis in the nineteenth century revolutionized notions of the personality. Over the past one hundred years, character has evolved as a manifestation of these nontheatrical rubrics. The popular pantomimic and comedic traditions in European theater that have long emphasized an external approach to character have never been a powerful component of American dramaturgy. Thus, the current profile of dramatic character blends Aristotelian agency or choice, psychological protocols, and thematic considerations that arise from given cultural conditions into an organic whole.

Even a strict Aristotelian such as David Mamet laments the speculative nature of dramatic character: "How equally foolish to wonder where Oedipus went to college, or if Big Daddy is the Kind of Guy Who Might Play Golf, or, finally, to vitiate any of the carefully constructed problems of the play by unconsciously positing and then accepting the existence of THE CHARACTER, as if the character were something other than a series of actions delineated by the playwright" (1990, 38). Indeed, as a common practice in development of new work, playwrights will be asked by the director or actors to provide "back story" to characters they have written. These fictional biographies flesh out the dialogue on the page. Playwrights are compelled by traditional protocols to answer all actors' questions regarding intention and motivation. What is lost in these extrapolations of the "internal life" is any sense of the character's theatricality.

A broader dramaturgical view, which includes popular forms such as vaudeville, melodrama, the musical, commedia dell'arte, and pantomime, demonstrates how core theatricality can provide the root of character. New playwrights, in styles and formats as diverse as that of Suzan-Lori Parks from that of Len Jenkin, build upon a theatrical construct of character that is shaped externally through their patented use of language. In other words, the new playwriting combines a novel concept of how language and theatricality can combine in the shaping of character.

## THE CARNIVALESQUE CHARACTER

Mikhail Bakhtin's dialogism is related to his influential construction of the carnivalesque—a period of transformation and overturning of societal norms. Bakhtin described carnival, traditionally the period between Epiphany and Ash Wednesday, as a time when normative functions were suspended, and serious culture was turned upside down—anything was possible.

Carnival promotes the strange juxtaposition of events and characters, and delights in the unexpected and the magical. As such, the carnivalesque offers a metaphor for character in the new playwriting. The carnivalesque character uses the gestural body, delights in vivid and sometimes ambiguous speech, and is often at the margins of the mainstream. The carnivalesque allows for sudden turns and identity transformations (see the discussion of Overmyer's equivocal character in chapter 6). Most significantly, the carnivalesque character is an ensemble character playing roles in the larger scheme of the play. There is rarely the sense of one character dominating the action.

## CONTINUUMS OF CHARACTERIZATION

Most playwrights following prescribed methods of characterization will establish characters along psychological lines based on need, desire, or goals. As a result, playwrights avoid conceptualizing along the lines of a showing, gestural character, deeming the thinking or emoting character more worthy of attention. Playwrights write these characters "off the line" (as indirect, oblique, implied), allowing the actor significant latitude in forming a subtextual approach. The more the subtextual level of character interiority is featured, the stronger the matrix—the actor has become the character (see chapter 11 for more on matrixing). On the other hand, new playwriting tends to be "on the line" (as in, say what you mean), and when it isn't, the formulation is more often an ironic "take" rather than internalized subtextuality. As a result, the matrix between actor and character flips, since the writing style demands a more externalized performance approach. Plays like Len Jenkin's *Poor Folk's Pleasure* encourage a broader, more gestural and visceral performance style than the method-based norm. Table 4.1 delineates several differences between the traditional and new writing approach from the actor's view.

**TABLE 4.1  Traditional versus New Approaches to Character**

| ACTOR BECOMES CHARACTER | ACTOR PERFORMS CHARACTER |
| --- | --- |
| emotional, psychological identification | external, gestural projection |
| integral traits; one character | contradictory traits; one actor may play several characters |
| matrixed (actor hidden) | dematrixed (actor exposed) |
| subtextual | surface textuality |
| off the line | on the line |
| interiority | virtuosity |

While this table is by no means exhaustive it illustrates differences that establish what the new playwriting is all about. Wellman posits that any poetic or language-oriented style will demand a heightened performance style. Overmyer links himself more to the poet/playwrights of the classicistic eras than to the canonized godheads of the American stage, Tennessee Williams, Arthur Miller, and Eugene O'Neill. The playwright needs to understand that the demands on the actor will differ in new writing. Nonetheless, I stress that there is a broad range in this continuum, so that the actor playing in Wellman's *Murder of Crows* may opt for a more externalized approach than those approaching Jenkin's *5 of Us*, or his recent *Like I Say*. In this regard, several second-generation playwrights (e.g., Neena Beber, Matthew Maguire) of the so-called language playwrights school can be seen to bridge the internal and external approaches often in the same play.

## THEMATIC-BASED CHARACTERIZATION

Situated in the gap between traditional approaches to character and external theatrical approaches (discussed below) is the thematic charac-

ter. In *Angels in America* playwright Tony Kushner blends a fairly traditional aesthetic of characterization with thematic ideas by shifting the balance
between the character's emotions and rhetorical impulses that purport an
ideological message. Kushner describes himself as a committed playwright—by definition, one who advances a political message. The playwright committed to a cause walks the tightrope between advancing the
action and advancing the agenda. In *Angels* (parts 1 and 2), the line
between what a character thinks and what Kushner feels about an issue is
blurred. Indeed, there are moments in *Perestroika* (the angel monologue),
or in *Millennium Approaches* where rhetorical monologizing overwhelms
(or at least stresses) the dramaturgy. These speeches cause a caesura in the
pull or forward dynamic of the play, foregrounding theme over the agency
of character. This has to be handled deftly, or results will appear heavy-
handed or clunky. In general, American audiences prefer getting their
political opinions elsewhere. The exception may be theaters that have an
audience constituency with shared values, often representing a specific
cultural, racial, or ethnic group. For example, New York City's WOW Café
produces shows by and about feminist culture for an intended female
audience (the acronym WOW stands for World of Women). In Britain, on
the other hand, the tradition of political playwriting has been much more
politicized through playwrights like Howard Brenton and David Edgar.
David Hare, in 1999 the most produced British playwright on Broadway,
began his career by successfully integrating politics with traditional characterization. However, in 1999, Broadway audiences packed in to see *Blue
Room*, an erotic adaptation of Arthur Schnitzler's *Le Ronde*, which starred
celebrity Nicole Kidman in various stages of undress.

Aristotle discussed the tragic play without character—what we might
call melodrama. If character represents agency, or choice, the play without character is like a nineteenth-century melodrama in which evil versus
good is personified in the villain and hero. Thematic-based characterization, which has become a mainstay of many contemporary playwrights,
"telegraphs" a certain thematic message or point-of-view from the playwright without fully integrating it in the aesthetic construct. The adept
playwright uses techniques of humor, irony, or song to get the message
across. Bertholt Brecht remains the master ideologue because he knew
that the message had to be aestheticized and theatricalized through
music, poetry, or well-known forms like the fable and allegory.

## DIALOGIC VERSUS DIALECTIC

Should playwrights disguise thematic concerns so as to avoid "telegraphing" a message? Perhaps this is one dilemma of so-called serious theater.
If the play or major character represents an ideology or belief system, discovery becomes less interesting or aesthetically challenging since it is a
given circumstance. The early plays of Heiner Müller, a force in the

European avant-garde of the 1970s and '80s, represent a move from a post-Brechtian epic theater to a dialectical theater in which character represents a given ideological point of view. Müller's early plays, written within the strictures of East German censorship codes, contain proletarian characters drawn along ideological lines, representations of the dialectical forces at work within the communist system. These committed plays serviced common societal ends, similar to the socialist realism plays of the 1920s Soviet Union. In his later works, Müller evinces the mature synthesis of thought with theatricality, and these works invite the director to explore a broader landscape of character. Müller collides place, genre, and era in the dialogic, rather than dialectical sense. In Müller's signature plays, like *Hamletmachine*, he leaves it to the audience to glean a difficult or conflicting message—one that resists telegraphing. The dialogic is interested in establishing the opposing forces with ends that are less determinate than those of dialectical theater. Dialectical theater attempts to arrive at a specific determined end as the result of conflict between forces, one of which is both privileged and predetermined. This strategy leads to a didactic theater and is related to a committed political or social praxis. Probably the most effective and successful venue for didactic theater today is children's theater: we want our children to hear positive messages and develop caring, humanistic values. Moreover, children's theater allows for the most innovative flight of the imagination. Small wonder that Jenkin, Wellman, Overmyer, Congdon, and other new playwrights have all written successful plays for the childrens' theater.

Two British plays widely produced in the 1990s have reflected a kind of thematic/character dialogism. Characters in Tom Stoppard's *Arcadia* "instruct" the audience how to interpret what the play is doing. The rhetorical mode of character, which emphasizes teaching or persuasion, takes over. Yet, as embedded in its dialogic structure, *Arcadia* reflects the juxtaposition of historical eras and discourses. David Edgar's polyvocal play *Pentecost* explores the tumult around a Giotto fresco found in a medieval church. The church has just been reconverted within a postcommunist Eastern European country, which is overrun with foreign entrepreneurs, prostitutes, and displaced individuals. The dialogism between language, cultures, and political forces creates a multilayered, thematic landscape that is reflected in the dramaturgical structure. Edgar confirms Bonnie Marranca's premise (1996) that this multilayered, theatricalized relationship between cultures, voices, and themes is the future of drama.

## SATIRICAL APPROACHES

Some plays advance a politically unpopular message through a character. Wallace Shawn's risky decision to place an apologist for Nazism at the center of *Aunt Dan and Lemon* provoked audiences and created some outrage. The primary interest in the play was its eerily ironic treatment vis-à-vis the

Nazi phenomenon. Was this satire? Did the playwright support these positions? Mac Wellman, in *Murder of Crows*, deals with the problems of toxic waste in a play that is more blatantly satirical—acid rain actually falls on characters in raincoats and hats. Satire embodies thematic intent within genre. It is more theatrical than most committed plays, because it relies upon the exaggeration and typification of characters. In *Sincerity Forever*, Wellman ridicules the Ku Klux Klan through repetition and silly wordplay. Wellman's *7 Blowjobs* offers an incisive satire on scandal cover-ups at the senatorial level. Wellman cloaks serious issues in bizarre humor or silliness, using comic strategies to veil his political beliefs.

The challenge for playwrights, then, is to recenter the thematic character within the theatrical aesthetic. Rather than foreground a sociocultural message that a character posits or volunteers, playwrights must establish characters along theatrical or external lines whereby the core theatricality of the character balances or juxtaposes the ideological framework that the playwright wishes to establish. As Brecht said, theater *theaters* everything. We need to explore that which is inherently theatrical for its potential to transform the theater. What appears strikingly new in ways reformulates solid theatrical practices of the past.

## TOWARD A THEATRICAL CONSTRUCTION OF CHARACTER

*PREMISE: Theatricality supersedes the dramatic function as the root of characterization in the new dramaturgy.*

Theatricality defines a self-evident condition of the theater that distinguishes it from literature: the live actor who inhabits character, the actor-audience dynamic, the living gesture, and the visceral and evanescent engagement with the collective audience. Theatricality is about what "works" as theater: the plasticity of language, the immediacy of action, the spatial/temporal imagination, and the virtuosic performance. It is about surprise, wonder, and daring, the reckless, the strange, the visually arresting, and the erotic. The playwright integrates or juxtaposes these elements, constructing character as an aesthetic—not representational or thematic—construct. Developing characters from a theatrical aesthetic rather than a psychological base represents a fundamental shift in the assumptions behind good playwriting.

Playwrights, but also dramaturgs and critics, need to recognize that this root shift changes the dramaturgical standards as they are currently applied. Terms like *conflict, through line, arc,* and *subtext* may be relegated to a subordinate position or be less viable. Recognizing the theatrical dimension as an essential component of characterization will revitalize the art of playwriting.

### The Twelve Tenets of Theatrical Characters

1. **Characters are larger than life, often exaggerated, extreme or heightened beyond the normative.** As such, they rip the reader/audience out of

the comfort zone of predictability. Consider, for example, the character Gogol in the opening scene of Len Jenkin's play by the same name:

> GOGOL: Welcome, I am Gogol. I am not lights and shadow. I am not the mountain or the lake below. I am not a stick, not the ashes, I am not an ape. I am not a hummingbird. I was born a man, and that has not changed, no matter what I do.
>
> I am not mother, I am not teacher, I am not a hero or a thief. I do not make paper snowflakes or count stars. I am not funny, I am not poisonous. I am not joking. I am Gogol, cloud and mud. I am extinct. I run the roller-coaster at night. I am a go-go dancer and a fool.
>
> I have an excellent notion of why you've come here. Let me assure you that each thing you expect to happen will happen. And less. And more. I am Gogol. Believe that, and I will tell you another one.
>
> (Wellman 1985, Gogol, 5)

In this opening monologue, Jenkin establishes an obviously heightened character based in negatives and absences (what he is not, and what he does not do) before he identifies himself. Even Gogol's identity is problematic ("Believe that, and I will tell you another one"). Gogol, in fact, is not actually based on the Russian playwright. He becomes a loose cannon, a self-deprecating oddball who if nothing else is unpredictable. As the playwright, Jenkin demonstrates a confidence in his directness and clarity of purpose. While unpredictable, the character is risky, edgy, and sharply drawn.

**2. Characters are formed externally rather than internally.** External form suggests that there is no subtextual basis of character. An analogy could be made to the masked character whereby the subjective and the psychological are de-emphasized and the gestural is heightened.

**3. Characters can be inserted for texture or strange juxtaposition, or to create a counterdynamic in the play.** For example, an eighteenth-century character Capability Brown is inserted in Len Jenkin's *My Uncle Sam*, presenting an iconic strangeness juxtaposed to the central action. Capability Brown serves a dramaturgic rather than dramatic function.

**4. Characters are drawn from a number of source materials, not simply imitations of life, or to service familiar roles (fathers, wayward sons, and so on).** As such, they are given the capacity for heightened language. Often marginalized, these characters find their lot through, and in, language, *as if language in new playwriting substitutes for traditional character traits and subtextual concerns.* Beyond his characters with lost dreams (see chapter 5), Len Jenkin draws characters from pop icons like comic books, hack detective novels of the 1940s, and carnival hucksters; Jeffrey Jones lifts pop celebrities and juxtaposes them to historical personae in strange combi-

**5. Characters are seldom built along thematic concerns or to forward an agenda in a play.** To this extent, new playwrights suffered during the "politically correct" eighties and nineties by not allowing their work to be appropriated by any special interest groups. Critics, as well as theater insiders, jump in on this bandwagon: Suzan-Lori Parks has been criticized for her characters and plays not supporting traditional black themes. Critics (and, it would seem, most dramaturgs and literary managers) implicitly prefer characters to represent thematic values, to serve as mirrors or spokespersons of or for popular culture. Perhaps a major reason that Overmyer's *Native Speech* went a long time without a production was due to the presence of the irreverent character Hungry Mother. Here was a disc jockey that substituted a "drugs on the street report" for the normative weather or stock report. Hungry Mother is a white character imitating a kind of black dialect. Potential producers would be wary of offending the conservative Right while the politically correct, left-leaning liberal groups would consider the use of black dialect by a white disc jockey an explicit form of racism.

**6. Characters transform, change, fragment, or deconstruct.** There is often a tension between the performer and character in these plays. In Overmyer's *The Heliotrope Bouquet,* Scott Joplin's wife transforms back and forth to and from his lover, becoming what I discuss in chapter 6 as the *equivocal character.* Here, a character dynamically serves as the theatrical corollary to Joplin's thought processes. Overmyer demonstrates how a theatrical stage device can underscore a thematic, psychological concern by projecting an absent personality on someone present. By actually showing the change in front of the audience, Overmyer makes the actor (and costumer) work to achieve a memorable theatrical "moment."

**7. Characters may be unnamed or nonhuman.** In Wellman's monologue plays, such as *Terminal Hip* or *Three Americanisms,* there are no character titles presented; rather, the audience formulates an image of the character based on the language and performance choices of the performer. For example, Mel Gussow's *New York Times* review of *Three Americanisms* described three very individualized characters that in the script are blandly listed as Man 1, Man 2, and Woman. Gussow "created" the individuals through their use of language, and by their presence and dress onstage (fronts). Wellman has used actors to portray aliens, crows, dogs—even shadows. Jenkin's use of props and animals adds a sense of charm and humor to the beginning of *Gogol.* The stage directions read, *A giant turtle enters, moving very slowly. It has a small saddle on its back. As it passes behind Gogol, he mounts it, facing the audience. The turtle never varying its pace carries him off.* (Wellman 1985, *Gogol,* 7).

**8. Grotesque and/or grossly satiric portrayals define characters that advance causes or serve as representatives of maligned groups.** There is no attempt to cure societal ills through the characters serving as moral agents. Nor does new writing draw sympathy directly to any of these characters. For example, the eccentric father/victim of toxic waste in Wellman's *Murder of Crows* seems eerily synergized within his sulfurous, contaminated world. Wellman's political satire *7 Blowjobs* presents Senator Armitage as a feckless, grotesque politician.

**9. Characters are archetypes.** Characters are larger than life, represent the ideal of their type, or assume an aspect of American mythos. They stake out territory that suggests specific actions and traits. In some cases, this is evident in the naming of characters: in Jenkin's *Dark Ride* The Translator, Deep Sea Ed, and The Thief could be considered archetypal characters. Dr. Mesmer, based on the inventor of hypnosis, in *Gogol* becomes the self-stated archetype of the charlatan, even drawing the analogy between the snake "wine" cures and his bogus remedies.

**10. Characters are stage figures.** A stage figure is a formation in which the actor creates a certain shape, pattern of movement, or gestural sense that the audience recognizes as a definite identity and imbues with traits that would not otherwise be evident. The audience builds the character by projecting its image of the ideal upon the stage figure. For example, an actor who mimics the gait and dress of Charlie Chaplin is seen as Chaplin or as Chaplinesque, and as such, the audience endows the figure with other traits. Stage figures can be created by costume (Dracula, Superman, other pop icons) or physical attitude (carnival showman, disoriented professor). This too is like the commedia dell'arte, whereby a character like Harlequin was imprinted upon the audience through mask, dress, and physical attitude. The audience anticipated and expected his preordained physical and psychological predilections for food, thievery, and laziness. The figures of Babe Ruth and the Joker from Jenkin's *Kid Twist* represent American versions of the stage figure. Babe Ruth is an icon from America's pastime (baseball) but eclipsed the sport as an American hero representing power and consumption—embodied in the epithet "the Sultan of Swat." The iconic Joker is immortalized in his bouts with Batman in comic books and in recent movie adaptations. Jenkin's *Kitty Hawk* includes the James brothers, the Wright brothers, and the Smith brothers (of cough drop lore) as characters. Sometimes the stage figure is rendered as a symbol or emblem. For example, Man with a Scythe in Wellman's *Bodacious Flapdoodle* is the standard iconographic symbol for the grim reaper.

**11. Characters may be dematrixed.** New playwrights use dematrixing techniques. The actor/character is dematrixed when he (1) fractures the mold of a specific character; (2) directly acknowledges or addresses the presence of the audience; or 3) foregrounds the presence of the actor over the character. Dematrixing utilizes some level of metatheatricality by calling attention to the artifice of the stage. In Wellman's *Energumen*, Megan is rehearsing a story while prompted by Jacques, who cajoles her: "Remember how it was in acting class?" He is calling attention to the dynamic between actor and character. Here the effect is doubled: Megan within the matrix of character rehearsing a role; Megan the character as actor in training, in "acting class."

**12. Music and sound as character motivators**. Jenkin uses music as a prod to character formation in the early stages of the writing process. In production, Jenkin and Wellman utilize leitmotivs to define an absent or approaching character, often to a comic end. All of these playwrights rely on highly amplified sound and music in production as determinants to a character's choice of action, or to shift the direction in a character's speech. The eerily haunting repetitive melody of "Who put the Y in YBOR" in Wellman's *Fnu Lnu* serves as a choral interlude that marks the structure of the play. Jenkin uses nightclub singers to create ambiance and define character in *My Uncle Sam*, and the club duo in his recently reproduced *Dream Express* weave music in and out of the action of the play. Music or sound can be seen in its structural or textural function rather than as primarily supportive or evocative.

Sound is often used in rehearsals or workshops to "get at" character, or establish the basis of a character. Characters are required to sing, even if not well, in a number of plays. Jenkin seems fascinated by this notion of the singing character who is untrained vocally. (As a director of his own work, Jenkin experiments in rehearsal with sections of text that may be sung, although these sections may not be indicated in versions of the script.)

These twelve tenets are useful descriptors that demonstrate how the playwright can build theatrical characterizations. The key link is usually between theatricality and language. This poetics (or artistic making) need not be tied to strict imitation (mimesis). But it may cause those in the dramatic process to ponder the origins of the word *mimesis*, which Aristotle sought as his basis of action. Characters in classical tragedies were masked, usually with features extraordinarily exaggerated or typified. We think of Antigone and Oedipus now as fully realized individuals who can be analyzed psychologically, but in antiquity their masks, costumes, and even footwear inculcated them with a magical theatricality.

## HISTORICAL COROLLARY: THE MASKS OF THE COMMEDIA DELL'ARTE

A useful analogy links the characters of the new playwriting to the masks of the commedia dell'arte. The commedia dell'arte used fixed character types determined externally by masks, physical traits, dialect, and function.

For playwrights Jenkin and Wellman, characters may be as archetypal as a Harlequin or Pantalone. While the language focus of the new playwriting differs from the unscripted scenario sketch of the improvisatory commedia, the new dramaturgy contemporizes commedia's rhetorical strategies such as tirades (in Wellman's haranguing monologues, for example), or *sproposito*, which means "nonsense speech" (Wellman's transrational monologues could also be related to the sproposito, which were usually given when the character was overcome with madness brought on by grief or inebriation). Wellman's blustering, pompous Senator Armitage simulates the self-aggrandizing Dottore type. The Ruzante-like characters who talk to themselves in Jenkin's *American Notes* are all marginalized, displaced, and in an ongoing stream of self-talk. Commedia and new playwriting monologues exemplify the role of the virtuosic performer, who orchestrates sharp turns in intention, or dialect, with gestural thrusts and parries that leave audiences astonished—and breathless. This freeing of language from psychological implications or thematic intentions makes for the vivid moment-to-moment excitement that represents theater at its optimum.

What does a sixteenth-century Venetian Pantalone or Arlecchino from Bergamo have to do with contemporary characterization? The external, iconic, and comic approach to character in Len Jenkin's plays simulate the commedia tradition of charlatans, con men, and hucksters of various ilks, usually with a full bag of props. Case in point: Jenkin's character Uncle Sam is a novelty salesman with props like goozeleum glasses, poop cushions, and illuminating crucifixes. Jenkin's characters bulk actions of deceit, chicanery, and thievery, with colorful slang-laden lingo, laced with double-entendre and innuendo. Similarly, in Wellman's early play *Harm's Way*, the character Crowsfoot is the quintessential mountebank, selling quack cures and paraphernalia to whoever is gullible enough to pay. This rascal-dupe dynamic is the essence of street comedy, circus (recalling P. T. Barnum's "a sucker is born every minute"), and the topical style of the commedia. The snake-oil peddling charlatan on a makeshift platform with the sexy "inamorata sidekick" (contemporized in *Harm's Way* as the character Isle of Mercy) is at the heart of the first commercial theater. Marginalized salesman in Jenkin plays such as *Poor Folk's Pleasure* or *American Notes* reflect these traditions, nowhere more evident than in the Lightning Rod Salesman figure in *Limbo Tales*.

In Wellman's production of *Murder of Crows* at Primary Stages in 1995, the central character, played by actor Stephen Mellor, used makeup in such a way as to suggest a mask, exaggerating his ghoulish features. The use of the face to indicate heightened states is typically seen in performances of works of the new playwriting. The chorus of crows (in crow costumes) harkens back to the bestial tradition of the commedia pastorals. New playwrights utilize animal-like costumes to achieve comic ends in a carnivalesque vein. Jeffrey Jones's *Seventy Scenes of Halloween* orchestrates scenes of the unraveling marriage with the intrusive silly masked figure that moves the play toward a farcical romp. The argumentative beats between the husband and wife skew into a reflection of the lover's quarrels (*contrasti*) of the early commedia dell'arte. Indeed, the director and actor who are exploring new playwriting for the first time should consider the commedia approach of performance as a more effective playing style than traditional internalized methods.

The commedia tradition has several premises that find their corollaries in the new playwriting, as the following list indicates.

1. The creation of a theatrical antiworld:
    a) a world usually in between a simulated reality and a kind of "otherness" (science fiction, as in Wellman's *Albanian Softshoe* and *Whirligig* or Constance Congdon's *Tales of the Lost Formicans*; worlds created by characters);
    b) a world of man and beast, aliens, and so on.

2. A sense of artifice rather than a representation of real life:
    a) external rather than internal or psychological form (surface, stylized dimension, textural);
    b) characters derived from genres, tradition, icons, and pop culture.

3. Fixed types and normative parts in the same play:
    a) cameo-like roles, types from various genres or periods in history;
    b) a dissonant ensemble of characters, marginalized rather than mainstream (broken dreams, economic fringe);
    c) a task-oriented and moment-to-moment existence rather than one that is arc-oriented and changed by circumstance.

4. The use of carnival-like language to create a sense of the bizarre, strange, or comic:
    a) a mixture of high and low levels of language (colorful, playful);
    b) words as attractors and shapers of character and destinations

5. Gesture- and movement-specific work; an aspect of gesture related to function:
    a) the relationship between man and beast; iconographic configurations (the part-man part-beast Crabboy in Jenkin's *Poor Folk's Pleasure*, or the hypnotizing Mesmer in his *Gogol*).

6. The work requires a virtousic, expressionistic interpretation by the performer.

This list represents a paradigm for characterization, the cartography from which an entire character ensemble might be constructed. Many of Jenkin's ensembles are built with a commedia-like company of specific types that are fundamentally interchangeable. These types are defined by role, as specific character names change from play to play. As commedia drew its fixed characters as much from the culture as from literary antecedents, so too are Jenkin's characters heavily drawn from pop culture, B movies and private-eye fiction. Yet, filled with spirit and brio, they are neither flat nor two-dimensional in realization.

## THE STOCK COMPANY OF LEN JENKIN

A Jenkin "stock" company would have the following fixed types (commedia corollary in parentheses):

1) professor (Dottore)
2) reporter
3) artist
4) salesman (Pantalone)
5) master of ceremonies or showman
6) shadow (Brighella)
7) detective
8) shaman (Charlatan)
9) thief (Harlequin)

Notwithstanding the absence of detectives or reporters in the commedia tradition, it is nevertheless compelling to note the similarities. These stock types weave into the action with normative figures; travelers, or journeymen with destinations; and a variety of narrators or storytellers who clue us in to the story. In chapter 5, we will probe this matter further.

## INTERTEXTUAL DIALOGISM

This comparative reference to the commedia dell'arte should be taken either as a point of contact or a point of departure. For those who seek a solid historical link and theatrical formulation, commedia is one persuasive benchmark. Other less familiar external traditions with historical implications are applicable here: for example, Eric Overmyer's Chinese characters in *In Perpetuity throughout the Universe* reflect the tradition of Peking opera in movement and formulation. The idea is not to get bogged down in recreating old forms, but to lend historical credibility and information to a different way of making theater.

## CREATING MASK AND SHADOW

Italian theater historian Roberto Tessari demonstrated that the commedia dell'arte mask carried with it many associations, including those connected to the devil, the notion of an antiworld, death, and the afterlife (1981). The external form of the mask is imbued with powers that create fascination and wonder. The mask relates to an audience on a primitive level, stirring the imagination in various ways. Tessari recognized that the mask's association with carnival meant that it signifies the overturning of norms, a kind of "anything goes" frame of mind. Moreover, the mask functions as a leveler of status, class, and even gender as it removes or effaces the individuality of the person wearing it. The mask neutralizes the distinguishing features of the face and eyes—the soul of the personality. It presents us with the "other," elements part man but also part beast. The mask forces the site of engagement with the audience away from the visage, to the gestural body in motion. Thus, the mask removes the psychology from the character, replacing it with an immanent theatricality that is edgy and immediate.

A playwright inexperienced with mask work can quickly recognize its potential for theatricality in the exercise that follows. The mask serves as a point of entry for the playwright interested in exploring external characterization.

## EXERCISE:
### Masks

This exercise is an excellent way to introduce playwrights to the notions of the external character. Typically, commedia dell'arte masks should be used for this exercise, although you can use whatever is available. Commedia masks are useful because they define a specific shape, color, and set of corresponding traits. For example, the curvilinear Harlequin masks suggest a circular sense of movement and gesture, as opposed to the angularity of Pantalone's. The green color of Brighella's mask is related to deceit and scheming. This exercise requires pairs of playwrights.

1) Approach the mask with great care. Study it carefully; sense its texture, form, and attitude. Hold it out at arm's length, then bring it toward your face, attempting to feel its power or energy transfer itself to you. Apply the mask slowly, feeling your way into it; let it "work" on you, directing you toward movements and gesture. Stand and walk about, then proceed to the next step.

2) One playwright wears the mask while the other jots down associations. The wearer of the mask should move about, play with gesture, sense the attitudes of the mask. As the other jots down associations, she should attempt to come up with an idea of character.

3) Reverse the roles and repeat the first two steps.

4) Based on experiencing and observing the mask, both playwrights should write a monologue together about a character who applies the mask. We should sense a transformation or transference that takes place at the moment the mask touches the face. Work your way to the transformation by exploring the various associations you came up with in step 2.

COMMENT: After some character work with the mask, you will have a more confident approach to an exploration of theatrical character in the new playwriting.

## CHARACTER CLASH

In formulating a character, most playwrights work from the basis of key relationships and the forces that are in conflict within a character's life. Typical in American dramaturgy is the dysfunctional American family, a continuing topoi through the plays of Eugene O'Neill, Arthur Miller, Tennessee Williams, and Lorraine Hansberry, to Sam Shepard, August Wilson, Jon Robin Baitz, and so on. The family provides a shared language and interactional system in which the playwright can operate on terms "familiar as family" to an audience. The family is dramatically efficient because histories (and therefore subtexts) are shared, lessening the need for expository material. Moreover, the family provides an underlying structure, a "given" in which typical roles are played out, gauged, and tabulated. Dramatic interest emerges when this integral structure is threatened with upheaval or disruption through internal conflicts, power struggles, or external violation. Historically, the family carries with it the weight of myth: Oedipus, the king who kills his father; Orestes, the son who kills his mother; Medea, the mother who murders her children. Modern playwrights, particularly within the confines of realistic drama, have resorted to these "mythic" models.

New writing, on the other hand, tends to look at nonfamilial subject matter, exploding the site of the play out of the living room. The recognizable system in which the play operates as an integral whole can be altered significantly by the intrusion of elements outside of the expected norm. For example, in Constance Congdon's *Tales of the Lost Formicans*, seemingly normative, integral characters become aliens when they don sunglasses. This breakdown in the integral character represents a fundamental break from realistic playwriting.

Traditionally, playwrights establish conventions of character that remain consistent throughout the piece. In the new playwriting, the terrain of character is shifting. In Wellman's *Albanian Softshoe*, normative characters become marionettes by act 2. In Jenkin's *Kid Twist*, scenes from the *Hindenburg* disaster collide against the surreal projections of the main character who is detained in a motel as part of the witness protection program. These manifestations of Kid Twist's dreams demonstrate new writing's affinity with surrealism, drawing sharp, satiric, and comic connections between the living and the dead. Further, the iconic characters of Babe Ruth, the Joker, and Kid Twist are juxtaposed in a visual, living collage that replaces traditional narrative. This clash of characters draws from American and German history, pop culture, and film noir gangster lore. The term *character clash* describes this collision of history, culture, or typology of character within play.

Several contemporary playwrights have experimented with character clash to achieve thematic ends. The spectrum is diverse, from Adrienne

Kennedy's early work, *The Owl Answers*, which juxtaposed characters from various historical eras, to recent politicized works such as *Pentecost* by David Edgar (see earlier comments in this chapter). In new writing, character clash involves the insertion of historical characters, pop icons, altered characters, aliens, and the like, juxtaposed to more or less normative characters. (*Normative* characters may be defined as reality-based.) This creates a polyvocality in the text, since neither "voice" is privileged. The result may be a hybrid, in which characters from opposing genres, cultures, or histories create a frisson in the text. This frisson sparks tension and forward movement that propels the play along, substituting for the traditional through line or progression. Len Jenkin's *Kitty Hawk* experiments with this idea of frisson by featuring the great brother acts in history: starting with the James brothers (Frank and Jessie); then to Orville and Wilbur Wright; and then to the Smith brothers of cough drop fame. Each new entrance creates a clash among contexts, voices, and histories in which a shared language had to be found and then re-formed as each new fraternal duo was introduced. The term *clash* is accurate in describing a conflict of worlds and histories that these dual characters embody.

Character clash provides the play with a nonlinear dynamic that interrupts or aborts a trackable, traditional narrative within a representational system. The creation of an antiworld parallel to our own world is central to new writing, insofar as it short-circuits any notion of an integral representational universe. The play becomes a heterogeneous landscape of figures, cultures, and histories. These figural polarities create a rich topography that is an innovative, and underexplored, dramaturgic strategy. In actuality, this polarized topography is more representative of current culture than the traditional homogenous landscape.

Character clash raises the aesthetic principle of *interruption*, a concept I will develop further in dealing with equivocal character in Eric Overmyer's work (see chapter 6). Interruption occurs at the point at which one theatrical world or one voice is eclipsed by another. At the moment of interruption, the spectator or reader is forced to consider the work in its entirety and is in effect thrown into a closer relationship with the text. Len Jenkin utilizes interruption through the character of Capability Brown, the eighteenth-century botanist who invades the "present" in *My Uncle Sam*. The insertion of Capability Brown impedes the sense of linearity or representational objectivity. Mac Wellman utilizes another form of interruption in *Albanian Softshoe*, when actors consecutively (and arbitrarily) change characters in the first act. Similarly, Constance Congdon's *Tales of the Lost Formicans* employs the technique as normative characters split into aliens. In the gap, or moment of transition, the audience is made to recognize or discover something about the character and the play. For playwrights, the beat of recognition is one of the most powerful dramaturgic tools, because it defines a point of entry during which the audience completes its relation to the text.

The principles of character clash are as follows:

1. It creates a unique theatrical environment in which normative relationships are altered or skewed through the use of

   a) characters from different historical periods;

   b) characters from different genres of literature, film, television;

   c) characters with diverse sexual identities or peccadilloes.

2. Characters are defined in relation to "other" rather than in the traditional protagonist/antagonist sense. The self is continually reshaped in relationship to the "other" rather than existing as a self-integrated entity.

3. Characters may be nonhuman or partially human.

4. Characters clash on the level of language, attitudes, goals, discourses.

## EXERCISE:
### Character Clash

### Exercise A

1) Select two characters, one from a foreign or exotic locale, the other a comic-book figure.

2) Establish one character as a traveler, the second as an expert or guide of some sort who has needed advice or information. A variant of the expert or guide is the omniscient character, such as a shaman, priest, or seer.

3) Create clash through shifting language levels and patterns.

   a) How well do the characters understand or misapprehend each other?

   b) Establish some common ground in language, or through visual properties.

4) Write a scene that marks a transition in the traveler's perception about herself. At the same time, the traveler's interaction with the guide or expert embodies an external change in the action.

### Exercise B

The next exercise is popular with playwriting students. It involves a rewrite of the above exercise. Here, you add a new character.

1) Write a short scene with two characters in a conflict or win-lose situation. The outcome is that one character will win, the other lose.

2) During the scene, establish one character's interest or obsession with some historical character, or choose a character from a particular genre of literature or film. Use visually identifiable means, such as clothing, hats, and accoutrements to theatricalize this character.

3) Find a point of entry for the historical character to come into the action.

4) Rewrite the scene with the inserted "genre" character taking the side of one character against the other.

1) Students should cut out pictures of characters from magazines or other topical source materials, then construct the above-described scenes with these visual models for inspiration. This step can be a preliminary to exercise B, above, but take full advantage of its use in the workshop, where it will stimulate all the students. Visual sources promote a theatrical mindset—at the heart of the externally constructed character.

COMMENT: Experiment with character clash to get a feel for a theatrical mix that creates immediate surface and dynamic interest. The interaction itself can stimulate a dynamic that is immediate and potentially comic. Students with broader theatrical training can muse on the notions of characters wearing masks, or on the old commedia troupes that clashed dialects, masks, costume, and gestures to create an intensely popular form.

Let us now turn our attention to three different formulations of character in the new playwriting. In the following three chapters, premises and modes of conceptualization will be targeted. Then, specific applications and exercises will follow.

# 5

# Len Jenkin's Dramaturgy of Character:
# From Stage Figures to Archetypes

*Stage figure* is a term first coined by the Prague semiotician Jindrich Honzl. He used it to distinguish the function and operation of the fixed characters of the commedia dell'arte from the traditional idea of character. Honzl asserted that "stage figures like Harlequin or Pantalone were transferred from one scenario or play to another, and exhibited traits that conditioned—even dominated—the events of the plot" (Quinn 1988, 330–31). Honzl suggested that since stage figures could be identified by specific codes of gestures and dress, they could be instantly recognized in the "intertextual" sense. The intertextual figure is a hallmark of the plays of Len Jenkin, and an effective determinant of his dramaturgy.

Typically, the portrayal of the stage figure is iconic; in other words, the image of the figure "speaks for itself." For example, if we see a performer in a superman outfit we automatically associate distinctive traits (flying, invulnerability) based upon our recognition of, and past experience with, the figure. An actor can readily simulate the figure of Superman, who is the archetype for invincibility and heroism. However, in Jenkin's plays the stage figure is not usually as locked-in as Superman, the Lone Ranger, or Harlequin, with their specific costumes and prescribed traits. Rather, they evolve from the fractured archeyptes at the seamy margins of the American mythos: the fast-talking carnival showman, the fried-out cantankerous professor in search of UFOs, or the failed salesmen of lightning rods and dime-store novelties. In *American Notes*, the reporter figure does not work for the *New York Times* or even the local paper; rather, it's the less reputable tabloid *Flying Saucer News*.

Across Jenkin's plays we find recurring figures: the thief; the con-man; the showman or master of ceremonies; the cop; the professor; the artist; and the reporter. Jenkin may change their proper names and specific actions in each play, but like the masks of commedia dell'arte, their actions and traits are to a significant extent predetermined. As intertextual figures they express a resemblance to precursors in American popular culture found in pulp detective fiction, comic book lore, and the B-movie film noir fare of the 1940s and '50s. Jenkin formulates his stage figures by skewing the archetypal image that exists for the audience—Kid Twist is a member of the Jewish, not Italian Mafia, for example. Then, he personalizes each character through careful attention to eccentricities, particularly in the use of language. Despite their pathetic, dated, or alienated core, the figures are humanized as each develops a distinct identity. The characters emerge without commentary. Indeed, Jenkin never uses his figures for blatant social commentary or to telegraph the message of the play.

While allowing for the variations and deviations in a given play, Jenkin's figures proffer an innate theatricality that guarantees appeal as well as audience recognition. As stage figures, their juxtaposition and interaction establishes pretexts and possibilities that determine the plot. In this sense, his plays are character driven, often with several figures at the wheel—like the ensemble performances of commedia dell'arte. The archetypal nature of the characters focuses their given actions, but it also gives latitude to the range of language. Language overwhelms the mold, never allowing it to consume or demean the unique individuality of the figure. If they appear at a distance like cartoon figures or cutouts, upon closer scrutiny the figures are fully dimensionalized. Jenkin dialogizes his characters to create a multiplicity of voices and figurations within his polyvocal theatrical landscape. We can now examine how Jenkin makes this work.

## JENKIN'S STAGE FIGURES

The stage figures in Jenkin's work present iconic and linguistic variations of well-known archetypes:

1. *The professor* usually specializes in some exotic subject, often whacked-out, and of suspicious intent or legitimacy. The character Driver in *Limbo Tales* is a lecturer on Ancient Mayan culture. Botany professor Finley in *American Notes* feeds young female students to his man-eating Amazonian plant that he has cultivated. See also *Gogol* and *Pilgrims of the Night.*

2. *The reporter* is on the margins of the reputable. Mrs. Lammle in *Dark Ride* is a finder of coincidences and has recorded them from all over the world. In *Kid Twist*, The Reporter recalls the hard-bitten 1940s style of reporter cum gumshoe.

3. *The artist* is often a struggling character within the various arts, sometimes a "wanna-be," or someone who is given to selling out for a buck: Mark in *5 of Us* writes porn; Viva is an ex-dancer in *Pilgrims of the Night;* the club duo in *Dream Express.*

4. *The salesman.* There is a novelties salesman in *My Uncle Sam;* the Resurrection Man in *Gogol,* a gravedigger who sells stiffs to researchers; and the Lightning Rod Salesman in *Limbo Tales.*

5. *The emcee, pitchman, or showman* are charlatan-like characters who nevertheless believe in what they are pitching. In *Country Doctor* the

Pitchman opens the play with a strange optical device that allows one to see around or behind oneself. The Pitchman in *American Notes* is a carnival barker who sells tickets to see Bonecrusher, The Monster of the Nile, actually a dead American Alligator. Crab Boy, in *Poor Folk's Pleasure*, is a legless man who has two digits on each hand that simulate claws. He exhibits himself to pay off a private eye who is tracking his daughter.

6. *The detective.* This character is right out of the pulp novels of the 1940s, or the film noir hard-boiled variety. See Sarge in *Kid Twist*, the Plainclothesman in *My Uncle Sam.*

7. *The thief or criminal.* Jenkin seems fond of his crooks. See *Kid Twist*, or the Thief character in *Dark Ride*. The act of stealing a jewel becomes the object of a search in *Dark Ride*.

Together, and in their multiple variations, Jenkin's figures make up the playwright's "stock company." Indeed, his plays would have fit well within the nineteenth-century format of the "lines-of-business" repertory company.

## ARCHETYPE VERSUS STEREOTYPE

The archetypal character can be distinguished from its negative counterpart, the stereotype. Stereotypical characters are uninteresting because they lack variation or individuality. Familiar traits or responses are repeated or represented without any distinguishing flair. Often the stereotypical character functions as a thematic extension of the playwright's bias. It may conform to a standardized mental picture shared by a specific interest group. In traditional dramaturgical terms, the playwright is telegraphing his message—speaking directly through the character's voice. While it is a transparent error, it is a common shortcoming in conceptualization. The flaw is most evident in television writing, particularly in the movie of the week format where characters must be quickly identified as victims, villains, persecutors, or saviors. The audience knows who to root for and against; the plot seems to drive the character, rather than the reverse.

## EXERCISE:
### Playing with Stage Figures

Jenkin starts his scenes off with a narrator figure who simply begins to tell a story. As the story unfolds other characters begin to enter into it, often with the narrator figure entering into the story in some role. Jenkin often uses writers, reporters, or translators, language specialists, who may be describing something they are writing or translating.

1) Using several of the above figures as models, create a sequence of scenes that involve an action suitable to the particular eccentricities of the characters.

    a) Use their archetypal actions as points of departure. For example, show your professor/teacher in the lecturing or professorial mode.

    b) Select a narrator figure from this group to begin the scene, allowing the other characters to enter as manifestations of the narrative.

    c) Allow these figures to frame subsequent scenes toward creating the sequence.

    d) Utilize at least one recognizable stage figure from comic-book lore.

2) Using Jenkin's archetypal model, adapt the notion to create your own archetypal variations (for example, athletes, models, nuns, politicians, announcers, and the like).

    a) Marginalize the character by making her a "has-been" or "wanna-be," for example.

    b) Give the character some eccentricities or bizarre behaviors.

    c) Create a monologue for each character that explores these sensibilities.

    d) From these monologues select a story line that integrates the figures.

COMMENT: Appropriate characters from fiction, comic books, and various pop media, then endow, imbue, or alter them with personalized and individuated traits. Explore techniques for rounding or flattening characterization. A rounded character possesses depth, dimension, and complexity. A flat character possesses limited, individuated traits, operating within a functional range.

## DOMINANT FIGURES

In general, Jenkin constructs his plays around dominant figures and archetypal stock figures. The dominant figures control the story line, as narrators alongside the action, or as characters in the center of the action. Structured within the framework of travel or journeys, his dominant figures play out that action in search or quest of someone or some object. This restless, wandering aspect of their nature stimulates the movement of the play (his plays are character driven), through an array of bizarre settings and encounters (e.g., the mise-en-scène of the carnival sideshow or wax museum). Jenkin's characters are American adventurers, romantic individuals struggling for a larger share or a better "take" on the whole; or, they are simply trying to escape the present. In some cases, it is a search for an individual, as in the Author's quest for his Uncle Sam in *My Uncle Sam*. Sometimes the voyage is mundane and comic, as in the Guest's search for the wedding in *The Country Doctor*. The dominant figure keeps the play moving. The fact that the mover is in crisis, and presented with obstacles or distractions, provides a dramatic grounding or level of interest, however absurd the crises may appear. The traveler figure is by nature an *outsider*, and being outside of his element creates the tension or energy in the play. When the movement through place is dramatized, the term *journey play* is accurate and helpful.

    Sometimes the traveler can take the more traditional form of an intruder figure: in *American Notes* the traveler figure is grounded at the roadside hotel. The sense of the temporary situation is sound dramaturgically because it creates tension for the character and the audience with built-in mystery, intrigue, or danger: is this the end of the line? In underscoring the stranger in a strange land, Jenkin examines the failed quest of the American dream and the poignant sense of aborted expectations. The topos of the stalled journey is present in a number of plays in which the traveler figure is used.

Here are some profiles of Jenkin's travelers:

1. The traveler often lives in a hotel or has other temporary arrangements. (*American Notes, Limbo Tales, My Uncle Sam*).

2. The terrain of the traveler maybe real space and time, or the product of memory and dreams.

3. The traveler is usually a male character, although there are exceptions (*Careless Love*). Often there is more than one traveler (*Pilgrims in the Night*).

4. The traveler is a character struggling with a dilemma, looking for a better life or deeper meaning but not really knowing what he wants.

5. The traveler is in conflict about a certain relationship; the journey works through some of these questions.

6. By the end of the play, the traveler arcs to some extent, reaching a deeper level of discovery or wisdom, or poses a deeper premise.

## SHALLOW VERSUS DEEP TIME

When the traveler moves forward in a linear way, from point A to point B to point C, the passage of time is shallow. Shallow time is immediate and forward-looking, not self-reflexive or past oriented. When the character is reflective of the past or saturated in consciousness the time progression is temporarily halted or moves deeper in the temporal sense. Playwrights should be aware of this difference in attempting to manipulate time factors in their plays to the best advantage.

## THE STORYTELLER

A second figure that serves a dominant function is the storyteller. Jenkin's theater celebrates the storytelling tradition; his characters like to talk or spin yarns. Using the techniques of direct address, Jenkin's storytellers "frame" the action and serve as the threshold through which the audience experiences the play. After setting up the frame, the storyteller enters into some dramatized context that elaborates on the givens established in the narrative.

Frequently there are stories within stories requiring a constant shift of perspective and voice. The multiple storytellers within a Jenkin play can confuse an audience who expect to follow the story through Jenkin's primary narrator. Jenkin's narrators are never tracked, but take turns spinning the story. The disturbing loss of context in *Dark Ride*, for example, is suggested in the play's title, but it may not be until the end of the play that the audience accepts the multiple layering and narrative levels. The standard character-related question of "Whose story is this?" is problematic in Jenkin's work because Jenkin categorically works against this dictum. To critique the body of Jenkin's work against a canonical premise of traditional playwriting would do disservice to his extraordinary talent.

### The Storyteller and the Frame

Framing is an essential component of Jenkin's figures. Usually, it involves direct address to the audience to set up the givens of a scene that subsequently unfolds in action. (It is a common strategy in current playwriting; Paula Vogel's *How I Learned to Drive*, Warren Leight's *Sideman*.) This metatheatrical device calls attention to the play's structure, and the matrix of the actor/character. Strategically, it marks the character with the dramatist's function—that is, emplotment. Jenkin's plays are character driven, but not in the traditional sense. Multiple characters zigzag us through to the conclusion. There is never a case of a single narrator (like Salieri in Peter Shaffer's *Amadeus*, for example) pitching a particular take across the entire play. *Amadeus* represents the picture-frame model in which the narrator straddles the frame. Salieri brings us in as participant; he steps back out to reflect, to lick his wounds, and only then does he advance the action. His emotional and affective presence mitigates the problem inherent in drama that is episodic, as most biographical plays are. Salieri provides structural unity. In *How I Learned to Drive*, Lil' Bit provides a similar function to that of Salieri, although Vogel fractures the chronological framework.

Conversely, Jenkin's plays are more like boxes within boxes, or layers of an onion: the first narrator who opens the frame will lead us to other narrators who open frames. For example, in *Pilgrims of the Night*, Tom begins by telling us a story about a group of people who are telling stories, and then these subsequent characters frame and enact the series of vignettes that follow. *Dark Ride* begins with the Translator having difficulty translating a text, from which characters appear and enact the action discussed. These characters then frame subsequent actions.

The relation between character and space is represented either as a manifestation of dream, fantasy, or memory—as in *Kid Twist*. A character may appear as the manifestation of a story in a text, as in the Thief in *Dark Ride*, or within travelers telling stories on a trip, as in *Pilgrims of the Night*. As such, characters seem to control the action by creating frames for other characters to appear as manifestations of something they are reading, a dream they once had, or a memory that consumes them.

This character dynamic in Jenkin's plays can be understood in the relationships between dominant and stock figures. The difference may be clarified as a matter of function more than form. Indeed, distinctions are not always clear-cut; the thief in *Dark Ride* is in the realm of a stock figure, yet is dominant in the progress of the play.

## EXERCISE:
## Creating the Ten-Minute Frame Play

The ten-minute form is becoming increasingly popular in contest formats. It actually works quite well in the character-driven frame format, since a fair amount of structural density or complexity can be allotted to a relatively brief piece. Moreover, the journey or travel action allows the character a kind of through line to a destination point, and a successful or unsuccessful outcome. Strong dramaturgical components involving the relationship between character and structure are built into the format. This is an excellent class or workshop exercise, since several plays can be read in class during a typical one-hour period. With the increasing popularity of the ten-minute form, this exercise is an excellent way to break into the genre.

1) Start by establishing a dominant figure, either a traveler or storyteller. This figure may or may not be a member of an archetypal group.

   a) This character provides the opening frame and must thrust us into some trip, search, or examination. It should be objective, rather than a trip into the psychological realm, for example.

   b) This framing character enters into the main action.

2) Determine two to three archetypal figures that enter into the story or provide obstacles for the dominant figure. They should also serve as actors in the story.

   a) Allow at least one of these characters to provide an inner frame within the main story.

3) Don't allow the play to go beyond 10 or 11 pages. The dominant figure should reach some kind of payoff or payback at the end of the piece.

4) Allow the characters to move through space and time as needed. Keep in mind that you are writing for the stage. Try not to demand large realistic set pieces. Study Jenkin's *Country Doctor* to determine how to handle these on stage.

Each character and figure should believe totally in what she is doing, or what she is about. They're working on it, even if it looks hopeless, or they're inept, or others doubt them. Always keep in mind the archetypal relationship between the character and the action. In a sense it's single-minded and purposeful. Use strange props or visual elements as much as possible.

Be sure to use "theatrical characters." Refer to the "Tenets of Theatrical Characters" as a guide.

Write fast, in a stream-of-consciousness style, then go over and refine, rewrite, refine. Or, as Eric Overmyer says, "hone, chip, sand, rub"—and finish. Once you are comfortable with using frames and sequences, attempt to write a one-act of around twenty-five to thirty pages.

## JENKIN'S PERFORMATIVE CHARACTERS

A playwright can benefit greatly by studying Jenkin's figures and archetypes. Replete with eccentricities, his stage figures offer the actor an array of performative choices. The performative character emphasizes gesture, movement, and expression over psychological insight or subtext. In practice, Jenkin often develops his characters by including actors in his creative process. In the workshop, the physically trained actor responds quickly and effectively to this external approach of characterization, providing real insight to the playwright in the construction of the play. Moreover, in the ten-minute format the playwright can thoroughly workshop the characterizations with actors in a relatively brief amount of time. For optimal results, this strategy should be implemented as soon as an early draft is completed.

# 6

## Eric Overmyer: Some Principles of Character Transformation

In several of his plays, Eric Overmyer's characters are drawn as much from psychological or biographical profiles as from archetypes. *The Heliotrope Bouquet* is based around the historical figure Scott Joplin and his sole collaboration with the unheralded yet enormously gifted pianist Louis Chauvin. The play captures a poetic rendition of the peregrinations in Joplin's mind as he recalls the past, particularly his heartbreaking relationship with Belle, the mother of their deceased child. These moments are vividly realized as the transformations of his current wife Lottie into the "image" of his former lover, Belle. The transformations in Joplin's mind, brought on by a late phase of the "pox," are thus theatricalized in a most cogent rendering of his fragile mental state. Lottie resents these shifts in Joplin's mind, and her devaluation as the important figure in his life. Overmyer establishes the convention early in the piece by moving from dream to "real" sequences. The merging or juxtaposition of reality and consciousness provides the essential structure of the play. It allows different historical periods to fluidly dialogize in Overmyer's typically baroque style.

### INTERRUPTION AND THE EQUIVOCAL CHARACTER

Overmyer presents a paradigm of the equivocal character in his rendering of the Spanish Mary, Belle, and Lottie character troika. If the equivocal character can be defined as one actor shifting between two or more significations, *The Heliotrope Bouquet* presents three. Spanish Mary in the first scene becomes Lottie; Lottie then switches back and forth with Belle. The equivocal character has the capacity to transform, or switch from one character to another—or back and forth between two or three characters. Unlike a true transformation, Lottie neither transforms entirely into Belle nor vice versa. Rather, the switching mirrors the structural dynamic of the play—the movement back and forth across time periods. In the play, the characters Belle and Spanish Mary are deceased in terms of Joplin's "real time" presence. His wife Lottie represents his current relationship. The play seeks to capture the elusive past with its ambient sense of hope and promise, contrasted against a tone of bittersweet resignation in the present.

The effectiveness of the equivocal character is reliant upon the *trigger mechanism*, the device that motivates the transition from one character into another. Overmyer establishes one major transformation of the characters with a carefully disguised bundle. The transformation of the bundle from his former child with Belle back to a bundle of now spilled plums echoes the transformation from Belle to Lottie in Joplin's mind. These expressionistic projections of Joplin's mind are fully theatricalized by Overmyer:

(*BELLE appears behind JOPLIN. She is holding a bundle.*)

BELLE: Oh Joplin.

JOPLIN: Belle. I'm so sorry.

BELLE: Coughed herself right out of this world and into the next. Poor creature. Tiny thing. Never knew a word.

JOPLIN: I'm so sorry. If I could find my work. If I could just find my work.

BELLE: What work? What are you talking about?

JOPLIN: The *Guest of Honor*. My opera. My ragtime opera. Mislaid. Misplaced. Where's it gone? Help me find it. If I could find that work, if I could just find that work, I could bring our baby back.

BELLE: Don't talk foolish.

JOPLIN: We could start over.

BELLE: I can't stay here.

JOPLIN: We'll go away to Chicago.

BELLE: You'll go.

(*JOPLIN grabs her*)

JOPLIN: Don't go. Don't go. Don't go.

BELLE: I'm sore Joplin. A walking bruise. A lame dog and a broken wheel. Singing never saved a soul. Singing never brought nobody back. Once you're dead you're done. I'm done. I'm done, Joplin. Dead on my feet. I got no love for you or any man. Love died with my baby.

JOPLIN: Don't go. Don't go. Don't go.

(*He shakes her. She drops the bundle and screams.*)

BELLE: Joplin.

(*The bundle hits the floor and scatters: plums roll across the floor.
Lights change. Belle becomes LOTTIE and stands before JOPLIN.*)

LOTTIE: Joplin. Look what you made me do.

(*She scurries about and picks up the plums.*)

LOTTIE: They were perfect. And now they're bruised. Ruined. Just like life. Like getting old. You make me tired. Old man, you called me Belle again. Damn you.

JOPLIN: Sorry.

LOTTIE: Now sit.

JOPLIN: So sorry, Lottie. So sorry.

> (*He sits at the piano. LOTTIE puts the plums in a bowl and sets them before him. SPICE enters with coffee.*)

(Overmyer 1994, *The Heliotrope Bouquet*, 246–247)

Lottie's existential plight is established through equivocal characterization. She can never achieve her identity in this marriage amongst the vagaries of the dottering Joplin, and her frustration is palpable: "Old man, you called me Belle again. Damn you," clearly marks the volatile passive/aggressive dynamic at the core of the marriage, as do "You make me tired," and later, "Now sit." The plum bundle provides a semiotic doubling of this transference. By utilizing the bundle as the image of the baby, Overmyer is setting the audience up for a surprise discovery. The spilling of the plums provides the perfect sound and visual metaphors (small, vulnerable ripe fruit of a red purplish hue)—representing and exposing Joplin's denial of the infant's death, but also Belle's fecundity, and of course, female genitalia, elements that Joplin gropes for longingly. For Lottie, the action of picking up the scattered fruit is the corollary to her picking up the pieces of Joplin's life, and marks her inability to capture a sense of wholeness about her life with Joplin.

Indeed, once the audience or reader catches on to the back-and-forth shift in the play, we come to expect, or at least anticipate, points of interruption. Belle floats out of Joplin's reveries and it is the move from Belle to Lottie that seems, from Joplin's perspective, like coming down from the high point of a drug-induced state to the world as it is. But Overmyer allows Belle to appear by linking *place* to Joplin's mental projections. In Belle's last appearance Joplin introduces her from her deceased, albeit heavenly climes:

JOPLIN: Still to be heard in the ether and the House of God. Chauvin's piano ringing ragtime in the House of God.

> (*BELLE appears.*)

BELLE: Wondering where you are.

(Overmyer 1994, 254)

Joplin's tag, "House of God," establishes the credible point of entry for Belle's character. In the final moments of the play, Overmyer weaves between the two characters as though each were vying competitively for a stake in Joplin's world. Lottie's dilemma is that she is trapped by history and circumstance, whereas Belle is the actualization of memory, and not held to spatial/temporal restraints:

JOPLIN: Belle.

LOTTIE: Oh, Joplin. No, not Belle.

JOPLIN: She was here.

LOTTIE: This is Lottie. The second one. The one saved your sorry life, remember?

(Overmyer 1994, 255)

The paradox of interruption creates a unique aesthetic response in the spectator, in fact enhancing the emotional involvement rather than aborting it. It calls for a particular approach to performance—an affective aspect that the playwright should be aware of and know how to utilize. There are points when Belle takes over the Lottie character; the emotional connection to the character continues, or is immediately heightened, right at those moments of transference. This gap of interruption or "between-ness" causes the audience to question where it is at that given moment. Rather than drawing us away from the piece it causes us to affectively enter into it more deeply. The equivocal character is experienced dialogically, as a theatrical conflation/divergence between two characters. Neither character achieves full absence or presence, and at the point of interruption the actor may suddenly be foregrounded over either character. Ultimately, meaning is determined at the point of interruption and deferral.

In Overmyer's use of the equivocal character, we can recognize the universal tendency to project the other on a present character—a particularly common component of love relationships—and a notable source of conflict. Obviously, it allows us to appreciate the aesthetic values in the play rather than just being taken on a linear ride in which our own expectations or presumptions are allowed free, dominant reign.

## FROM CRITICAL EXPLANATION TO CREATIVE IMAGINING

For playwrights, the above analysis explains what's going on in the text. The question is, How can this technique be used creatively? Two familiar aspects of contemporary playwriting involve memory and dreams. Either or both constitute an important facet of characterization because they target the soul or truth of an individual. Moreover, any manipulation of the character's relation to time should add depth to characterization. Memories of experiences provide the foundation for narrative, while dreams have been fundamental components of the drama since the classical era. The equivocal character provides the playwright a key to unlock these elements dialogically through theatrical means. Otherwise, we become absorbed in self-indulgent ruminating or extrapolating—neither "holds the boards" very well.

There are several ways to approach writing the equivocal character, but it may better to consider some scenework you've already begun, or in the revision of a drafted play.

## EXERCISE:
### Equivocal Character and Interruption

1) Write or revise a short three-to-four-scene piece that involves equivocal characterization.

2) Start from a likely premise: rebound situations are viable, where one character

(A) recently lost a romantic interest (C) through death, divorce, to another, and so on.

3) Begin with the projection of (C) on character (B). Then move to the "real" time relationship between (A) and (B).

4) Target the points of interruption, where (C) become (B) and vice versa. What visual signifiers can pass from one character to the other? (The plums offer a good example.)

5) Strive to differentiate traits (C) from (B) and differ the responses of (A) to each character. For example, Joplin seems far more enraptured with Belle than he now is with the dutiful and pragmatic choice of Lottie.

6) What does it all add up to? Is it about winning and losing? The inherent possibilities at closure are multiple, from (A) overcoming his manifestation of (C) to (B) accepting (C) as a component of the relationship, even if the portrayal is relegated to a role-played distancing. How you work the scene determines the relative strength or weakness in each character.

NOTE: Step 3 is important. Overmyer shows us the soundness of establishing a convention early, then reintroducing it at points throughout the play. The points of interruption in step 4 are major moments in the play. In production, we witness the actor work this magic to create great interest. Dramatically, the playwright provides the contour that will govern the ebb and flow of the scene.

## IN PERPETUITY

Another example of equivocal character occurs in the shift between the characters Dennis Wu and Tai-Tung Trahn in *In Perpetuity throughout the Universe*. Tai-Tung Trahn establishes the exoticism of the piece with his pantomimic opening—a hodgepodge of a tai chi master meets Fu Manchu type meets Peking opera type while dressed in a business suit. The movement patterns and apparel allow him to nonchalantly transform into the acculturated Asian-American writer Dennis Wu. Tai-Tung represents a common topos of American films from the Fu Manchu series to *Chinatown*—the Asian character as a subject of intrigue and dangerous cunning. In this conflation between the somewhat normative Dennis and the exotically theatrical Tia-Tung Trahn, Overmyer offers the actor a virtuosic turn that in production is highly theatrical. By allotting Trahn the traits of a businessman, Overmyer maintains a link and moment of ambiguity between the two characters, and this "interruption" in clarity draws our attention as an audience. Tai-Tung becomes the objectification of the thematic, subject matter at the center of the play. A third tier publishing enterprise that employs Dennis Wu on its staff is built upon its publications of Orient-based conspiracies.

## CHARACTER DOUBLING

While the equivocal character and the notion of interruption are powerful dramaturgic components of Overmyer's characterization strategy, there are situations where it may be more effective to simply double characters.

Character doubling should be indicated by the playwright on the character page, and should have a dramaturgic payoff. In a multicharacter play, doubling is always a pragmatic concern: the fewer actors involved in production, the better the chance that the play will be produced. Generally, actors appreciate the challenge and financial bonus of doubling; directors and producers benefit by the savings in time and money. Overmyer achieves a dramaturgic payoff through the Babcock/Nizam double in *Dark Rapture*. Babcock is present throughout the piece; Nizam appears in one strikingly powerful scene where he is assassinated for his supposed connection (as a Turk) to the slaughter of Armenians early in this century. In a dramaturgic sense, Nizam provides the ironic and cynical Babcock character with a sympathetic resonance that carries over in production. On the other hand, there is no device of transformation or visible moment of "between-ness" since Nizam appears once in the play out of Babcock's range.

Playwrights must duly hesitate before writing a character who appears in only one scene. The trend in the profession is to bulk parts whenever possible. This applies to functional characters. A current remedy is to have one actor play a serial array of functional characters, giving each a distinct flavor through movement patterns, dialect, and degree of gestural activity. Audiences enjoy the theatrical dialogism that emerges as the actor gives life to various cameolike roles. The notion of doubling in its various modes has become a staple of contemporary playwriting technique.

## EXERCISE:
### Bulking Parts

1) Revise a play so that one actor plays a sequence of functional roles (for example: taxi driver, waiter, bellhop, masseur, etc.).

## IDENTITY AND GENDER POLITICS

The increasing practice of doubling characters may be related to the growing interest in the politics of identity, including the relation between sex and gender. In the early 1990s, Craig Lucas won a Pulitzer Prize for his play *Prelude to a Kiss*, which explored the switching of souls from Peter's wife to an Old Man who arbitrarily crashed their wedding. After this point, the play turns from a whirlwind boy-meets-girl romance to an exploration and search of recapturing past identities. That the piece was far more interesting as a play than in its film version bears testimony to the fact that theatrical immediacy makes this doubling device viable.

Another of the most often performed plays in the early nineties, *Tales of the Lost Formicans*, explores identity issues in a satirical comedy of manners. The playwright Constance Congdon doubled human characters as aliens by simply having them don sunglasses. The move from human to alien was thus easily accomplished and established as a convention from the beginning of the play. Note that in *Formicans* the aliens present an outsider's "take" on the everyday—what we consider the mundane becomes fascinating or talismanic in their eyes.

In Brechtian terms, Congdon would be creating an alienation effect insofar as once the human characters are dissembled as aliens they force the audience to see or experience them in a different, more objective way. Doubling, in this case, precludes a high level of empathic involvement from the audience. Conversely, in *Prelude to a Kiss*, the switching of inner souls creates a sense of pity and loss, as Peter recognizes the futility of continuing a marriage in which the "other" or Old Man character has taken over the identity of his wife. The poignancy of the play is that its implications extend beyond its story, so that audience members can reflect on the forces that change the people in their lives, and how relationships are continually challenged and reshaped.

The theatrical extremes of character doubling are found in the one-person show. Performed in male drag, Peggy Shaw's *Menopausal Gentleman* is a tour de force that probes the tumult of a women going through menopause. Not only does Shaw explore dynamics across sexes (and within her own gender as a role-playing lesbian), but she also effects a dialogic tension between ages: in drag, she takes on the look of a thirty-something man. The gaps and conflations between sexes, genders, and ages offer numerous opportunities for commentary and humor.

## EXERCISE:
### Playing with Gender and/or Identity Doubling

1) Begin by reading both *Prelude to a Kiss* and *Tales of the Lost Formicans* to achieve an understanding of this principle.

2) Write a monologue in which you establish a primary character in a major dilemma: whether or not to leave a lover, to go on the lam, to undergo an operation, and so forth.

3) Now write another monologue from the standpoint of a double: alien, lover, opposite sex—whatever provides a level of contrast. This character must have a definite "take" on the primary character's monologue.

4) Allow the character in step 3 to inject, insert, or embody the primary character from step 2. Weave together and edit the monologues into a scene in which the doubled characters interact. The shift in the primary character should be noted on a physical, psychological, and spiritual plane. The style or mood can shift, but comic aspects should be exploited.

The doubling technique can be central to a dialogic dramaturgy, as it is to Overmyer's. Nevertheless, the playwright must consider each choice carefully: strive to gain a dramatic edge through doubling characters rather than bulking them to meet bottom-line expectations.

# 7

# Mac Wellman:
# Language-Based Character

## THE EUCLIDEAN CHARACTER

Mac Wellman's consideration of character in traditional theater is worth quoting. As he writes, "One of the most striking features of American dramaturgy is the notion of 'rounded' character. This creature of theatrical artifice with its peculiarly geometric—nay! symmetrical—aspect is so like an object from a math textbook; and one finds it so frequently onstage (and nowhere else) that I have dubbed it the Euclidean Character. Every trait of the Euclidean character must reveal an inner truth of the same kind about the personality in question; each trait must be perfectly consonant with every other trait" (Wellman 1984, 34).

Wellman is clearly resisting the traditional approach to characterization. He rejects notions such as character-specific dialogue and subtext, two benchmarks of the Euclidean character. Wellman's Euclidean Character is ensconced within his screed on the American theater, "Theatre of Good Intentions," insofar as this formulation of a character intention revolves around a relevant sociocultural mission that binds the thematic message of the play. According to Wellman, this "liberal" agenda has privileged the Euclidean character in American dramaturgy since Clifford Odets.

Wellman's distrust of this construct is entrenched in his quintessentially modernist view of the theater artist, a view that he integrates with breakthroughs in chaos theory, fractals, and the philosophy of language. As a modernist, Wellman is the master of each inimitable universe that he creates. The actor, rather than "representing" as character, is the "plastic material" that can become whatever Wellman wishes him to be. No one questions the abstract artist for not creating representations of reality, but because the playwright's "material" is the actor, there is the built-in expectation of similitude to characters in real life. Wellman deflates this notion by celebrating language as his primary material and character as a configuration of language, rather than vice versa. An apt corollary might be to the abstract French painter Olivier Debré, who created what he termed *signes-personnages* (figurative or character-like signs) and *signes-paysages* (landscape signs) (Debré 1999). Debré posed these highly evocative signes-personnages in oblique relation to each other, suggesting various relation-ships. The human entities perceived from the shapes were associational simulacrums rather than representational bodies. The landscape signs formed a similar phenomenon, inviting the spectator to form conclusions through association. In his extensively monologic works, like *Cellophane* and *Three Americanisms*, Wellman uses language to create transient charac-ter-like signs and landscape signs in an aesthetic manner that recalls Debré.

As a playwright, Wellman projects language through the speaking fig-ure, but the language is doing double or triple duty (Wellman 1996). By combining unique syntactical choices with striking sonics, Wellman's lan-guage creates a force field that is stronger than that of any current play-wright. Moreover, because language is innately culturally bound, and the figure of the actor is necessarily perceived by the audience as a given sociotype or class, Wellman's characters seemingly emerge from the lin-guistic heat. During these moments his language delineates a certain scale, as well as an architectural, spatial, or iconographic field in which the figure operates. The figure can rage like an Aeschylean hero or squeal like a deposed corporate guru. The phenomenon of character is created in a stunningly dialogic manner by the figural presence of the speaking, ges-ticulating actor conflating with the associations resonating from the lin-guistic force field.

## CHARACTERS WITHOUT NAMES

In several plays, Wellman has abandoned any traditional notion of char-acter. Characters may not even be named, as in *Terminal Hip*, a kind of free-form monologic blast, or more recently, *Three Americanisms*; both plays provide the conflation or merging of discourses. Most individuals shift levels of language depending on whom they are interacting with. Mac Wellman provides an interesting twist on this multivocal character in his monologue plays. The end result is kind of character by distillation. In Mel Gussow's review of Wellman's *Three Americanisms*, he notes the emer-gence of three distinct characters confronting aspects of contemporary American culture. When no character names are provided whatsoever, the formation is up to the performer in performance, and the perceptions of audience members. *Three Americanisms* provides us with three distinct characters never mentioned by name, only as Man 1, Man 2, and Woman for the benefit of the script reader.

## EXERCISE:
### Creating Character from Language Models

1) Begin by reading *Terminal Hip* and *Three Americanisms* and viewing paint-ings by Yves Tanguy or Olivier Debré.

2) Sense two or three figures as a shadowy presence, not exactly human but as figures are seen in the paintings of Tanguy or Debré. Envision a kind of otherworldly space and locale.

3) Free write or associate on a pad idioms belonging to a certain ethnic, cultural, or cultish group.

4) Create a list of architectural terms and forms, as well as terms that might be described as shaping or configuring.

5) Attempt to concoct a different blend for each of the three figures by varying syntax, syllabic structure, and idiomatic choice.

6) Write three or four monologues for each character over about 10 pages, allowing the figures to interact at various points. Make no effort to identify the characters by traditional names, biographies, or histories—just let language lead the way.

Note: This exercise is much more helpful if you provide the visual sources as indicated above.

## TICKET NAMES

Wellman's range of characterization is broad and complex. As a result, the Wellman concept of character is more difficult to pin down than that of either Jenkin or Overmyer. It seems more experimental in some cases, but Wellman's political series of plays, *Professional Frenchman, Bad Infinity,* and *7 Blowjobs,* employ satiric characterizations where characters are named in a somewhat traditional sense. Wellman's "ticket name" approach is traditional, and rings of classicism à la Ben Jonson or the melodramas of the nineteenth century. An early play, *Harm's Way,* uses ticket names (Crowfoot described a carnival huckster, for instance) and hip thematic phraseology (By Way of Being Hidden, and Isle of Mercy) to name characters. Beyond these somewhat human figures Wellman delivers alien characters and puppets (in *Albanian Softshoe*), animals (in *Murder of Crows*), and oddities (the fur balls in *Sincerity Forever*). The importance of character naming is often overlooked by writers, or confined in terms of its scope. Wellman's choices remind us that a character's name may offer an interesting sound quality, a relation to a societal question, a way to "point" a script, or establish class or mental state. Ultimately, the sum total of the character list helps to create the overall mood or flavor in a particular piece.

In some cases, Wellman engages character ensembles (the crows in *Murder of Crows*) as a kind of Greek chorus, thus continually invoking and reworking theatrical conventions in his plays. This aspect of Wellman's writing regarding character should be noted: the reliance and reworking of past traditions long forgotten, or seldom used, in the American theater.

# LANGUAGE AND THE CREATION OF CHARACTER

The philosopher Ludwig Wittgenstein was the first to reassess the relationship between character and language. In traditional dramaturgy the character has a motive that is expressed in language specific to that character: in sum, the notion of character-specific language. Character-specific language is a rubric that posits a causal relationship between an individual's sociocultural class, education, motive, and level of speech. Play developers have fallen in love with character-specific rubric, denouncing the character that violates "how that character would really speak." This notion rules television and film writing, wherein the dialogue may be almost schematic, allowing the actor to bulk subtextual muscle into the character-specific framework. The problem with the character-specific approach is that it limits both variety and the imagination. Wellman posits the multivocal character, since, as he states, we all change our language styles, and even speech genre, according to a situation. Conflated speech styles may have more impact than the words themselves would indicate: 1960s lingo can jumble with the market-speak of Wall Street, earmarking political views and biases, or demonstrating guru savvy. Variety in speech is as dependable as the passing of time, and is often contingent upon it. Thus, once slang or speech style falls out of favor it becomes more interesting for the playwright to shape character nuance, background, and ideology without resorting to dreary exposition.

Wittgenstein noted that instead of language being the *result* of character, language was actually the *cause* of character. In everyday life we assess individuals according to their level of speech, vocabulary, syntactical choices, and mastery over jargon, cant, or slang. Regional background, level of education, literary influence, and age are concluded almost immediately. Wide groups of the population are earmarked by certain linguistic predilections, whether Cajun, redneck, valley girl, sorority sister, rapper, discourse-driven academic, or "politically correct" politician. Soundbites favored by the media have penetrated everyday conversation. Talk show psychobabble is readily worn on the sleeve and delivered off the cuff. Language frames character: it establishes the context in which the individual operates. We can sense this presence of language in the new playwrights, this sense of playful grafting of "realspeak" with the imaginative and inventive, to create the delightful idiosyncrasies of character.

In the following exercise, attempt to establish various figures, phrases, or flourishes that designate various characters. It is important to note how the language serves as a mask or reveals, establishes an emotional place, and so on. It can then be readily manipulated to meet the playwright's ends. For example, the speech genre of a therapist, the jargon of self-awareness, would be about relaxing the consumer toward opening up and revealing certain truths.

## EXERCISE:
### Language Shaping Character

1) This exercise can be used in revising a work, or in developing a character in a scene.

2) Envision a particular character: environmentalist, academic, hip-hop rapper, conservative politician, fundamentalist preacher, anchorwoman, or mortuary owner.

3) Make a list of jargon, expressions, phrases, terms, figures of speech that earmark this character.

4) Determine how each term or expression might be used dramaturgically: to conceal, reveal, to get what the character wants, to create color, to distract, to seduce. In other words, while the language itself is defining an aspect of this character in relationship to the other characters in the play, the language is also functioning in creating a second, strategic level of interest.

5) Write a scene that conflates at least two of these language systems within one character. While not necessarily naming the character, provide a strong passion that governs the character's logorrhea.

6) Create several more or less functional characters utilizing ticket names to describe the characters' main actions.

## CONCLUSION

As we have seen, the plays of Jenkin, Overmyer, and Wellman challenge traditional approaches to character. Perhaps, the future of character will bring about the convergence of language-based and psychological models toward some new definition. Indeed, the recent plays of Matthew Maguire (*Throwin' Bones* and *Phaedra*) point in that direction. Whatever the outcome will be, there can be no doubt that these novel strategies of character have already affected and influenced the playwriting mainstream.

# PART II

---

*Strategies
of Structure
and
Form*

# *8*

# The Dialogic Beat

This chapter explores how dialogism shapes the creation of beats in a play's script. It examines how the component beats in the script interact to create interest. The concepts and techniques feature characteristics common to plays of the new playwriting. In a number of cases, they expand upon traditional approaches and, as such, should stimulate craft development and dramaturgical acumen. Rather than impose a formulaic way of writing, each playwright can assimilate and adapt these strategies toward novel configurations.

## CONSIDERATION OF TECHNIQUE: THE DIALOGIC BEAT

*PREMISE: The play in itself is a dialogic system. The basic structural component in playwriting is established in beat juxtaposition. The playwright envisions the script as an interactive mechanism in which each beat is in "dialogue" with other beats.*

Beats constitute the smallest identifiable units of language, action, or thought in the play. They represent the fundamental building blocks of the playscript. In traditional playwriting, beats generally cohere to form an overall unity of intention in the play. The causal linkage of beats provides a consistent progression of action that is considered a benchmark of good dramaturgy. From this perspective, the beat is the fundamental means toward the larger end—the finished play. This relegation subordinates the potential of the beat in the immediate moment to how it services the wholeness and unity of the play.

Conversely, in new playwriting the beat is given its due; the direction of the play exists or is discovered from moment to moment. The beat becomes the site of innovation, shifting the direction of the character or play, and by doing so, contradicting the expected or conventional. Means and ends are no longer hierarchal distinctions since juxtaposition supplants linear progression as the prevailing structural scheme. The dynamic meaning of the play occurs at the interface or junction between beats. This strategy is paramount in new playwriting: Constance Congdon's shifting character/aliens in *Tales of the Lost Formicans;* Eric Overmyer's use of languages that "osmose the future" in *On the Verge*; Len Jenkin's shifting narrative and dramatic voicings in *Dark Ride*; Jeffrey Jones's juxtaposed "strips of found language" in *Der Inka von Peru*; Peggy Shaw's split-second gender shifts in *Menopausal Gentleman*. It helps to visualize this effect as if it were a synapse operating within the larger nervous system of the play. By definition, the synapse is a charged impulse interacting between two or more nerve cells. The dialogic move is synaptic, providing an energizing, nervy impulse between beats. The more striking the dynamic shift between beats the more impulses are awakened in the text.

Beats offer the potential for *disruption*—for immediate shifts in intent, purpose, and narrative. To write the polyvocal play, the playwright must be open to the beat's capacity to shift the language or action. This move against monologism requires the writer to share the authorial function with this "second voice." This expansion of the beat's function concomitantly allots more indeterminacy in writing the play. The playwright actualizes his dialogic relation to the script, *pro-acting synaptically* (like a synapse) rather than *reacting synoptically* (with a view of the whole). This notion of energy is similar to the actor's unleashing psychic and physical associations located in the body through exercises or games. The dialogic playwright responds to associational shifts across the text, crafting them to maximum advantage. New playwrights like Peter Mattei (see the opening scenes of his play *Tiny Dimes*), or Matthew Maguire (*Throwin' Bones*) are experts of this nervy use of the beat to affect a sense of spontaneity in the text. The playwright, open to the "second" voice, is empowered to break free from dramaturgical orthodoxy and fully release the potential energy of the script. Table 8.1 distinguishes the beat in new playwriting from its use in traditional dramaturgy.

**TABLE 8.1 The Shifting Beat**

| TRADITIONAL BEAT | NEW PLAYWRITING BEAT |
| --- | --- |
| 1) Language (word) as part of system | 1) Language (word) as free radical |
| 2) Language toward coherence | 2) Language discoheres or innovates |
| 3) Language as meaning | 3) Language as sign or sound |
| 4) Conventional syntax | 4) Unconventional syntax |
| 5) Gesture dependent on language | 5) Autonomous gesture |
| 6) Synoptic: gives view of the whole | 6) Synaptic: partial, immediate |

In new playwriting, the play is negotiated in the moment. This primary emphasis of the beat as shifter focuses the playwright's intuition and imagination toward language and character explorations as the primary building blocks of play structure. In effect, the shifting beat simulates real life better than realistic or traditional methods. We constantly change roles and levels of speech to fit the given situation. Our lives move at "e-speed": we key in a word and we can instantly access places and information across

is the shifter, where language takes on protean characteristics, providing the material means for transition and transformation.

## EXERCISE:
### The Beat Shifter

1) The objective is to create reverberations in the script through rapid shifts in direction. To begin: consider the shifting beat in relation to language; then, explore possibilities with character, or theme. Trigger the shifts with resonant words and reactions to established "givens" in the play. Givens can include physical surroundings, physical props, mood states, time of the day or night, and so on.

2) Shift the vocal level from high-toned to lowbrow; or move from a plaintive state to a wildly exuberant condition (see Santouche in Mac Wellman's *Harm's Way*).

3) Use a mundane topic to trigger a furious interaction. Then, shift to a topic of huge import or consequence (see the early scenes in Mattei's *Tiny Dimes*).

4) A peace-loving character rapidly shifts in a beat of radical violence. Locate a trigger word or phrase to set it off.

5) A seemingly innocuous "given" element in the play triggers a character's impulsive action.

6) The beat as interrupter: give one character the action "to interrupt" the established flow in the scene. Find a word that serves as the interrupter.

Interruption is a fundamental beat-shifting strategy. By interrupting a series or progression of beats, the playwright forces the audience out of its comfort zone to "work" at the play, actually increasing rather than decreasing its involvement. Interruption is akin to the formalist device of "impeded form." Bertholt Brecht used the device to redirect audiences from emotional to intellectual involvement. Breaks in continuity compel the audience to "see anew." The beat of interruption *energizes* the play, as it shifts focus and direction in the script. (Interruption is discussed at length in chapter 7, particularly as it concerns the move from character to narrator or from one character to another.)

## PAROLE VERSUS LANGUE

Since this is a probing of language playwriting, it may be helpful to describe the shifting beat in the terms of linguist Ferdinand de Saussure. Saussure used the term *langue* to describe how current conventions and rules within language and culture give it coherence and understanding. Changes in langue are gradual; once competence is achieved the individual operates within the system without giving it a second thought. Traditional playwriting is oriented toward langue, since it applies familiar conventions (representational, fictional matrixed characters), which are familiar to the majority of audience members (competence). Conversely, one reason mainstream audiences have not embraced the new playwriting has to do with their lack of "competence"; quite simply, as the familiar moorings are unloosed or parodied, the audience is made uncomfortable, or is uncertain about how to react. The dramaturgy of the traditional play as a system of langue aims for coherence over formal innovation or disruptive experimentation. In this sense, it does not favor the beat as the site of innovation.

Saussure used the term *parole* to describe "how" a word means in actual practice—in its endless variety of contexts, intonations, and syntactic arrangements. As such, parole suggests the potential for innovation or deviation from the conventionalized system. Over time, these innovations (in fashion, usage of slang, foreignisms, etc.) become assimilated into langue as conventional or mainstream parlance. Eventually, slang dates itself and passes out of general parlance. At some later point it becomes historicized, and is then useful to designate a particular feeling or mood about a given period. The new playwriting favors parole in its capacity to innovate; for example, Mac Wellman's unique syntactical choices extravagate how language is configured in current American culture. Moreover, new playwrights rebottle historicized slang to establish variations on American character types.

## BEAT VARIATIONS

The following techniques, examples, and exercises are designed to create more immediacy in the construction of beats. For the most part, these are language-based strategies that open you to your "second voice."

### Riffing

*Riffing* occurs when one character "picks up on" a phrase or line of dialogue, then embellishes it, rephrases it, or emends it. The concept derives from blues or jazz music in which a short musical phrase is repeated with continual variation or embellishment. Overmyer's use of the effect in *The Heliotrope Bouquet* is mostly lyrical; although it serves the story function of identifying the brothel the women work in, The House of Blue Light. This beat occurs in the middle of scene 1, labeled "Joplin's Dream":

SPANISH MARY: There's a lacy breeze.

HANNAH: Lacy breeze fluttering.

SPICE: Lacy breeze.

JOY: Spanish moss lacy in the live oak trees.

FELICITY: Fluttering.

JOY: Morning, morning, morning.

FELICITY: Morning in the House of Blue Light.

(Overmyer 1993, *The Heliotrope Bouquet*, 231)

This beat riff functions lyrically, poetically interpreting everyday phenomena. The first four characters repeat the word *lacy* in various manifestations and probable intonations; the fifth character's "fluttering" refrains the second character's "lacy breeze fluttering." Riffing links the characters through sound and expressive intent, while maintaining a sense of immediacy in the moment. Overmyer's characters simulate the music of Joplin—the variance in phrasing has its corollary in jazz or ragtime.

Overmyer's riff divulges lyrically what would otherwise be a tediously labored expository scene. In traditional dramaturgy, the women would "volunteer" information about setting, time, and action that the playwright felt necessary for the play to progress. The scene's placement at the beginning of the play would probably ensure that there would be some discussion about the major characters about to be introduced. Overmyer's riffing approach transcends the cliché, and in doing so proves that most expository information is unnecessary, or at least can be handled in a more aesthetically satisfying manner.

## EXERCISE:
### Riffing and Exposition

1) *Exposition* is generally defined as the information needed for the play to progress effectively. To be effective dramaturgically, exposition must appear unforced and earned; it should be sprinkled deftly throughout the playtext, and not simply "front loaded" in the beginning of the play. In traditional practices, expository material works best when delivered under pressure, as the result of conflict and complication. Otherwise, the divulging of information will appear gratuitous or contrived. In new playwriting, the two prevalent forms of handling exposition are either through riffing variations or the point-of-view character. Playwrights such as Eric Overmyer, Matthew Maguire, and Jeffrey Jones favor the former, whereas Len Jenkin and Tony Kushner favor the latter. The point-of-view character usually has an ironic or politicized take on expository material that includes significant commentary. This exercise gets you through some tedious exposition by exploring riffing variations.

2) Character A reacts to a word used by Character B that relates to something expositional [consider this in an associational manner, as in the Overmyer scene in chapter 6 where *lacy* ends up at the place indicated]. The expositional beat should relate to an offstage character, an event, or place.

3) Character B embellishes on Character A, varying the phrase by repeating and reforming or transforming the word. The riff can rhyme, or disclose etymological derivations or foreignisms that provide onomatopoeia, and so forth.

4) How does the riff serve as the shifter in the scene?

5) Find an end or stasis point in the exchange. Note how the riff should be doing double duty, accomplishing both expositional and lyrical functions.

**Wellman's Solo Riffs**

In *Whirligig*, Wellman's character Girl engages in lengthy solo riffs:

GIRL: [a fragment of her speech] Zero the ozone layer. Zero the Museum of Natural History. Zero the pink tennis shoes. Zero the green hair. Zero the heroes, Ollie, Poindexter, rolling uphill, are dead, blast, brightness nothing.

(Wellman 1994, Whirligig, 149)

Wellman configures shifting phenomenon and places riffing off of the trisyllabic ([*Zero the*] ozone layer. [*Zero the*] Museum of Natural History, etc.). The repetitive riff provides coherence, grounding the freewheeling conflation of unrelated phrases and terms. The associations ultimately release into Wellman's point of departure, after "Zero the heroes." The repetitive riff accumulates energy in the text that now flows in another direction. This riffing technique is analogous to a typical musical composition by Philip Glass, which builds through subtle variations and accumulations. Glass's music from his collaboration with Robert Wilson, *Einstein on the Beach*, is a good example. Following these examples, the playwright can repeat a rhythmical phrase or motif and then allow associations to come forth. Moreover, the repetitions produce a mantra-like effect that mitigates the intrusion of the self-censor, freeing the playwright to explore dynamic shifts and juxtapositions.

### Turns and the Shadow Riff

Turns relate dialogue to pairs of speakers. Turns concern the structure and dynamic of dialogue between speakers and responders. Turns are weighted toward power dynamics: a question from leader to subordinate demands an immediate response, whereas a question from subordinate to leader might be deferred without protocols being violated. Other rules apply. Speakers are expected to take their turn in everyday discourse. For example, a greeting that is ignored or met with silence might be considered insulting, rude, or indicative of an underlying antagonism between speakers. On the other hand, turns often reflect a mirror-like patterning whereby one speaker mimics, questions, or reiterates the utterance of the other. This pattern of repetition is called *shadow riffing*. The shadow riff is a variable type of turn. It may involve the responder "topping" the speaker, or permuting what is said. The shadow riff foregrounds the surfaces of language as it probes the subtle power plays that underlie conversational exchanges. For playwright David Mamet, the shadow riff is a signature stylistic feature that offers flexibility through shifting intonation, context, and pace. The following example from *Speed The Plow* is indicative:

FOX: I just thought, I just thought she falls between two stools.

GOULD: And what would those stools be?

FOX: That she is not, just some, you know, a "floozy."

GOULD: A "floozy" . . .

FOX: . . . On the other hand, I think I'd have to say, I don't think she is so ambitious she would have to schtup you just to get ahead. (*Pause*)

That's all. (*Pause*)

GOULD: What if she just "liked" me? (Pause)

FOX: If she just "liked" you?

GOULD: Yes.

FOX: Ummm. (*pause*)

GOULD: Yes.

FOX: You're saying, if she just . . . liked you . . . (Pause)

GOULD: You mean nobody loves me for myself?

FOX: No.

GOULD: No?

FOX: Not in *this* office . . .

(Mamet 1985, I: 35–36)

Gould shadows Fox's statement regarding "stools," with the question, "And just what would those stools be?" The statement shadowed by the question is a trademark of Mamet's dialogue style. The phoneme intoned (oo) in stools riffs into the alliterative "floozy," an anachronistic descriptor. As an anachronism, the word is foregrounded while both men take pleasure in the sound play. Then, in a turn reversal, Fox shadows Gould's limpid, "What if she just 'liked' me?" with his sarcastic take, "If she just 'liked' you?" Here, intonation provides contextual and rhythmical variety through the shadowed "liked," in quotes, preceded by affirmations and followed by negations. The riff pays off with Fox's punch line, "not in *this* office"—the follow-up to Gould's setup, "You mean nobody loves me for myself?" Mamet's shadow riffing reflects the gaming nature of language in *Speed the Plow*. Rather than character-specific dialogue, Mamet orchestrates the sequence to suggest subtle moment-to-moment advantage between the characters. The power dynamics disguise the underlying formalism of the shadow riff and the necessity of careful crafting to maximize its effect.

## EXERCISE:
### The Shadow Riff

The shadow riff exercise is particularly helpful to young playwrights who generally have difficulty keeping their dialogue "in the moment." The stratagem simulates the "mirror game" that actors play as one speaker provides the language for another actor to copy, mimic, and extrapolate upon. The playwright should maintain the surface level of language, while exploring the subtleties of power relationships. One character must strive to gain some advantage over the other or the riffing will sound mannered and strained.

The shadow riff exercises should be read in the workshop in order to heighten the variables of intonation and rhythm.

1) Characters A and B discuss a third offstage character C.

2) Establish a key word or phrase uttered by Character A.

3) Character B shadows the phrase of A in the form of a question.

4) Character A answers by restressing the phrase, after several turns of spacers (umm, uhh, ahh) or affirmations; negations reinforce the shadowing.

5) Character B mimics, embellishes, or "reframes" the shadow.

6) A conclusion is arrived at regarding Character C.

VARIATION: Alter the above sequence by riffing on expository material rather than conflict or action material.

COMMENT: The shadow riff will go where it wants to go, and is not predetermined by the playwright. Allow the characters to enjoy and engage the moment without overt interference or "forcing it." An overly controlled shadow riff will sound stilted and calculated, rather than light and quick-witted.

### Dictionary Stop

The introduction of external language sources to redirect the course of the play is characteristic of the new playwriting. In Dictionary Stop, an exercise devised by Mac Wellman, a word is selected at random out of the dictionary and inserted into the text. The character or characters riff on the word as it ineluctably shifts the scene in another direction. Wellman vaunts about the effectiveness of the technique in his own plays, particularly as a means to mitigate writer's block. He draws the corollary with physics: the inserted word is the free radical that creates a fission-like reaction within the text, releasing the stored energy in the script.

## EXERCISES:
### Dictionary Stop

## Exercise A:
### Solo

The purpose of this exercise is to unlock writer's block by freeing the playwright of the responsibility to produce language. This dialogic engagement embraces the "other" and reorients the putative notion of "ownership" in the playscript.

1) You have come to a temporary impasse in writing dialogue. Go the dictionary and randomly select a word (however obscure). Insert the word into the character's dialogue at the point of impasse.

2) The dictionary stop becomes a free radical pivot beat. Have this character and others riff off of it, allowing it to lead or channel the scene in a different direction.

COMMENT: This exercise always yields unexpected results. As the dropped-in word piques the curiosity of the playwright, the imagination is awakened with new possibilities. The playwright relaxes, allowing this "second voice" to motivate the direction of the script.

Use this exercise in the playwrights' workshop with up to eight to twelve participants. The entire exercise is conducted in the workshop or classroom.

1) Begin writing a two-character scene with a simple premise, such as: one character attempts to get the other character to leave (a room, a house, a car, etc.).

2) Make a list of terms or bring in the dictionary, and at two- or three-minute intervals stop, then drop the word in a line of dialogue.

3) Pass the paper to the left or right. Give from thirty seconds to one minute for the next playwright to read the text, then continue the process of writing and passing the text, stopping at regular intervals to drop in another word.

4) When you reach your time limit (ten to fourteen minutes), direct the final playwright in the sequence to finish the scene with the instigating character accomplishing or failing the objective.

COMMENT: This exercise builds camaraderie and trust in the workshop. It also takes "ego" out of the mix and involves multiple, often indiscernible voices in the text. Do not overly emphasize the narrative thread; the playwrights should focus on how the inserted word motivates the script.

### Speech Acts or Performatives

Many beginning playwrights have difficulty making dialogue sound immediate or in the moment. Typically faulty dialogue is overly expository, has too many ideas per speech, or expends excessive time describing offstage events and characters. As a result, scene work lacks presence and verve. One effective way to correct this problem is to employ speech act beats. A *speech act* is a word, phrase, or sentence that suggests immediate or deferred action. It is dialogic because it requires the "other" to respond; moreover, the speech act inherently conflates word and circumstance. Playwright Richard Nelson, who is well known for both his original plays and adaptations of classics, considers the speech act the sine qua non of writing for the theater: "There's this wonderful English philosopher, J. L. Austin, who conceived what he called the 'speech act.' He was asking, 'When does speech become an action?' For example, if I'm in a marriage ceremony and say, 'I do,' I become married. That involves an action, an action beyond the act of speaking. Theater is one giant 'speech act.' That's its very nature." (Nelson 2000, 25–26).

The speech act takes a number of forms, but here are some examples:

1. **The threat.** When character A threatens character B, apprehension and suspense are created. The tension is immediate and sustainable because the speech act defers to the moment that the threat will or will not be realized.

2. **The promise.** When a character makes a promise, she sets up

anticipation. If the promise is not delivered we learn something about the makeup of the character. If the promise is delivered we have a plot point.

3. **The command.** The power move demands an immediate response. Those characters receiving the command are compelled to react. This reaction determines the relationship of the characters at the moment of utterance. What is the power dynamic in the play? How will the commanded respond? What is the potential for reversal?

4. **The vow.** A vow establishes a bond of trust between characters, or between character and audience. It calls to question the credibility of the character making the vow.

5. **The strategy.** Planning an action keeps the play in the moment. Characters must role-play as leaders, followers, instigators, and soon. The relationship between the plan and the outcome establishes a dynamic tension. The sequential nature of a strategic plan provides ready-made plot points.

Most speech acts are considered truth statements until broken. Unless a playwright establishes the character as untrustworthy, the audience will accept characters at face value. Playwrights can manipulate this "tacit bond" to create interest and surprise. On another level, there is a "force" potential to the speech act—how it is said, and with what intonation, and in what context, are crucial to its effectiveness (Petrey 1990, 15).

A speech act demands a performative response. It is neither ideation nor idle chat, but must involve behavior. When reactions are conflicted, the speech act beat accelerates the rhythm of a scene. If character A says, "Get up!" then we will anxiously await character B's response, which plays out in the form of an action: to comply, to resist, to defer, to ignore; and in a certain manner: rashly, sluggishly, or distractedly. Speech acts are playable for actors since they externalize intention. Harold Pinter was a master of the speech act, using it to threat, intimidate, accuse, and browbeat, thereby creating a sense of menace in the plot and characters. His early works like *The Homecoming* or *The Birthday Party* are indicative of this usage of language as weapon.

## EXERCISE:
### Speech Acts

To curtail the impulse of young playwrights to describe past events, telegraph internal states, or simply front load expositional material, undertake a scene that utilizes various speech acts. To avoid diluting the force of the speech acts, require that the playwright limit individual speeches to one sentence or phrase.

1) Initiate a brief two-character sequence (made up of three to four beats). Character A utters a speech act that compels Character B to respond. Examples include: threats, promises, agreements, vows, denials, commands, directives, and orders.

2) While responses may be immediate (to commands, orders, etc.), other speech acts anticipate later results (promises, vows, or threats); Character B thus has a number of options in responding.

3) At the end of the sequence determine the "truth quality" of the speech act. In other words, was it a bluff, a lie, a subterfuge?

4) How does this "truth quality" inform us about the character?

5) What were the varying degrees of *force* for each speech act? What was done with the dialogue to create shifts in intonation?

### Beat As Gesture: Quotable Gestures and Utterances

Although we have considered language beats primarily, a beat may also be a gesture. The influential Marxist critic Walter Benjamin said that Bertholt Brecht's plays offered the actor the potential for the quotable gesture, one that could recast an earlier moment in a different light. The quoted gesture interrupts the present context (Benjamin 1977, 7), thus causing the script to be self-reflexive. In doing so it calls attention to itself, revealing the underlying form of the dramaturgy. The gesture may be repeated or "shadowed" from another character, and thus is related to the beat variations we have referred to above. In productions of Mac Wellman's plays, performers can formulate extreme gestures, particularly to clarify or amplify sections of monologue (in plays like *Three Americanisms, Terminal Hip*, or *Bodacious Flapdoodle*). The gesture provides a frame for the segment of text, as it reinforces the dialogic relation between text and physical action, two autonomous systems that converge and mediate with each other. For example, gesture can provide intention to beats of nouning or syntactical phrases that would otherwise defy categorization. As gesture marks the text with intention, it provides a performative structure that stands side by side with the text. Actor Stephen Mellor has been the most adept at bringing a gestural intention to the language beats in Mac Wellman's plays. As Mellor scans the play text, he determines an external gestural form to link passages in the text. The acting approach conflates the heightened spirit of an Eastern model such as Kabuki with Western Grand Guignol stylization. Both styles feature exaggerated, physical gestures and facial expressions executed with style and formal precision. Mellor uses makeup to exaggerate or shadow features of his natural visage, emphasizing a strange, macabre quality that seems the perfect complement to Wellman's verbal assaults. Moreover, this "masking" promotes a broader, gestural interpretation of the text.

A gestured beat can quote itself to create a structural link or unifying device. For example, a gesture that is repeated several times within an act will serve as a linking device across the act.

## Tag Lines

In effect the *tag line* is a "quotation"—the character is quoting himself. Since the content of the beat, or in this case, tag line, is shifting through the course of the play, the beat is dialogic. In the same way, a "running gag" will provide a topos of unity in a comedy, and it will adjust to the given circumstances to build a laugh. Odd syntax, slang, or maxims can serve as interactive links, serving the larger purpose of defining a character. The character becomes associated with a certain rhetorical phrase or style. It is really in revision that quotable beats are first discovered, then honed and reshaped, to maximize their affect. In revision, examine your script at ultraclose range: explore the beats; then, exploit their dialogic potential.

## Spacer Beats in Dialogue: Pauses and Ellipses

The function of *pauses* or *ellipses* is often misunderstood by beginning writers, who overuse them in an attempt to seem profound or mysterious. Aping the "Pinter pause" will bring detrimental results. In Pinter's dramaturgical scheme, pauses relate to shifting power dynamics, a truth submerged under the spoken lie, or they further a sense of menace and terror. As in real life, the lack of a verbal response may be construed as an insult, or may at least frustrate an antagonist. These actions are *produced* by the pause. Each pause has a definite, calculated, and often subtextual reason for being there. Conversely, beginning playwrights use pauses indiscriminately or gratuitously, and rarely with a sense of strategy or dramaturgic purpose. Pinter's complex dramaturgy involves a system of dialogue breaks of varying duration: the brief *ellipsis*, the one- or two-beat *pause*, and the protracted *silence*. The multiple beats of the silence represent a plunge into the abyss, and theatrically may exact a period of total stasis.

Playwrights should be wary of the interpretive latitude that pauses and silences afford the director. The pause is a gift to the actor, offering, in the moment, a sense of the improvisational, particularly in terms of gesture, movement, or stage business.

The playwright utilizes pauses the way the composer incorporates the rest—for rhythmical syncopation or alteration, to set up a payoff, or to interrupt and refocus. However, there are differences to be noted as well. For example, a pause in drama often reflects an awkwardness, or inability to verbalize, whereas the same cannot be said of music. Moreover, in the theater it is impossible to be as precise in assessing duration, since composers provide a definite metrical rate. Nevertheless, both the pause and the rest affect timing and pacing, and are therefore reliant on feel. The pause provides a spacer not only for actor and director, but for audience as well. By interrupting the flow of dialogue the pause draws attention to what has been said. The pause allots the audience a moment to reflect, to anticipate, or to renew interest. Pauses must be paced judiciously or the results will be static, awkward, and overly stylized (not appropriate for a realistic or naturalistic approach, but potential fodder for an antinaturalistic play). Auteur-director Richard Foreman in the production of his play *The Cure* used stylized pauses and rapid shifts in pace as a means to juxtapose various sequences in the play.

Mac Wellman's pauses frequently indicate a gestural response, a chance for the body to rearrange itself. When used in succession, the pauses allow a director to orchestrate a series of movements, whereby each beat can be specifically focused in rehearsal. Wellman also uses pauses to set up tag lines, buttons, or punch lines in longer speeches. This short segment from *7 Blowjobs* indicates how the pause opens up space for the actor, as it establishes, or refocuses the action:

EILEEN: BAG IT DOT!
 *Pause.*
SENATOR: Cool down, Eileen.
 *Pause.*
        And get him out of here.
 *BRUCE comes to.*

(Wellman 1994, *7 Blowjobs*, 232)

Eileen's command, "BAG IT DOT!" freezes the moment. The pause acknowledges the shift in energy, and the senator's response, "Cool down, Eileen," addresses the momentary vacuum. Because the pause creates a vacuum, it serves as an attractor. Wanting to be filled, a shift in the rhythm or dynamic of the segment now occurs. In the first pause, the senator takes control of the scene. In this sense, the pause can be an important dramaturgic factor in establishing power dynamics in a scene or act. The pause puts matters "up for grabs." The second pause places the senator in charge, as he shifts focus from Eileen to Bruce on the floor. Physical options are made available to the actor during this pause.

Overmyer and Jenkin utilize pauses less frequently than Wellman. Overmyer is specific about the effect of his pauses, as a passage from *On the Verge* indicates:

FANNY: The postal system is worrisome, Mr. Coffee, but not yet hopeless.
 (*Pause. Fanny Understands.*)

(Overmyer 1993, *On the Verge*, 89)

The effect during this pause simulates the illuminated lightbulb in old cartoons—Fanny sees the light. This is a normative usage of the pause: as a transition in thought, the beat of recognition.

## Jenkin and the Dialogic Ellipsis

Jenkin frequently employs ellipses to achieve structural goals such as linking speakers or scenes. At the end of scene 2 in *Dark Ride*, the translator, whose translation establishes the action of the play, reads a passage from his work:

> TRANSLATOR: [*At the end of his speech*] I quote. "Margo lies back on the couch in her apartment, and opens a book. She turns the pages slowly until she finds her place. Her lips move slightly with the words she reads, like a child. . . ."
>
> (Jenkin 1993, *Dark Ride*, 65)

The ellipsis provides the transition into scene 3. Here, MARGO takes over, as the scene shifts locale:

> MARGO: Chapter Nine. At the Clinic. [*Her speech continues*]
>
> (Jenkins 1993, *Dark Ride*, 66)

The beat of the ellipsis serves the structural function of shifting the theatrical environment. It is dialogic because it bridges the "present" world of the translator with some distant past literary world that he has translated. Jenkin's ellipsis is a connector—a dialogic conduit between the two ontological levels. This use of the ellipsis represents a dramaturgic innovation.

## The Ellipsis As Interrupter

While the ellipsis may function as a connector, it may bring about a beat of disruption or interruption. In part 3 of *Limbo Tales*, "The Hotel," Jenkin sets up two audio speakers, stage right and left. These two sound areas represent the adjoining rooms to the center chamber occupied by the character, named Man. As speakers they simulate typical noises from the adjoining room, thus interrupting the narrative of Man:

> MAN: [*At the end of his speech*] I was sending money home all the time, so Eileen must have liked the other guy a lot, cause the money must have made her feel bad . . .
>
> SPEAKER C: [*Humming of a little song, coughing, very soft, . . . continuing and fading . . .*]
>
> MAN: . . . She should have, too, cause all I thought of on the road was her and the kid.
>
> (Jenkin 1993, *Limbo Tales*, 42)

Jenkin uses the ellipsis to show the points where Man's train of thought is interrupted—then renewed. The in-and-out-of-focus aspect of the Speaker C intrusion serves several functions: (1) creation of tension and anticipation; (2) reorientation of the audience's attention; (3) rhythmical interpolation; and (4) theatrical use of sound and space. The disruption ultimately draws attention back to Man's reaction.

Wellman's use of the ellipsis is often related to the pause, as the opening of *Whirligig* indicates:

> GIRL: I dreamed I had a wicked sister . . .
>     *Pause*
>     She was a girl Hun.

(Wellman 1994, Whirligig, 143)

In this example, the opening line, "I dreamed I had a wicked sister," establishes the premise and narrative thrust for the entire play, while the ellipsis is the continuant, open-ended frame for the story. The pause represents the transition into the body of the play.

**Conventional Uses of the Ellipsis**

Playwrights have used ellipses to simulate telephone conversations, the " . . ." that is the convention for the voice of the other. Another traditional use is to simulate doubt, vacillation, and quick shifts in thought, where the ellipsis defines the transitory mind. The ellipsis is thus a playwright's tool for dealing with a character's inner dialogism. When taken to extremes, the ellipsis presents the opportunity for the multivoiced character to emerge: witness Hungry Mother's levels of language in Overmyer's *Native Speech*.

## EXERCISE:
### Ellipses

1) With the excerpt on page 108 from *Dark Ride* as an example, use the ellipsis to segue from a character's closing line of dialogue to a subsequent line of action that is begun by another character. Envision the ellipsis as if it were a relay-race baton: Character A hands off a phrase or sentence to Character B, who channels the play in a different direction.

2) With the above excerpt from *Limbo Tales* as an example, utilize ellipses to frame an intruding character that interrupts Character A. After the interruption, allow Character A to continue his speech.

COMMENT: What are the effects of these two exercises on your sense of playwriting structure. Do they open up certain possibilities? Sequence and points of transition ultimately define structure. Structure is about the interrelationship of parts.

### *The Asterisk and The Slash*

Wellman's signature punctuation mark is the asterisk (*). Anyone who reads his plays is initially baffled. Wellman explains, in the notes to

*Whirligig,* "The occasional appearance of an asterisk in the middle of a speech indicates that the next speech begins to overlap at that point. A double asterisk indicates that a later speech (not the one immediately following) begins to overlap at that point. The overlapping speeches are all clearly marked in the text" (Wellman 1995, *Whirligig,* p. 142).

This section could be included in the chapter on monologue, although it is clear that the overlapping creates a kind of dialogic dissonance, a more aural than semantic phenomenon. Its use is similar to Caryl Churchill's application in *Serious Money,* in which the forward slash (/) indicates the point in a character's dialogue that is overlapped by the subsequent character's speech. Overlapping or dovetailing dialogue is a regular phenomenon of general discourse. The collision of speeches on stage can be highly effective.

## EXERCISE:
### Collision of Speech

1) Transcribe a taped conversation between two persons. The persons should not be aware of the taping which should last 5-6 minutes. Note in the transcription points where voices overlap before the first speech is concluded. Other aspects to consider:
   a) the use of pauses;
   b) paralinguistic spacers like well, hmmm, and uhh;
   c) how beat shifts and changes in topic correlate.

COMMENT: This transcription exercise demonstrates how speakers interact with no expository material; limit speeches to short phrases; overlap and interrupt each other.

## EXERCISE:
### The Asterisk and the Slash

1) Revise some turns (dialogue pairs) in a script by inserting the slash at key or intentional words.
2) Use the asterisk in several long speeches or monologues that are sequential; note the effect of density in the text.

We can now turn our attention to the larger building blocks of the script, the most significant of which is the beat segment.

### THE BEAT SEGMENT

The building of several beats around a given action or topic constitutes the *beat segment.* It would be nearly impossible to form a play that was based

solely on isolated beats. Perhaps the futurists could be considered, since
their plays (really fragmentary sketches) lasted seconds in real time. The
sequential quality of the play script mandates certain organizing factors.
The beat segment groups beats together, providing a grounding from
which the playwright can establish larger units within the play. The beat
segment can vary in length from several beats to a dozen or more; thus, it
is a significant structural component in the development and later revision of the playscript. Sometimes the beat segment is the same as a French
scene: defined by a character's entrance or exit. (While the term *French
scene* is useful to pinpoint entrances and exits, under this system of nomenclature, the French scene is more akin to the beat segment. Thus, the
term *beat segment* is used in this context.) The following beat segment from
Jenkin's *My Uncle Sam* is typical of the latter approach:

> [*The MANAGER is gone, The LITTLE PERSON in the dirty yellow vest
> appears; The PERSON is carrying a box with holes in the top.*]

LITTLE PERSON: Got a Butt?

YOUNG SAM: It's you again. Who are you?

LITTLE PERSON: I'm nobody. Who are you?

YOUNG SAM: My Uncle Sam, Hey . . .

LITTLE PERSON: Just kidding . . . I'm in show business. Show's in
here.

> [*Holds up box.*]

Rats. I run a rat theatre. But the show's not in A-1 shape. Yesterday,
we were doing a matinee of Romeo and Juliet when a dog broke into
the show tent and ate the cast. These are only the understudies.

YOUNG SAM: You been following me.

LITTLE PERSON: Or vice-versa. I'll put my cards on the table. In fact,
I'll put my cards on the floor. You got troubles ahead. Go to the
church of St. Christopher. Watch out for Lila.

YOUNG SAM: Lila?

LITTLE PERSON: Then go to the Blowhole Theater. Gotta run there's
the travel agent.

YOUNG SAM: Hey—wait . . .

> [*The TRAVEL AGENT appears with his female ASSISTANT as the LITTLE
> PERSON runs off.*]

> (Jenkin 1993, *My Uncle Sam*, 184–185)

How is the above a typical beat segment? It is marked by the entrance and
exit of Little Person, and several internal beats: the introductory "Got a
butt?" and the questions of identity, and then the rat theater show, with
the preposterous rejoinder that the rats are indeed understudies. The rat

theater is foregrounded in the beat segment. After that we return to essentially narrative information—"You've been following me"—to specific directions that take the form of speech acts. These speech acts are most effective tools of dialogue since they not only suggest a present action, but anticipate the future: "Watch out for Lila," which can be construed as a warning, or threat; "go to the Blowhole Theatre" is a performative command or direction that anticipates Young Sam's actually going to the theater. Little Person's quick exit ends the beat segment with a build of suspense and interest. The structure of this beat segment contains a clearly marked beginning, middle, and end.

The beat segment can also establish a rhythmic or gestural thrust and parry. In *The Bad Infinity* Wellman utilizes labels and pauses that establish an interesting form of dialogism, a kind of call and response. Near the end of the play, as Sam prepares to leave the Chef and the forest, there is the following exchange:

CHEF: What will you find? Will you find
   love in the city? Bah!
   Love is for children. For idiots.
   A beautiful woman is a false
   beautiful woman.

SAM: But she is still a beautiful woman.

CHEF: True.

SAM: I'm going now.

CHEF: Clown!
*Pause.*
   Compromisist!
*Pause.*
   Tool of the bourgeoisie!
*Pause.*
   Fascist!
*Pause.*
   Pessimist!
*Pause.*
   Gourmand!

SAM: I've got to get out of this place.

   *He Exits.*

(Wellman 1994, *The Bad Infinity*, 100–101)

The Chef's scurrilous labels attempt to demean or villainize Sam. Wellman sets up a gestural parry in each pause, although it can only be inferred that some response from Sam is indicated. Each label and pause represent a beat in this segment that can be isolated from other beats and staged accordingly. Sam's exit concludes the segment, so the beat segment in this case is tantamount to a French scene.

## Beat Segment Overview

Examine some of your recent scene work in different plays. If you have not reached the stage where you have a body of work, then simply look over several scenes. Begin by defining the beat segments with adhesive notes or flags if you have a hard copy, or use word processing bookmarks if the script remains on disk. If you choose the latter approach, be certain to save a copy of the working draft before you begin to cut and paste. Len Jenkin favors this method of revision by segment.

1) How many beat segments are there per scene? How much variance in the number of beat segments per given scene? For example, does one scene contain twelve segments, another scene one or two?

2) How many beats are there per segment?

3) How does each segment affect the progress of the scene?

    a) Number each segment or give it a letter designation.

    b) Note which segments are keys to the scene and which segments float.

    c) How are segments juxtaposed? Are transitions smooth or arbitrary?

4) Alter the sequence of segments: cut and paste (hard copy or on disk).

    a) Which segments seem superfluous, no longer serve the play?

    b) What are the "synapses" between segments?

    c) In an early draft, the playwright will often construct transitional segments for her benefit—as a means of getting to beat segment 3 from 1. Once the scene is written, however, 2 may become superfluous, and the jump from 1 to 3 may energize the script.

    d) Consider how the juxtapositions of segments might work after revision.

5) How does each beat affect the progress of the segment?

    a) Which beat gives the segment some punch or pull?

    b) Which beats seem to wobble, wander aimlessly, or feel (to you) awkward or uncomfortable? Why?

    c) Highlight where you really detect a synapse between beats.

As a rule, the more variance from segment to segment, the more interest will be created in the script. Richard Nelson's *Bal* is a good example of how beat segment variance can be effective. Some of Maria Irene Fornes's plays (*Mud*, for example) rely upon beat segment arrangement to create the sense of structure.

Because it interacts dialogically with neighboring segments and across the play, the beat segment is a key structural component. Therefore, in early drafts one should "rough in" the optimal sequence of segments, before polishing the specific segment. It is useful to determine whether the segment is primarily working within a scene, an act, or across the entire play. Never in isolation, its variable nature allows the segment to be moved, shortened, lengthened, or deleted entirely. The beat segment must be mastered for the playwright to effectively write the polyvocal play.

Once these chops are developed, the playwright can orchestrate juxtapositions, conflations, and transitions with more confidence and speed. Now let us turn our attention to some major components of the beat segment.

## Contour

Each beat segment suggests a certain definable shape, or *contour*. While the *beat segment* is a structural term, *contour* is primarily a stylistic consideration since it describes how or in what manner the material is handled. Jagged, sinuous, flat, rounded, straight-ahead, angular, S-shaped or elliptical are metaphoric descriptors that are used to describe contour. The contour for a given playwright may vary somewhat from play to play, and contours can vary throughout the play. However, there is usually some benchmark present in most of the playwright's work. Contour throughout segments of Anton Chekhov's plays could be described as elliptical or sinuous. Segments of *Three Sisters* and *The Cherry Orchard* seem to flow into and out of each other without sharp breaks or delineation.

The above beat segment from *My Uncle Sam* has a jagged contour: information is given or asked for, but conditions remain mysterious; a gratuitous story is told, then there is a sudden shift: "You been following me." This jagged contour of the beat segment reflects in microcosm the action of Young Sam's search, and suggests the overall contour of the play.

Contour can be varied or manipulated by altering the rhythms and tempi of speeches. The playwright who is adept at contour will influence the breathing of the actor, since contour is akin to lyrical phrasing in music. Contour is paramount in determining the effectiveness of monologues, providing clues for the actor and more engagement for the audience. Hungry Mother's monologues in Overmyer's *Native Speech* demonstrate zigzag contours that propel us forward with hairpin turns and rapid shifts. So while the character's speeches appear longish on the page, in performance they play quite fast, with vertiginous effect. Overmyer considers his writing to be poetic prose—the modern corollary to the iambic pentameter of William Shakespeare, or the Alexandrine hexameter of Molière, or Jean Racine. Overmyer crafts his words toward specific "shaping" effects. Contour provides a discernable signature of the master playwright.

### Contour and the Designer

To understand contour in your own work, ask a stage, lighting, or costume designer to read and respond to the contour of your play; the feedback is of a different ilk than you will receive from directors, actors, or dramaturgs. Designers are trained to think and speak in terms of line, shape, form, and mass. For production designers, contour will manifest itself in intuitive terms, a feeling about the shape of the text that emerges over several readings. Follow up by asking the designer how the contour of your work would affect a production design.

## Contour

1) Write several two-character beat segments, using no more than four words per phrase, sentence, or utterance. How would you describe the contour of shape of the segments?

2) Insert a third character into these segments whose utterances run on without punctuation containing many words in a single breath. IMPORTANT: These insertions should not be monologues, but contain between seven and twenty words that can be spoken fluidly.

3) How does this insertion affect the sense of contour across the segments?

4) How can pauses and ellipses affect contour?

### *The Marker*

Each beat segment finishes with a *marker* placed at or near the end of the segment. The marker can be an exit, an exit line or button, a pause or stage direction that underlines or defines a transition. Markers are signals for the audience that suggest a change in direction or character; an anticipation of forthcoming events; a key name or identifying characteristic. The marker is a signpost for the reader/audience and, as such, is a definable structural unit. When Little Person in Jenkin's *Uncle Sam* says, "Watch out for Lila," the audience not only receives future character information, but an anticipation of suspense, danger, or threat. So the speech act— "Watch out for Lila"—combines a character marker with one that is plot related. A skilled playwright like Jenkin is able to provide markers and fascinating beats that digress (the rat theater story) within the same beat segment. Markers are the playwright's pact with the audience. They allow the playwright greater latitude to experiment because they give the audience some clear indicators to follow.

Markers provide directors and actors with focal points as well. For the actor, the marker represents the crucial moment in the character's arc where an important action or discovery is registered and made, or a change in direction is indicated. For the director, the marker provides the opportunity for directorial choice, and production coherence. Without attention to each marker, the production will appear unfocused, as the director will have neglected making choices in the script.

In traditional playwriting, markers could be as easily notated in a scenario or synopsis as they are in the script. If language is the marker, it resists reduction because the marker is embedded in itself. For example, to produce Mac Wellman's language plays effectively, the director and actor must predetermine markers based on shifts in the intention of the language. These shifts in intention are reflected onstage in dynamic changes of rate and intensity involving voice, gesture, and movement.

The following comparison (table 8.2) demonstrates how markers function in traditional versus new playwriting.

**TABLE 8.2 Markers in Traditional versus New Playwriting**

| TRADITIONAL PLAYWRITING | NEW PLAYWRITING |
| --- | --- |
| **Story markers**<br>advance the story<br>create exposition and backstory | **Story markers**<br>advance and/or reiterate the story<br>create divergent stories and narratives |
| **Plot markers**<br>advance the plot<br>provide progression | **Plot markers**<br>advance the plot<br>create interruption and shifts<br>break causal schemes |
| **Character markers**<br>provide vital information<br>are consistent | **Character markers**<br>provide vital information<br>provide breaks and shifts within beats |
| **Language markers**<br>are metaphors and figures<br>are a means of drama<br>are historical | **Language markers**<br>create structural links and/or levels of<br>   discourse<br>are the material of drama, are devices<br>are historicized and dialogized |

In traditional, plot-oriented dramaturgy, dialogue represents the link between markers—the means of getting from A to B. This tracking rationale lends more credence to the scenario approach, as it diminishes the importance of language in the play. Countering this tendency, language playwrights rescued language by foregrounding interruption, repetition, intonation, and other devices that stressed the importance of language as a component of dramaturgy. Foregrounding, as discussed earlier, has several connotations. It can (1) be manifested as a word, speech, or object taken from the background and thrust into a closer, more immediate range; or (2) as a device is given special emphasis to make it stand out from surrounding factors or circumstances. The goal of foregrounding is to alter our perception about a word or object by extricating it from a familiar context. In new playwriting, foregrounding devices are themselves markers, just as the V-effect would be considered a marker in the dramaturgy of Bertholt Brecht. As these devices become more dominant in play making, they shape the dramaturgical aesthetic toward formalism.

In Wellman's and Overmyer's plays, character utterances are continually shaped or reshaped by earlier dialogue. Repetitions, reiterations, and variations provide a sense of form to the script. In the opening of Wellman's *Sincerity Forever* successive speeches are reiterated almost verbatim, yet by different characters. In Overmyer's *In Perpetuity throughout the Universe* the continuing action of throwing first unlit, then lit matches into a bowl with items from a list occurs across several scenes. The tag line first spoken by Christine and later by Dennis creates a doubling or compounding effect across the play. The line is each time accompanied by a similar stage direction. Close to the beginning of the play, in part 1, scene 3, we read:

> (*DENNIS lights a match and tosses it into a bowl. The matches flare.*)

CHRISTINE: I love this list. This list is my favorite. People to kill after the revolution.

(Overmyer 1993, In Perpetuity . . . , 179)

Then, near the beginning of part 2, scene 22 ends:

> (*DENNIS lights a match and tosses it into a bowl. The matches flare.*)

CHRISTINE: I love this list. This list is my favorite.

(Overmyer 1993, In Perpetuity . . . , 211)

Finally, before the penultimate scene of the play, at the end of scene 34 (note how Overmyer sets up the character reversal) we read:

> (*CHRISTINE lights a match and tosses it into a bowl. It flares. An intense light erupts from the drawer suddenly blinding LYLE. He shields his eyes*)

DENNIS: I love this list. This list is my favorite.

(Overmyer 1993, In Perpetuity . . . , 225)

The above quotation suggests how the marker is used dramaturgically: the first two utterances by Dennis occur early in each act. The final toss is a reversal: Christine now tosses the match while Dennis utters Christine's phrase. In ritual fashion, the subsequent tossing of lists and matches into the bowl bonds these two characters. The reversal marks their dual/duel ownership of this action, as it closes the frame on the action of the play. Overmyer is, in essence, resorting to a structurally familiar principle of linking by threes; he is savvy to the reversal's inherent ability for variation and for topping what preceded it. The result of the surprise is the final stage direction, which describes an "otherworldly light from the drawer." Ultimately the markers establish a structural link through the repetitive dramatic action and the theatrical payoff of the otherworldly light.

A more compressed linking by threes occurs early in the first act of Wellman's *7 Blowjobs*:

> *Scene two: The SENATOR'S office on Capitol Hill. DOT, the busy receptionist, is answering a busy phone.*

DOT: Hello. Senator X's office. Hello, nothing of value inside, please,
Please don't steal our stuff . . .

> *Pause.*

Yes. No. Maybe.

> *She hangs up. Pause. Phone rings.*

DOT: Hello. Senator X's office. Hello, nothing of value inside, please,

Please don't steal our stuff . . .
> *Pause.*

Yes. No. Maybe.

> *She hangs up. Pause. Phone rings.*

DOT: Hello. Senator X's office. Hello, nothing of value inside, please,
Please don't steal our stuff . . .
> *Pause.*

Yes. No. Maybe.

> *She hangs up. Pause. Phone rings. There is a knock at the door.*

DOT: Phone. Door. At the same time, wow.

(Wellman 1994, 7 Blowjobs, 207)

Wellman uses repetition to establish the satirical/farcical nature of the theatrical world, but also to set up the punch line or payoff: "Phone. Door. At the same time, wow." While providing exactly the same lines in each case, Wellman recognizes that intonation, or actor inflection, will alter the meaning in each delivery of the same utterance. The above beat segment is a marker, since it represents a microcosm of the entire piece: to director and actor, the slant to the writing suggests a farcical, exaggerated mode of performance. For all he is due as an imaginative and innovative playwright, Wellman is also a master craftsman playing familiar theatrical tricks for a payoff.

### Dialogue, the Marker, and the Principle of Intonation

When a marker is repeated, particularly when an utterance is repeated verbatim, dialogism is present through *intonation*. Intonation distinguishes dramatic dialogue from other literary forms including the novel, essays, and so on. How a word or phrase is spoken means a great deal in performance. Intonation allows a semantic shift to take place, even though an utterance or phrase appears the same on the page. Obviously, there is a pitch shift between Christine's and Dennis's delivery, above. The shift in intonation changes the meaning entirely. An ironic, parodic, or mimetic interpretation can offer a startling variation on the original utterance. In performance, these ramifications are indicated by the director's and actors' choices. The playwright should not underestimate the strong dramaturgic effect of varying intonation.

In conclusion, the marker carries with it another signal—the playwright's level of craft. Markers are the playwright's clues or imprints; they focus the audience's perception, guiding the spectator through the play. For this to be effective, markers must be deciphered and interpreted by the director and actors, allowing these collaborators to make sense of the play for an audience.

A truism of playwriting posits that dialogue is meant to be spoken, not simply read. While this fundamental precept seems obvious, it gives function and purpose to the staged reading: if we as playwrights were certain how the script sounded, the process would be more direct from page to stage. In new playwriting, the playwright is creating a secondary linguistic system that offers its own set of rules and challenges to the audience. The test upon hearing experimental work comes in understanding what language is doing in the play, and what you as the orchestrater must do to improve it, whether that means eliminating sections of text, adding new beat segments, rewriting segments, leaving it alone, or beginning anew.

# 9

## Scenes, Acts, and Revisions

### SCENES AND POINTS

A *scene* is made up of one or more beat segments that come to a *point*. The point could be described as the *super marker*, revealing something of crucial significance in the scene. The *point* is the culminating moment of emphasis or action in the scene. It indicates the purpose or function of the scene in the play. Generally, in new playwriting, it is more accurate to describe the play in terms of scenes and points rather than acts and climaxes. Screenwriters use two or more plot points to describe first the inciting incident at the end of the first act and then the major reversal or change of fortune—the climactic point that ends the second act of the three-act screenplay. In new playwriting, however, the point may define aspects of major emphasis unrelated to plot. Rather than the traditional peripetia, the point may be a device of language or form that functions to provide linkage or coherence. In Eric Overmyer's *On the Verge*, scene 4, "The Mysterious Interior," Fanny's machete whacking leads to the discovery of an "old-fashioned egg beater," which had not yet been invented by the starting date of the play's action (1888). The women assume it may be a talisman, totem, amulet, or marsupial's unicycle. The point represents Fanny's discovery, which connects to the point in the first scene, Mary's "Trekking in Terra Incognita." The point in the first scene focuses the forward movement of the play toward the discovery of unknown lands. This point in scene 4 establishes the gulf between objects and language, which underscores not only a specific action but clarifies the thematic direction of the play.

Good dramaturgy dictates that every scene come to a point—no matter how brief the scene. For example, scene 22 of Len Jenkin's *Dark Ride* consists of two words of dialogue:

22.

(*The Ballroom. Music. All characters except the* THIEF *appear.* COOK *emerges from his cage.*)

DEEP SEA ED: Edna!

DEEP SEA EDNA: Ed! (*A stately dance, during which the THIEF arrives, and places the diamond on a pedestal among the dancers. The dancers stop their movement.*)

(Jenkins 1993, *Dark Ride*, 117)

121

CHAPTER 9 SCENES, ACTS, AND REVISIONS

Here, the dialogue is incidental to the major action of the thief placing the diamond on a pedestal among the dancers. As the penultimate scene in the play, the action represents a culmination and merging of several facets in the play's structure. The unifying device, the dance, theatricalizes the convergence of the ensemble. This scene indicates the relation between the point and what theater practitioners describe as a *moment*. Every play and production should have its moments; this moment in the play is clarified by the transition from movement to stasis, and by the fulcrum-like effect of the pedestal among the dancers. This point is both a dramatic and theatrical moment, and becomes one of the primary images of the play.

Points, then, provide clarity and focus to scenes and can be described as a marker with greater dramaturgic significance. In new playwriting, points emerge during the act of writing and should not be overly predetermined in a scenario or synopsis. They are further clarified during the shaping and refining of the play.

As the play takes its final form it becomes important for themes or theatrical ideas to payoff in a point. Otherwise, the conceptualization will be incomplete. In revision, pointless elements can be identified and then, either reshaped or cut. If not, the playwright will be accused of "playing fast and loose" with themes and theatrical ideas. Ultimately, points are a barometer of what the play is about; the playwright thus needs to follow through and be selective.

## SCENE SEQUENCE AND STYLE

A scene establishes references to a specific place or time; it focuses on a given topic and demonstrates significant action. The arrangement or sequence of scene units determines the plot of a play. The nature of transitions from scene to scene will define the structural style. For example, when transitions involve leaps in time or space between scenes, the structure is *episodic*. Conversely, a *classical* style favors a more compressed time frame that promotes a logical or causal progression of scenes. The major scenes are linked causally or, at least, logically—sometimes with interpolated choral commentary. The time factor is compressed, limiting the range of action.

Ideally, the choice of the structural style is contingent upon the subject matter, and how the playwright feels it is best served. In general, a playwright gravitates toward a specific structural style, tending to shape content within a given style, rather than vary formats accordingly.

For the most part, new playwrights favor an episodic style. This format suggests loosely related, noncausal relationships between scenes. What is antecedent may have little or nothing to do with what follows; temporal and spatial conditions can alter with the turn of a phrase. The open-ended episodic approach offers numerous variations:

1. In the *serial episodic approach* the progression of scenes builds toward a climax or major point of complication. There are frequent shifts in time and place. Scenes are rarely extended beyond several beat segments. Generally, a central character provides a through line for the disparate scenes. Examples include *Dark Rapture* (Eric Overmyer); *Restless* and *Prelude to a Kiss* (Craig Lucas); and *Bal* (Richard Nelson).

   a. Journey plays as a subgenre are serially episodic. *On the Verge, Dark Ride,* and *Harm's Way* are examples from Overmyer, Jenkin, and Wellman, respectively. Usually, the journey structure provides linkage between scenes through transitional devices I explore elsewhere in this book.

2. In the *parallel episodic approach,* succeeding scenes disclose separate story units, but at some point in the story lines converge or characters intertwine. Some hybrids would fall into this category; see *Tales of the Lost Formicans* (Constance Congdon); *Der Inka von Peru* (Jeffrey Jones); *Angels in America* (Tony Kushner); and *American Notes* (Len Jenkin).

   a. Here the operating aesthetic is juxtaposition and fragmented sequence. Scenes are compartmentalized and self-contained. There are two or more story lines that may comment or inform each other. Historically, William Shakespeare perfected this multilayered dramaturgy. Kushner juggled several story lines effectively in *Angels in America;* His approach exploited the opportunity for the grandest sweep—the truly big play.

   b. This scene aesthetic is most effective when there is a convergence of characters or themes that link or interlace at a given point.

3. In *nonserial juxtaposition,* scenes are juxtaposed and individual scenes are repeated with variation. There is never a real sense of story lines coming together in a cohesive narrative. See *Limbo Tales* (Len Jenkin), *Albanian Softshoe* (Mac Wellman), and *New World Border* (Guillermo Gomez-Peña).

   a. The structure may be collage-like. The resolution or conclusion exists outside of the play. This style seems to be favored by performance artists such as Guillermo Gomez-Peña, Peggy Shaw, and Karen Finley. A strong thematic thread holds together the disparate scenes.

   b. Jenkin's *Poor Folk's Pleasure* establishes several basic scenes that are repeated with variations throughout the play. It is described by Jenkin as a play developed in a workshop, constructed as independent vignettes, then assembled as a whole. This approach can be most

effective in a thematic play: consider George Wolfe's *The Colored* 123
*Museum*, which uses independent scenes to satirize elements of
African-American icons and culture in current America.

The influence of television and film has been pervasive in elevating the
episodic approach. Increasingly, playwrights are writing scenes that are
more truncated than extended. This proclivity has led to plays that feature
frequent shifts in place, but along with it, numerous difficulties in handling transitions. New playwrights have innovated bold solutions to solve
problems of transition and sequence. (See chapter 11 for a discussion of
transitions in Jenkin's *Dark Ride*.) Nevertheless, the episodic format is difficult to execute effectively because the playwright must constantly
reestablish the "givens" for every scene. Moveable settings and wagons are
required to effectively establish a sense of place. Frequent scene shifts and
blackouts will appear awkward unless integrated into the dramaturgy.
Blackouts that exist solely to cover scene changes create more problems
then they solve. Playwrights can mitigate this problem by using narrative
or dialogue bridges that cover the change. Too often playwrights leave the
execution of transitions up to the director without fully recognizing how
the nature of transitions affects the overall structure.

## ADAPTING THE CLASSIC APPROACH

While admiring his colleagues who work in episodic formats, Wellman
laments that these difficulties with exposition and shifting scenery are the
reason he does not favor this style for his plays. Wellman points out (with
a wink) that he is simply writing in the grand tradition of classic, American
playwriting. Eugene O'Neill, Tennessee Williams, Arthur Miller, and
Edward Albee have all written major plays for a single, nonchanging unit
setting. Wellman, with notable exceptions, establishes a single environment for his plays: *7 Blowjobs*, *Bad Infinity*, and *Professional Frenchman*
progress sequentially from start to finish in one setting. Dissimilar works,
such as *Terminal Hip* and *Three Americanisms*, require a theatrical (not representational) environment and utilize only a simple unit set, which is
more suitable for the extended one-act format of Wellman's plays. In
*Murder of Crows*, the production requirements include a steady rainfall on
stage; indeed, any set changes would diminish this striking visual image.
Moreover, in *The Murder of Crows* premiere at Primary Stages the execution
of rainfall and proper drainage, as well as the insulation of electrical materials, mandated that the set be stable for the production. Unity of place
was not the only classical dictum Wellman was following. His use of the
crows to simulate a Greek chorus intimated a core tenet of classical dramaturgy. To this extent, Wellman's plays underscore the dialogic tension
between innovative approaches to language and character that are
grounded in established dramaturgical principles.

Wellman's commissioned pieces provide a variant of the single locale or unit setting: the award-winning *Bad Penny* was written as a site-specific piece and performed on the lake in New York's Central Park; *Crowbar* was written and performed as a site-specific play at London's Old Victory Theatre.

## CONCEPTUALIZATION: DIALOGUE AND SCENE

In traditional drama, dialogue is conceived and executed according to a general overall strategy. The following three categories, loosely derived from Jan Mukarovsky's studies on dialogue, are helpful in assessing the playwright's conceptualization of dialogue and scene. These categories are challenged somewhat by the new playwriting.

In the first category, the *conflict-driven scene*, the dialogue between characters A and B clashes with opposing viewpoints or objectives. It establishes a clear objective/obstacle situation that drives the scene. Dialogue may be written *on the line* when characters say exactly what is on their mind, or written indirectly, *off the line*, whereby characters mitigate, evade, or willfully ignore the present conflict. Indirect dialogue creates tension between the given circumstances and what is actually spoken. This tension translates into subtext for the actor, and is characteristic of psychological realism.

New playwriting relies less on the conflict-driven scene than traditional forms. In new playwriting, oblique rather than direct conflict is generally the rule. *Conflict,* in the traditional sense of the term, does not exist at all in Wellman's *Terminal Hip* or *Three Americanisms* and is not really relevant in Jenkin's *Poor Folk's Pleasure.* In plays with a central character—Jenkin's *Kid Twist,* for example—conflict is built into the circumstances (the criminal Kid versus the feds who hold him "under protection"). The character of the Author may face numerous obstacles in locating Sam in *My Uncle Sam,* but the conflicts are less than the core of Jenkin's dramaturgy. There is tension and suspense, yes, but not the classic high-stakes protagonist/antagonist struggle. Where conflict is central, and a protagonist is clearly defined, the conflict is embedded within bizarre antiworlds or the atmospheric picaresque. Wellman's breakthrough play *Harm's Way* contains straight-line conflict provoked by the violent aspirations of the lead character, Santouche. The setting is a carnivalesque otherworld, inhabited with con men, stiffs who talk, and oddly named characters like *By Way of Being Hidden* and *Isle of Mercy.* In Overmyer's *Dark Rapture,* the lead character Babcock flees pursuers across a shifting tropical landscape that promotes rapid changes in atmosphere (local color) and mood.

In the second category, the *circumstance-driven scene,* a dialogue can emerge from the speaker's reaction to prior events (back story), to circumstances, or better, to events that occur during an actual scene in the play. In other cases, the anticipation of impending circumstance or fate drives a scene. These conditions guide or shift the direction of dialogue. They are most powerful if they are introduced at or around the *point* in the scene. Because discovery takes place, this type of scene is almost always material to plot. When dialogue responds to given circumstances within the present environment, *deictic* dialogue is favored: a spatialized language that connects characters (*you, we, us*) and places and objects (*here, there, this, that*). Gestural indicators such as pointing or referring to objects present in the environment perform this function visually.

Len Jenkin's plays generally explore some longstanding condition facing a character that has in some way come to a crossroads or reckoning point. For example, the Kid in *Kid Twist* reexamines his life through dreams and imaginative flights as he is holed up in a rundown hotel room, interred by federal agents. The Translator in *Dark Ride* has come to a critical point in translating an arcane text, and has difficulty assessing the credibility of his findings. In *American Notes*, Jenkin combines an ensemble of feckless characters who seem to be at the "ends of their ropes." The dialogue in these plays explores the character's search for some meaning, or the hope of a new identity. The marginalized settings, particularly seedy hotel rooms, suggest a longing for roots and a legitimized identity.

Overmyer explores the onstage event as a recognition device in the opening scene of *Dark Rapture*. The character Babcock reacts to the fortuitous burning of his Malibu home, seeing it as a means to escape his present fate. The opportunity to burn away his old identity and create a new one is both theatrical and dramatic.

Wellman's characters often respond deictically to their environment: the acid rain in *Murder of Crows*; the televised football game in *The Professional Frenchman*; and the fur ball phenomenon in *Sincerity Forever*. The characters' responses to these given objects provide crucial texturing and coloring to the respective plays. Playwrights should note that references to onstage objects and events give dialogue presence and immediacy.

In the third category, the *belief-driven scene*, dialogue may also reflect thematic variables, ideas, or beliefs that form the playwright's or character's personal views. This type of scene might be about satirizing something or someone, or advancing specific ideological ends. Several of the above conditions are present to stimulate the dialogue in a scene. Christopher Durang uses consecutive scenes in *Betty's Summer Vacation* to satirize the overly talkative roommate, and then, the oversexed jock with limited brainpower. Tony Kushner utilizes the backdrop of a funeral and aids treatment area to launch into an exploration of current cultural mores.

In his "Washington D.C. play," *7 Blowjobs, Bad Infinity*, and *The Professional Frenchman*, Wellman satirizes aspects of Washington D.C. culture, just as successive scenes in act 1 of *Albanian Softshoe* satire sitcomia (see chapter 11).

A scene bears some relation to a specific spatial/temporal field. Language playwrights have been particularly effective in creating shifting scenes, usually in the form of landscapes altered and formulated by language. The seemingly desultory relationship between scenes is mitigated because language provides a structural linkage.

In part 1 of *Limbo Tales*, Len Jenkin establishes a scene with the anthropology professor, Driver, commuting to his girlfriend's house two hours away. Jenkin's stage directions require a miniature highway and landscape that illustrates the sights and sounds described in Driver's narrative. Phenomenally, we experience a shifting highway environment, although the scene itself situates Driver's relation to the action on the set piece: a miniaturized landscape featuring roads, street signs, lampposts, and the like. Jenkin's novel solution creates a vast changeable space reduced to the scale of an intimate stage. Moreover, the spatial distance between Driver and his destinations affect the character's mental processes; the comic effect is enhanced by the miniature representation of his car in a scale model.

Driver's academic specialty as a professor in Mayan anthropology is exploited during a subsequent scene. An ancient Mayan tomb is constructed on the miniature highway board, suggesting an interesting dialogic relation between cultures and histories. In this sense, we have a meeting or clash between present and past time, immediate and distant space.

## EXERCISE:
### Stage Space

This exercise is based on the use of stage space in *Limbo Tales*.

1) Develop several scenes based around the use of a miniature set board that contains a cityscape, an airport, or a train set, for example.
   a. Consider characters who regularly commute, and draw given materials from their particular line of work.
2) Have the dialogue in the scene interact with the space; a character might set off on a trip; another is on her daily commute, and so on.
3) Create the sense of wonder, as if a child playing with a train set under a Christmas tree.
   a. Introduce other characters on the board that your primary character interacts with.

## CAPTIONING

One device shared by language playwrights is the *captioning* of scenes with a telling phrase, quote, or, in the case of Overmyer's *On the Verge*, a journal entry. These captions mark the shift from scene to scene. This shift in locale indicates scenic movement or other design changes in lighting or sound. The journal entries in *On the Verge* provide the audience with guides throughout the play. Prior to scene 19 the entries are usually posted by one character. Overmyer then utilizes all three of his major women characters:

> MARY: Ladies—I believe we're on the verge!
>
> (*All three ladies do journal entry in unison.*)
>
> ALEX, MARY, and FANNY: We arrive in '55!
>
> (19) Paradise '55
>
> *Lights! A flashy sign, neon: Nicky's. Some palm trees and streamers: A gaudy, pre-revolutionary, Havana-style nightclub. Nicky rolls on with a piano and live mike. Does a splashy finish.*
>
> NICKY: Vaya! Vaya! Vaya! Vaya! Con! Dios! Wo Wo Wo Wo Wo—yeaaaaah! Pow!
>
> (Overmyer 1993, *On the Verge*, 97)

The caption sets the scene, opening on a fifties-style Havana nightclub, as Overmyer's language riffs establish the pre-Castro nightlife culture of Cuba. Since these captions establish the scene, they are considered *markers*. A designer, for example, would factor any shift or cueing signal based on this type of marker; it is a unit of transition.

Overmyer's *In a Pig's Valise* uses captioning to interpolate various musical numbers in the play. These titles, "Shrimp Louie," "Vegetable Medley," "Talent Scout," "Balkan Jam," "Prisoner of Genre," and so forth, serve to break the play down into scene-like units.

Jenkin uses captioning in a number of plays. The transition from scene 9 to scene 10 in *Dark Ride* is uncannily similar to Overmyer's use of it in *On the Verge*. The Thief character, here functioning as a narrator, establishes the segue:

> THIEF: But in case you people think I'm only interested in the sensational—there's another article in this magazine that's different. I been thinking about it—reading it over and over. It's by a Mrs. Carl Lammle, who is someone I'd like to talk to sometime. It's called:
>
> ALL: THE WORLD OF COINCIDENCE.
>
> 10.
>
> MRS. LAMMLE: All of you are, I'm sure, familiar with what I term the WORLD OF COINCIDENCE. In this world events seem to be more connected . . . than they are in our everyday world, where they most often seem, random, absurd—if not perniciously unrelated to each other. In the world of coincidence, however, the most common expression is:
>
> ALL: What a coincidence!
>
> (Jenkin 1993, *Dark Ride*, 82)

Again, the ensemble is called upon to serve an essentially narrative function: to establish the forthcoming scene. Captioning is a fundamental unit for implementing transition and sequence between scenes. The "world of coincidence" indicates or suggests a kind of theatrical "world" while not designating any specific place. The designer and director are prompted by inference rather than direction.

On the other hand, Jenkin may use narrators who stand apart from the action and announce the place of the scene. For example, scene 13 of *My Uncle Sam* begins with the narrator's indicative statement, which reflects the preliminary stage description:

13

> *The garden. The stage is almost bare. Green. DARLENE and YOUNG SAM. OLD SAM, alone, toward the rear.*

NARRATOR: IN THE GARDEN.

(Jenkin 1993, My Uncle Sam, 199)

Captioning is a theatrical function of language, serving several purposes: indicating, describing, suggesting or differentiating scenes; or dialogizing between levels of language. The use of a narrator, a theatrical rather than representational construct, allows the non-realistic language to work effectively on stage. In scene 2 of *My Uncle Sam*, two narrators parody the use of captioning:

> NARRATOR 1: Now's Lila's telling Sam she'll marry him if he'll find her brother.
>
> LILA: I'll marry you if you find my brother.
>
> NARRATOR 1: She's listing some people who might have some information about his whereabouts . . .
>
> LILA: A gentleman with a big book.
>
> YOUNG SAM: A big book—
>
> NARRATOR 2: A gentleman with a big book.
>
> LILA: A lady in a golden vest—
>
> YOUNG SAM: A lady in a golden vest.
>
> NARRATOR 2: A lady in a golden vest.
>
> LILA: A man with eight flags.
>
> YOUNG SAM: Eight flags.
>
> NARRATOR 2: A man with eight flags.

(Jenkin 1993, My Uncle Sam, 137)

By juxtaposing direct address (the narrators' captions) with the descriptive dialogue between Lila and Young Sam, Jenkin achieves a comic effect. Although this passage is more representative of a beat segment than a scene, I have included it here as an extreme example of captioning, one which also demonstrates the dialogic relation between narrative and dialogue passages that is at the heart of the new playwriting.

## THE NUMERICAL BREAKDOWN OF SCENES

The numbering of scenes is a device used to differentiate one scene from another. While the traditional approach has been to label in progression (scene 1, scene 2, etc.), many of the plays by Jenkin and Overmyer eliminate the word *scene*. By changing the traditional nomenclature the new playwrights are foregrounding, or at least compartmentalizing, the scene as a structural unit. If the traditional nomenclature suggests some linkage between scenes, the use of numbers alone isolates one scene from another. This numerical technique indicates an arbitrary change of locale in several plays. Locale is shifted in dialogue or language; each scene stands in dialogic relation to past and subsequent scenes.

In general, the independent scene, with its beginning, middle, and end (or at times, simply middle and end) remains the building block of not only the language playwrights but also more mainstream playwrights. In episodic structures, each scene takes on a vitality of its own, as the arranged sequence builds toward a climactic *scene à faire*, the major confrontational or "obligatory" scene. Tony Kushner's *Angels in America* is indicative of this trend to compartmentalize within the limitations of the episodic form. Separate story lines develop and intersect at various points in the play. The more separation and distinction between the worlds represented in each scene can create considerable dialogic tension. Kushner does this successfully in alternating Roy Cohn's McCarthy-era tough guy discourse with more contemporary and familiar discourses from gay society (a young Mormon character who is coming out of the closet; a flamboyant "queen" who serves as the nurse). The interweaving of spiritual realms, particularly in part 2, is in fact more representative of the dialogic principle at work.

Craig Lucas (*Reckless, Prelude to a Kiss*), Richard Nelson (*Some Americans Abroad*), Richard Greenberg (*Eastern Standard*), and for the most part, John Guare (*Six Degrees of Separation*) utilize the scene as the structural unit. The reason: unlike a sprawling act structure, evident in modernists first, like Eugene O'Neill (*Long Day's Journey into Night, The Iceman Cometh*), then Lanford Wilson (*Hot L Baltimore*), or Sam Shepard (*Fool for Love; Curse of the Starving Class*) the scene provides the writer with a limited scale. The playwright can work unit by unit. Entire units can be abandoned, or restructured to form the wholeness of an act, or play.

In politically committed playwrights (Tony Kushner, for example) there is an underlying thematic intention to dialogue in the scene. These thematic intentions construct the larger presence of the character in the scene. When characters represent an unpopular ideology, like that of Roy

Cohn in *Angels in America* we can expect that somehow these characters will be taught a moral lesson; that they will ultimately receive some psychic or emotional pain to address their actions.

## SCENES INTO ACTS

To a degree, the process described above for each scene can be expanded to serve as a microcosm for the act. Indeed, in some cases, the act may serve as a microcosm for the structure of the play. But this practice varies considerably; many plays of the new playwriting have radically different approaches to the acts. It is difficult for the playwright to consider an entire act until later in the evolution of the play. Range and breadth are too large. Nevertheless, the effectiveness of an act can be determined by (1) the quality and flow of the beat segments, particularly how they work together and interact; (2) the buildup or arrangement of points across the scenes; (3) the theatrical and dramaturgic effectiveness of the convergence point, or the major moment in the act; and (4) the sense of scale.

Convergence points provide major dramaturgic resonance because they establish points of contact across juxtaposed scenes and seemingly disparate narratives. The role of the act, after all, is to gather the scenes into an aesthetic or formal pattern that is dramaturgically effective. Convergence can happen when characters from disparate scenes share the same space, or even sing the same song, dance together, or are brought into some form of interaction.

After the first draft of a script is completed, elements need sharpening and clarification. It is in the revision or development of the script that dialogism is consciously considered. The buildup of dialogic units begins with beats, then proceeds to beat segments and markers; and then to scenes and points; and then to acts and "moments" of convergence.

Scale determines the crucial relationship between the volume or weight of the subject material and its dramatic treatment. In most cases, there will be too much material, and like the sculptor, the playwright will need to determine what needs to be chiseled off in large blocks versus what needs to be honed and buffed. The proper way to address this revision is by examining the effectiveness of each individual beat segment rather than lopping off a line here and there.

Scale may be a pragmatic consideration. Mac Wellman conceptualizes most of his plays as extended one-acts. The seventy-five- or ninety-minute play without intermission is somewhat anomalous considering that most Broadway plays run well over two hours. Wellman cites that it is difficult to do extensive work when rehearsal schedules are restricted and actors and directors often have other obligations. This is the reality of noncommercial theater in New York. If rehearsal means repetition, then Wellman prefers to have a more concentrated approach to rehearsal. The extended one-act allows the flexibility of either rehearsing the entire play or examining segments and scenes at close range during relatively brief rehearsal periods.

Scale should be a consideration whenever narrative and dramatic elements are interlaced. The attempt is to achieve a balanced weighting in the script. Examine, in particular, how the monologues are functioning in relation to dialogue sections. Since monologues create a sense of mass in the script, you need to assess if they are supported by the dramaturgy or balanced by sections of dialogue. Scale affects the size relationship between segments and scenes and is an important technical indicator in assessing the formal quality of the script.

## THE REVISION PROCESS, AND DEVELOPING CHOPS

At the New Wave Playwriting Festival in San Francisco (1996), Jeffrey Jones (*Der Inka von Peru; Seventy Scenes of Halloween*) was emphatic that the play develops from "stuff"—that is, from written play material. Jones was alluding to the rough draft, a species with a wide range of definitions, from a first go at the material to a script that needs a mere polish to become performance ready. Jones asserted that the real work of the playwright begins after a threshold of written material is reached. While some playwrights such as Sam Shepard seldom revise initial drafts, the opposite is more often the case: the play is "discovered" after numerous rewrites. Jones, for example, meticulously labels subsequent drafts during the revision process. His first draft provides the benchmark for the initial impulses behind the script. Later drafts offer significant room for expansion or deletion of characters, scenes, and so on. In this sense, Jones's drafts dialogize with each other in the creation of the ultimate script.

The playwright needs an approach to revision that will maximize chances of success. Many playwrights reach an impasse at this phase; students, in particular, will balk at the forecast of rewrites as tedious and frustrating. Many scripts fail to improve at this phase of the process. Part of the resistance and difficulty stems from traditional thinking that defines playwriting as linear and monologic rather than interactive and dialogic. The playwright who forces the play into the wrong mold will not only feel frustration, but will worsen the play in the process. The dialogic method seems more natural than prescribed linear approaches because it seeks to discover the optimum relationship between parts in a playtext. Once this format for conceptualizing the play is in place it is a matter of the playwright having the craft and stamina to execute the plan.

Stamina may be the most important attribute in a playwright's arsenal. First, it gives the playwright power to cut through lows brought on by frustration, rejection, and bad reviews, and to continue writing. Second, the play itself must have stamina to "cut it"—in other words, to hold an audience's interest over an hour or more. To this extent, a balance must be struck between imagination and solid dramaturgical craft. A great deal of stamina is necessary to complete revisions with attention to detail, while not losing the perspective of the overall play. Put another way, lack of stamina probably drives out more would-be playwrights than anything else. While every established playwright has several plays that were never completed, this prospect can be discouraging to the young or emerging playwright. Many promising new play projects never get finished or are half realized. This matter is compounded in new playwriting, where no effective criteria or methods can aid the playwright through the revision process.

With this factor in mind, the craft, or "wrighting," of the play is a foremost concern in the revision process. The demanding nature of playwriting often grinds down to the common denominator of craft. Craft is effective dramaturgy; it is the conscious application of form in the script. To effectively "hold the boards" a play must be well crafted; to be a masterpiece the crafting must be exquisite. Learning the craft is the most difficult step for young playwrights, and certainly the most humbling. Yet there is no way around the mastery of technique as a means to achieving potential.

The synergies of conceptualization, stamina, and craft equal *chops*. Chops, in music, have to do with the player's musical concept, sound presence, and, of course, confidence and facility of technique. In playwriting, chops separate the lesser playwrights from the truly great: the master playwright demonstrates a level of virtuosity that is signatory. Literary managers, dramaturgs, and directors recognize chops as technical execution and dramaturgical savvy, with something more—a distinctive voice. The building of chops is the byproduct of effective revision.

## THE REVISION PROCESS

*PREMISE: The beat segment is the primary site of revision. Effective beat segments and the optimum placement of markers provide the building blocks of form.*

In revising the playscript through the early drafts, the playwright must consider how each beat segment establishes markers, and what the relation between segments is, particularly for those segments that precede and follow. What is dialogic here? Beat segments interact with each other in the formation of scene. How effectively they interact determines the quality of the dramaturgy. Most playwrights, beginners in particular, make changes line by line without first determining or identifying the entire beat segment. The first step should be to define the marker of the beat segment. Once you understand how the beat segment functions you can proceed. At this point, you can choose to work to this marker from the preceding marker, or revise backward from this marker to the previous marker. You can also assess if the entire beat segment should be moved, deleted, or stored for potential later use. The revision process, rather than a sloppy and difficult procedure, can now be more efficiently accomplished. Developers who understand the workings of the beat segment can be more specific (and helpful) in discussing revisions with the playwright.

## EXERCISE:
### Revision

You probably have several fragments of plays that you have shelved, with the hope of returning to them at some future point. The following exercise encourages you to bring out one of your rougher works and give it a dialogic makeover.

1) Read through the entire draft (without wincing).

2) Since step 1 is not possible, read through the draft; indicate in the left margin each beat segment, numbering and bracketing them as you go along. If the segment has no marker this indicates a certain revision area.

3) Locate the marker in each beat segment. Identify what happens there. If the script is a full-length one get a separate sheet of paper and number and identify as above. This is your *aide-memoir*, so you don't forget what you've already written.

4) Assess each marker and its relation to the other markers that precede and follow. Are there shifts in direction? Can the marker be clarified? Should the contour of the beat segment be altered?

   a) Examine the potential of opposite outcomes in the marker. Is the opposite outcome better? What are the possibilities?

   b) Refer to your list. Can a beat segment be taken and shaped from another part of the text? To determine this, start back from the marker using only the material that you need; slough off the rest and place it in a file. Another option is to cut and storyboard the numbered beat segments, exploring possible configurations.

   c) Does the new arrangement release the energy potential of your script? Altering the contour across the various segments can release stored energy from the texts. Now move on to the next 10 pages.

5) At some point in this process, you will sense, or feel in your gut, a direction for the play that may have previously escaped you. Something in the dialogic relationship between markers, or the shifting contours of segments, will trigger a solution to the project. It may be the entry of a character, or a strategy of monologue, the introduction of song or music. *Keep yourself open to these possibilities.* You may see in the markers the key to subsequent scenes and excise whole sections of the script. Often, you will need to bridge old passages of script with newly written material.

6) Program your subconscious to trigger the ending of the play. Attempt to visualize an image at the final curtain. Think theatrically: Who is on stage? What has just happened? Does it conclude the script satisfactorily? Once you've determined the landing point you can rework the high points or the most important markers in the play. Endings shape the thematic matter conclusively. After the ending is determined, proceed with revisions. You will

have less trouble with the ending (a major stumbling block of young play-wrights) if you are tuned in dialogically to the markers in your script. Priming the subconscious is good because the answer may come from something that comes across your everyday life: a phrase, an image, and a dream. The best revision will come when the imagination tunes in to the dialogic process.

7) Before you begin polishing the revisions clarify the following, in order of importance: the curtain scene; the major markers that precede the curtain; the end of the first act (if there is an intermission); the beginning of the second act; the beginning of the play to the first marker. Most playwrights spend a great deal of time reworking the beginning of the play and categorically less on the second act than the first.

The mid-revision phase is where the *wright* in *playwright* demonstrates his craft and finesse. Too often playwrights lament crafting the script as dull, rife with writer's block, blind alleys—when actually it can be the most invigorating and satisfying part of the process. If you view the first part of writing the script as creating the raw material, then you won't feel the script is a failure, because you have to work at it before true form emerges. A number of texts on playwriting blame the failure to complete a script on lack of planning, but it may be the inability to discover what is inherently valid and worth pursuing in the given raw materials. In this sense, the playwright is in a dialogic relation to the material; the evolving script is in a very real sense in dialogue with him. This dialogism between playwright and the evolving text goes on night and day until the text is finished. Sometimes, an old script "calls" the writer back—the process is visceral and living. Could this be the muse, this seductive dialogue between text and writer, the desire to complete the text?

Too many playwrights send their work out before this phase is conclud-ed adequately, in a sense, hoping that someone "out in development land" will save their play. It rarely happens. You need to establish the craft in the play. Like the "eye music" that attracts the reader, an advanced level of craft provides the pleasure of form. Playwrights Jenkin, Overmyer, and Wellman delight us as much with their sophisticated handling of materials, which we will now probe as we look at some specific aspects of dialogue.

## EXERCISE:
### Dramaturgy

Read the following plays for craft purposes only: *Sincerity Forever* (Wellman), *Dark Ride* (Jenkins), and *In Perpetuity throughout the Universe* (Overmyer).

1) Pick ten pages of text at random from each play.

2) Repeat several steps from the above revision exercise: include beat seg-ments, markers, points, contour, and the dialogic relation between beat segments.

3) Play close heed to the transitions. What's happening to create shifts, movement, and so on?

4) Analyze the ending of each play. What is the relationship between the ending and the ten pages you selected? Is a sense of dialogism apparent? How were certain markers drawn to conclusion?

## REVISING DIALOGUE

Most playwrights would envy Sam Shepard's approach to writing dialogue which is to let the first draft stand as it hits the page. In actual practice, dialogue undergoes a metamorphic process during the vetting of the script.

*Metamorphosis* is an apt term because it describes how the early drafts molt away, leaving a more evolved form. The script, as the more experienced playwright knows, becomes an active player in the changing process. The writer's mental engagement with the material activates it toward its optimum form. Throughout the process, the writer will undertake both *the revision* and *the polish*; the differences between the two are shown in the following table.

**TABLE 9.1 Revision/Polish**

1) The revision shapes the material into form: the play takes on life.
2) The revision should remove the awkwardness from the play.
3) The revision deals with beat segments and establishes the markers and points.
4) The revision opens up the potential of the play. The theme or project becomes clear enough so that subsequent work can be targeted.
5) The revision reveals the inherent dialogism at work.

1) The polish hones, buffs, and waxes the material into a refined state. Sharpness and clarity of attack are made apparent.
2) The polish reveals the elegance and expertise of the craft and craftsman, respectively.
3) The polish deals with each beat and the point of attack of each line of dialogue (see below).
4) The polish realizes the potential of the play. The material of the play is worked toward its greatest fruition.
5) The polish reveals the sharpness of the dialogue.

*Point of attack* usually refers to the moment in the story where the playwright begins the play. Early point of attack means that most of the story unfolds before our eyes, and mandates a longer passage of time and greater space. This favors the episodic style of writing. A late point of attack occurs within a compressed time and space and often is a response to events that occurred prior to the beginning of the play. The late point of attack suggests a more classical style.

In referring to dialogue, *late point of attack* refers to the latest possible point at which to begin a line of dialogue. Note the following example: *I think I will come to see you soon* versus *I'll see you soon* versus *See you. Soon.* Clearly the last version sharpens intention. In polishing the point of attack, cut back compound verbs and conditional verbs (would, could, should) as much as possible. If the "I" or "you" is implied then it can be eliminated. Generally, unless it is utterly mandated, avoid the subjunctive or the conditional if the indicative will do. This is simply the language of presence versus the language of ambiguity and absence. A skilled actor can play on the line or against the line. The actor can manufacture subjunctive qualities (hesitancy, uncertainty, speculation, etc.) through intonation or behavior. The intention of the language should make this clear.

Polishing dialogue happens from beat to beat. Nevertheless, the polish helps to determine the contour of the beat segment and the dialogic relationship between markers. Contour emerges more clearly as dialogue is sharpened and honed. Indeed, contour can provide the modus operandi for the polish insofar as the shaping of lines creates a desired pace. The contour should generally reinforce the action of the beat segment. In other words, in a romantic seduction scene the playwright might strive for a sinuous sense to the contour, versus a staccato angularity (though the latter approach might be appropriate in creating a stylized or comic handling of the same material).

Usually, a polish will decrease the distance between markers in a scene. The rate of the play will appear to quicken, as extraneous material is vetted. This compression will affect the contour across the beat segments and may change the quality of the scene. At this stage, you should arrange a reading of the script to monitor how the revisions have affected it. A brisker pace is usually preferred to the alternative. If the pace is too fast, consider inserting character-oriented beats, or even digressionary material related to the givens. Rather than slow the script, these inserts can add impact and immediacy as the character notices some object, or has a revelation that is prompted by the givens of the scene. These beats can include pauses as well as spoken dialogue. Pay close attention to what your characters are wearing: jewelry, charms, or more mundane items can be worn, transferred, lost, or provide comic relief. Wellman is a master at this technique. A broken watch spring in *Harm's Way* provides a major impetus for Santouche's action.

In a polish, you are *detailing* your script—honing it to its optimum degree. Because the new playwriting is reliant on language to a greater degree than traditional dramaturgy, it is essential for the playwright to execute the polish with precision and care.

# 10

# Foundations of
# Contemporary Monologue

"Show us don't tell us" is the most widely used caveat directed at playwrights. It demands that good dramatic writing be present tense, immediate, and interactive. While it remains an operative strategy for playwrights, a casual glance at any play anthology suggests that the adage is untrue. Often guised as the single monologic voice, narrative elements in play texts have been present since Thespis. Take your pick from the historical canon of plays: the reportage of the Sophoclean messenger; the soliloquies of the Shakespearean hero; the caustic commentators of John Webster; the rhetorical moralists of John Dryden; the lamentations of Anton Chekhov's characters; the self-absorbed ruminations of Tennessee Williams's women; the backstories of Peter Shaffer's narrators; or the ideological tomes of Tony Kushner's tormented characters, to mention only a few. These playwrights, and most contemporary dramatists, employ monologue as a significant factor in their dramaturgy.

Moreover, during the past ten years, the use of monologue in the theater has increased significantly, spurred by the growth in popularity of the one-person show. This type of monologue in performance differs from traditional monodramas in which an actor would become immersed in the biographical portrait of a well-known historical character (e.g., Mark Twain, Emily Dickinson). Rather, these one-person shows are built extensively from autobiographical materials—the author and the performer are the same person. Drawing upon a format successfully developed by Spalding Gray, theater performers and others are branching out to create their own, self-contained studies of contemporary life and culture. Because of the cost-saving features of the one-person show, the format has been effective in bringing marginalized groups to a wider audience. Peggy Shaw, founder of the lesbian theater company Split Britches, won an OBIE award in 2000 for her cross-dressed performance of *Menopausal Gentleman*. Shaw was exploring the ravages of her own menopause—ironically, as she pointed out—dressed as a man who looked twenty years younger—a dead ringer for Sean Penn. Similar to most one-person shows, Shaw's conflated numerous elements in a pastiche that contained references to Frank

Sinatra, her own childhood, stories about her father, lip-synched music of the 1960s, and 1940s zoot suits. Guillermo Gomez-Peña has brought the issues of multiculturalism and "border psychology" to the fore with his award-winning *New World Border*. As part of this format, narrative, visual, and gestural elements are drawn from their respective subcultures. For example, Shaw utilizes lip-synching techniques drawn from her work with drag shows, while Peña underscores his narratives with the iconography and costuming of Mexican-American culture. If these one-person formats contain a variety of theatrical elements, their textual bases are in monologue; the principles explored in this and the next chapters will apply in most cases.

Current playwriting texts do not consider the practice and strategy of writing monologues. There is a need to cover some basic principles that govern the use of monologue, both as a linguistic strategy and on the stage. So while this text considers the monologue's use in new playwriting, it is at first necessary to briefly explore some traditional uses and applications of the monologue. Therefore, this chapter will examine the underpinnings of the monologue, and consider several contemporary functions of monologues in plays. The next chapter discloses how the monologue in the new playwriting represents a progress from its monologic aspect toward various forms of dialogism.

## THE FUNCTION OF MONOLOGUE IN EVERYDAY LIFE

In daily life, the monologue serves a transactional rather than interactional function. In transactional speech no conversational response is anticipated, as monologue pretends to be the last word. As a result, the monologue casts an air of authority, in spiritual realms and pulpits (from the voice of God to the sermon by the priest) or in more mundane offerings (the presentation by an expert, a lecture by a professor, or the scolding of a parent). The authority of monologue is related to its inherent resistance to interruption or disruption. As practical, everyday language, monologue possesses qualities that are static and planned; it knows where it is going, either in intent or ideology.

Narratology exists as a branch of linguistics that deals with transactional speech. This is to differentiate it from discourse analysis—the study of conversational patterns and strategies. As a relatively new subdiscipline, narratology considers contexts and outcomes where the speaker is largely uninterrupted. Some examples include taking personal histories (e.g., from medicine or journalism); using legal narratives such as briefs, affidavits, confessions, and testimonies; and using personal narratives entered into journals and diaries. There is a growing interest among playwrights to create plays based on these formats. Anna Deavere Smith based her entire award-winning play *Fires in the Mirror* on transcriptions after the fact of personal narratives from people involved in or affected by racial upheaval in the Crown Heights section of Brooklyn, New York, in the summer of 1991. Emily Mann has similarly transcribed trial testimony to create compelling characterizations in *Witness for the Prosecution.*

## HOW MONOLOGUE TRADITIONALLY FUNCTIONS IN A PLAY

Monologue's contrived aspect is featured on stage. Real-life, intense emotions actually trigger a lack of clearly articulated speech, but that is not usually the case in drama. The convention, in which intense character emotions trigger the articulation of carefully composed language, is at the heart of the contrivance. Most monologues use selective repetition and figures of speech, as well as negative space—clarified through pauses, silences, or ellipses. The monologue is composed, orchestrated for effect, and marked by a heightened, often formal level of language. In reality-based drama, monologue may theatricalize what Dorrit Cohn has described as the *transparent mind,* allowing audiences entry into the characters' consciousness: their motivations, history, or point of view. As Cohn posits, "If the real world becomes fiction only by revealing the hidden side of human beings, the reverse is equally true: the most real, the 'roundest' characters of fiction are those we know most intimately, precisely in ways we could never know people in real life" (1978, 5). This psychological "rounding" provided by monologue serves to texture the dramatized action. The Aristotelian action expands to include the articulation of thought processes, emotional states, visual metaphors, and so on. Who can think of William Shakespeare's greatest play, *Hamlet,* bereft of the soliloquies?

Before a live audience, heightened by lighting and staging effects supporting the force of the actor, the monologue's impact can be powerful. The theatricalized baring of the one before the many rivets an audience's attention to this character's moment of epiphany or intimate revelation. This convention of monologue remains one of the most tried-and-true elements of dramaturgy, and its effectiveness is reserved for the stage. Because of their essentially visual, image-oriented basis, neither the media of film nor television suffers long speeches gladly. In film, monologue is invariably formatted as a voice-over: a vocal narrative track that underscores a series of visual images.

Strict adherence to the "show us, don't tell us" dictum (i.e., the purely dialogue-oriented play text) may render subtextual meaning opaque or hidden. Novelist Thomas Mann lamented these limitations: "I confess that in everything regarding knowledge of men as individual beings, I regard drama as an art of the *silhouette,* and only narrated man as round, whole, real, and fully shaped" (Mann, quoted in Cohn 1978, 7). Mann's cavil targets the silhouetted "agent of the action" that marks the Aristotelian character. Monologue allows telescopic glimpses of characters beyond the capacity of conversational discourse, thus ensuring a greater possibility of "knowing the character" beyond the plot-limiting function as an "agent of the action."

In contemporary drama, monologue services the requirements of both actor and audience toward *explication and clarification of subtext*. Wendy Wasserstein, Tina Howe, A. R. Gurney, August Wilson, and Romulus Linney are virtuosos of this practice. After Anton Chekhov, Tennessee Williams may be the most important playwright to examine the psychological world of the character through monologue. Chekhov's current appeal may be partially linked to his characters' monologic rhapsodizing. Nevertheless, most experienced playwrights are keenly aware that overdoing monologues can lead to a very static dramaturgy.

In the traditional dialogue-oriented script, monologue expands upon the core of the play script, giving the audience more satisfaction, a sense of coloration, and clarity. As a by-product, the quality of its presence defines to an extent the writing ability of the playwright. Moreover, monologue's acceptance as a dramaturgical convention establishes playwriting as the most literary of the dramatic medium. To prove this point, attend several stage readings of new work and observe what audiences respond to. Invariably, they will single out monologues as examples of the playwright's ability to capture an essence or feeling, and as a measurement of their awe regarding the talent of the writing.

In traditional dramaturgy, outer motivations are realized through dialogue and dramatic action; thus, it remains for the monologue to clarify inner objectives, especially if those hidden forces run contrary to the more apparent external motives. The unbolting of strong emotions can reveal a sudden shift in intention. For the actor, the release of hidden forces is a clear point of definition for the character, representing a discovery or reversal. In backstage parlance, this point is where the character gauges the overall *arc*, or trajectory of the character's journey during the course of the play. Thus, the proper build to this point in the arc can be clearly orchestrated, giving the character structure and definition. Based on these observations we can arrive at the general premise that monologue serves a variety of expansionary functions, and its placement in the playscript generally indicates its purpose. The various functions can be (1) exposition or anecdotal diversion in the early scenes; (2) metaphoric or thematic analogue used to emphasize or clarify points of conflict in the rising action; and (3) character discovery, epiphany, or reversals located near the major crisis of the play.

Providing examples of the first two of those functions are the contemporary plays *Mud*, by Maria Irene Fornes, and *Wall of Water*, by Sherry Kramer. David Hare's *Secret Rapture* is an example of the third function. Characters in these plays are generally imitative of, or based in, real life. Thus, realism defines content rather than formal or structural elements of the plays. For example, in *Six Degrees of Separation* John Guare utilizes the well-documented scams perpetrated by the ersatz son of Sidney Poitier as the basis for the action in a play that utilizes time fragmentation and nonrealistic structure.

Fornes and Kramer interweave dramatized scenes with monologue sections. In *Mud* the central character Mae uses her monologic "moments" to provide exposition that details her relationship with her father and the rationale for her living arrangement with Lloyd. While Mae's readings to the illiterate Lloyd take the apparent form of a lesson, the subject matter of the starfish and hermit crab provides a thematic analog that informs the action of the play. Mae associates herself with the starfish, a symbol for hope and rebirth indicated by its ability to regrow lost appendages. Lloyd is the image of the hermit crab, one whose domicile has been invaded and usurped by Mae's new lover, Henry.

In *Wall of Water*, Kramer sets her characters' monologues in a bathroom, a place to withdraw and escape—the symbolic sanctuary for sharing (with us) their thoughts and desires. We consider the bathroom to be a safe, private space. Here, Kramer's characters expose their innermost thoughts, while the space itself offers a comic counterpoint. In both *Wall of Water* and *Mud*, the monologues have an interpolated structural quality, serving as a bridge between scenes of dialogue. While not advancing the action, they function to provide character detailing and thematic reinforcement.

## MONOLOGUE INTERPOLATION IN NEW PLAY DEVELOPMENT

In play development, monologue interpolation between sections of dialogue can provide an effective strategy for discovering a character's functions and thematic values without massive internal redrafting of scenes. Several years ago the New Playwrights' Program developed *Southern Girls*, a play by Dura Temple and Sheri Bailey. The playwrights nearly doubled fifty minutes of dialogue to about 100 minutes as each of the six characters (three black and three white) were given monologues that flashed from the present back to the 1950s, 1960s, and 1970s. These monologues segued through the historical periods presented in the play. While audiences relished these character moments, we were pleased that the monologues covered the structural breaks of time, and gave unity to the form. Subsequently, *Southern Girls* was chosen as best new play from the southern region of the American College Theater Festival.

## EXERCISE:
### Monologue Interpolation

A very effective exercise for any level of playwright, the following involves two playwrights working together.

1) Write a short, five-scene play that will be about ten minutes in length.

2) The group should use free association to profile the main character, who should fall within the realm of a persecutor or savior type). A saturated biography can also be manufactured for the main character; this provides a complete history of the character up to the point of attack (the beginning of the play).

3) Playwright A drafts three dialogue-oriented scenes.

4) Playwright B interpolates two monologues at key points interrupting the dialogue. Each monologue serves a distinct function.

5) Playwright B redrafts the dialogue-oriented scenes.

6) Playwright A revises and tweaks the monologues.

## EXERCISE:
### How Monologues Function: Creating the Ten-Minute Play

1) Write three scenes in dialogue involving a love triangle.

2) Target five scenes, either alternating two monologue scenes with three dialogue scenes, or two dialogue scenes with three monologues. In the latter format, start with a monologue from your major character; the second monologue comes from another character; the third involves the major character in a discovery, or moment of peripiteia.

3) One monologue uses the image of an animal or fish to describe the character analogically or metaphorically.

4) Play with the structure by interpolating the monologues between scenes of dialogue. What happens to the sense of sequence and transition? You will have to revise a bit to accommodate the monologues into the dialogue.

5) How and what do the monologues tell us about the character speaking, and the other characters?

COMMENT: This exercise has been successful with beginning playwrights because it accomplishes several important dramaturgical moves at once. The outcome of the exercise is usually a ten-minute play. The playwright will also notice an enhanced presentation of character. The alternation of monologue and dialogue scenes affects stage time, seemingly expanding a sense of duration while being read within the ten-minute framework. The concept of monologue as scene is made clear.

NOTE: Try both combinations of structure:

dialogue/monologue/dialogue/monologue/dialogue;

monologue/dialogue/monologue/dialogue/monologue.

Note the differences in the results.

# EXERCISE:
## The Relationship of the Monologue to Space

1) Select a common household space and integrate it completely into a scheme of character and structure.

2) Consider private or transitional spaces and write several character monologues; use closets, attics, foyers, and corridors, weight or exercise rooms, laundry rooms, and so on.

3) How does space inform the monologue? What feels safe to the character?

4) Attempt to build a brief one-act play around one of these transitional spaces. For example, think of the dramatic possibilities in a laundry room: its powerful image of clean and dirty and forgotten or ruined clothes. How can this visual reinforce the past, the present? The action of ironing or pressing clothes may trigger emotional responses. Corridors or stairways (i.e., transitional spaces) are seldom used by playwrights but impose interesting contextual frames. Playwright Kent Brown and others have written successful one-acts around garage sales. Obviously, items put up for sale have histories that inform us about the characters in a natural way. The space-event related action provides context for the play. Rummaging in an attic might border on the cliché or banal unless objects and memories become imbued with wonder.

# EXERCISE:
## Monologue As Study

Monologue can be used as a study of character; similar to the way an artist sketches several views of a figure before settling on the appropriate pose and disposition.

1) Have your major character write a letter to another character in the play. The attempt is to discover, then isolate specifics about the relationship, which your current draft may be glossing over. In addition to personal matters, the letter can explore thematic issues you wish to introduce in the play.

## HARE'S INTEGRATED MONOLOGUE

David Hare's use of monologue in *Secret Rapture* is completely integrated within the dramatic scheme. Isobel and her sister Marion's revelatory monologues in act 2 demonstrate each character's reversal in self-perception— their moment of perepeteia. Isobel's monologue near the close of scene 6, in act II, is particularly apt since its crucial placement heightens the impact of the character's epiphany and reversal through the dramaturgical shift to the monologic form:

ISOBEL: Paradise. I took off all my clothes off and walked along the beach. Lanzarote was paradise. But unfortunately no use to me. (*She laughs.*) You can't get away. You think you can. You think you'll fly out. Just leave. Damn the lot of you, and go. Then you think, here I am, stark naked, sky-blue sea, miles of sand—I've done it! I'm free! Then you think, yes, just remind me, what am I meant to do now? (*She stands, a mile away in a world of her own.*) In my case there's only one answer. (*She looks absently at them, as if they were not even present.*) I must do what Dad would have wished. (*She turns as if this were self-evident.*) That's it.

(Hare 1989, 2: 6, 69)

Hare's carefully constructed dramatic monologue concentrates traditional elements of play structure: *beginning* (exposition: sense of place and context, Lanzarote as "paradise"), *middle* (discovery, climax: realization that this resort offers her no panacea—"what am I meant to do now?"); and *end* (reversal, choice, resolution: "I must do what Dad would have wished"). Her sister and brother-in-law, while present, take on a quality of absence indicated by the stage direction "she looks absently at them, as if they were not even present." Jan Mukarovsky identified this characteristic "absence" in his book, *The Word and Verbal Art*, positing that a character's move to monologism occurs "by virtue of the fact that one of the speakers forgets his partner(s) and speaks "to [her]self" by indulging in recollection or by becoming absorbed in [her]self"(1997, 115). Of course, onstage this is accomplished with a subtle lighting special that illuminates the monologic moment in contrast to dimmed background characters and setting. The skilled director, and the actor playing Isobel, will find distinct beats in this monologue—emphasizing the transitions from beginning to middle to end—fully working the range of contrast and contour. In its entirety the monologue represents a beat segment with clear dramaturgical markers.

## EXERCISE:
### Utilizing the Integrated Model

1) Write a two-character scene in which the characters are bound in some type of relationship: a couple, business partners, siblings, parent and child.
2) One character should reveal some deep or hidden truth that will change or reverse the course of their relationship.
3) This revelation is accomplished through a monologue that has clear beat transitions for beginning, middle, and end.
4) Create a strong level of self-absorption in the character during the monologue.
5) The character should feel a strong change of horizon as a result of the monologue (a weight has been lifted). Clarify this marker with something visual, a rhythmic shift in speech, a pause, and so on.

COMMENT: One of the contrived aspects of the monologue and one of the problems in rehearsal has to do with the other person(s) who are listeners, but not participants. In fact, part of the effect is achieved by making these listener characters somewhat remote. It is easy for the silent character to inadvertently steal focus for example. It is even worse if that character appears bored or distracted.

Structuring the monologue with specific beats that indicate beginning, middle, and end is often quite difficult for beginning playwrights. The tendency is to get pulled off track in the middle of the monologue—usually with digressionary material that brings in other subject matter. A successful counterstrategy has the playwright construct the end first, and then begin the monologue keeping the target in mind. Just like the special ellipsoidal light beam that captures the monologue's delivery, the monologue must remain focused throughout, with a sharpness of attack and purpose.

### EXPLORATORY MONOLOGUE

The exploratory monologue is a means to flesh out a character or integrate backstory into the character's actions. Sometimes it can be used to recall sense experience in a particular episode of a character or author's life. It can also be used as a means to arrive at the above exercise, providing the raw materials that can be shaped accordingly into the requisite beginning, middle, and end.

### EXERCISE:
#### Sense Recall

This exercise was given in a workshop by Matthew Maguire, author of the award-winning *Throwin' Bones* and *Phaedra*. Maguire heads the playwriting program at Fordham University.

1) In a monologue, describe a true, nonfictional accident that happened to you.

2) Select the most intense moment of the accident, how you felt, what was happening around you, capturing as closely as possible the senses of the moment.

COMMENT: The accident represents a moment of hyperreality when time seemingly stands still, and life hangs in the balance. This sense of danger is the very stuff of theater. Keep audiences on the nervy precipice, off balance and engaged. Attempt to write rhythmically, withholding and restraining the monologue until the heightened moment of no return. At this point increase rapidity, by using truncated phrases, accelerated rate, and heightened pitch. Indicate with exclamation points and capital letters. Consider the breathing of the actor—from slow and sustained to ending in a pant.

### MONOLOGUE AND THE ABSENT "OTHER"

A fundamental skill of playwriting is the ability to effectively score monologues to offstage characters. Often, this convention of monologue involves the semiotization of the absent "other." When a character prays to an onstage statue, for instance, the statue is the visual stand-in for the actual saint, for Christ, or for an ancestor. *Semiotization* means one object stands in for something else, becoming a sign of that object. Perhaps the most prosaic example is the telephone, the use of which indicates and simulates that someone "absent" is on the other end. An empty chair can be just that, but when it is semiotized it could signify the person who just left, or even a deceased parent (as in dad's favorite chair). Tape recorders and answering machines have long been used to introduce characters before their entrance. The use of visual or iconic signs can be particularly effective, as when a character addresses a photographic image of a loved one, a painted portrait or bust, or even a tattoo of Mom etched into the flesh. Various symbols may portray the absent other: a piece of jewelry such as a locket, or a flower.

By using these devices the playwright can construct the monologue with confidence that the audience will "suspend its disbelief" regarding the nonpresent "other." For instance, in the familiar phone monologue, the playwright deftly disguises the monologue within conditions that are essentially dialogic, or interactional, by presenting disagreements, misunderstandings, and disruptions, rather than a chain of uninterrupted continuity or agreement. In writing the phone monologue the playwright must provide leading questions, followed by credible responses. This device has become increasingly popular with the ubiquity of the cellular phone, which can simply be pulled from the actor's pocket at the appropriate moment. Of course, the risk for the playwright is in overusing a technique that can grow predictable and stale; it can become as corny as the written letter that is gratuitously recited or dictated to a third party. We are now witnessing a current generation of plays with recited e-mail and chat room responses (for example, Patrick Marber's play *Closer*).

## EXERCISES:
### Monologue and the Absent "Other"

### Exercise A

1) Brainstorm over typical professions that use the phone often.
2) Write an opening scene that utilizes a phone device but creates a vivid sense of offstage characters. In other words, use the monologue to focus on the offstage character.
3) Give the offstage character insight into the behavior of the character that is speaking, thus creating a kind of self-commentary, which is ironic and effective onstage.

1) Have a character find the photo of another character at an earlier phase in his or her life.

2) Have a monologue develop the differences between the past and the present in terms of the character perceiving the photograph (the marker is the moment of discovery).

3) Some change of outlook or emotional horizon is indicated (shift the mood).

COMMENT: While the phone convention seems stale from a theatrical point of view, the Greg Mosher–directed production of John Guare's *Six Degrees of Separation* at New York's Lincoln Center solved the problem of the phone device by moving characters into individual spots when phone contact was necessitated in the script. While neither props nor miming were used, the semiotized lighting effect translated an old convention into a powerfully theatricalized realization. In the workshop, discuss some of the problems you had in managing this notion of semiotization so as to avoid the cliché and the obvious.

In sum, the key factor in writing effective monologues is to capture the character's transition in mental and emotional states. You need to provide markers for the actor to effect this end result. If you wish to improve characterization in your monologues, a good tool is to study portrait paintings, paying close attention to visual details in particular. In period portraits, you will notice iconographic elements that show us what an individual is about—profession, passions, and private concerns. An effective exercise that takes this visual aspect to the extreme involves the fetish object and the character. By showing the abnormal attachment of the character to a particular object, you unlock a level of visual interest for the audience while drawing a dialogic relationship between the fetish object and the character's emotional states.

# 11
## Dialogic Monologue:
## Structure and Antistructure

Phone devices demonstrate how the distinction between monologic and dialogic discourses can be blurred in the theater. As in everyday speech, transactional and interactional modes of discourse are simultaneously present in a state of continual flux. Generally, monologue and dialogue should not be conceived as two mutually exclusive forms of dramatic language, but as two approaches that struggle for predominance, even within a specific speech (see Mukarovsky 1977, 102). In drama, this struggle is evident when the addressed "other" is the audience.

Part 2 of Len Jenkin's *Limbo Tales* makes this point: Although the actor/character directly addresses the incoming spectators as the *emcee*, the conditions are fixed and monologic: the ad-libs are scripted and will stand without reply. Nevertheless, the opportunity for dialogic exchange is offered whenever the speaker "penetrates" the fourth wall and directly engages the audience. When the *emcee* introduces us to the cast of characters in *Limbo Tales* he becomes matrixed as a character in the play. Margaret Edson's 1999 Pulitzer Prize–winning play *Wit* makes a similar move; in the opening monologue, the actor playing Vivian introduces herself first as the actor in the play:

> VIVIAN: (*Waving and nodding to the audience*) Hi. How are you feeling today? Great. That's just great.
>
> (Edson 1999, 7)

Then, she sets herself into the character of Vivian:

> (*In her own professorial tone.*) This is not my standard greeting, I assure you. I tend to something a little more formal, a little less inquisitive, such as, say, "Hello."

The monologue then continues to disclose the character's profession, current patient status and obviously dire condition until the end of the speech, when the actor brings us back to the theatricality of the event: "I've got less than two hours. Then: curtain" (Edson 1999, 7–8).

These level shifts in language, intention, and matrix represent a form of internal dialogism. In both *Limbo Tales* and *Wit*, the narrators' voices shift between presentational and representational modes, giving the plays a dialogic structure. This dialogic shift is a benchmark characteristic of the new playwriting and it offers the playwright a variety of dramaturgic options.

In several examples from the new playwriting (including Jenkin's *My Uncle Sam,* and *Kid Twist*), the events narrated are different from those staged, with the speaker positioned at the interface between the audience and the dramatic event. Monologue's authority is undermined in its relation to the event onstage. Regarding contextual relativity in *The Dialogic Imagination,* Mikhail Bakhtin posited that "there is a constant interaction between meanings, all of which have the potential of conditioning others. What will affect the other, how it will do so, and in what degree is what is actually settled at the moment of utterance. This dialogic imperative . . . insures that there can be no true monologue (Bakhtin 1981, 246–47). This indeterminate quality of monologue is evident in plays that feature memory or the recall of past events. Harold Pinter uses monologues in *Betrayal, Old Times,* and *Landscape* that proffer the impossibility of memory to capture truths underlying shared events. Sam Shepard uses monologue similarly to Pinter: in the film version of *Fool For Love,* monologues become voice-overs to a different action than that suggested in the narrative. In this case, the dialogic clash is determined contextually rather than textually. This cinematic technique has been adapted by new playwrights, who innovate its use as a clash between the narrator's voice and the image of the mise-en-scène.

## NEW DRAMATURGY

The blurring of monologic and dialogic qualities predominates in the plays of Len Jenkin and Mac Wellman. In Jenkin's plays dialogue at times serves a narrative function, while monologue, upon which his storytelling techniques are established, functions in an interactional, dialogic manner. Conversely, Wellman uses monologues to subvert traditional syntactical and linguistic constructions. Strategically, Wellman establishes internal dialogism across several language systems within his plays. This focus on the syntactic and phonetic, an approach shared with playwright Suzan-Lori Parks, targets language itself rather than plot, character, or a traditional sense of discernible meaning as the thematic. As discussed in chapter 2, Parks's unique phonetic approach to dramatic language contains immanent links to African-American dialect and history without overtly stating or reiterating traditional black themes. Wellman conflates slang from different eras into neologisms or new combinations, as in *Whirligig.* A monologue play such as Wellman's *Terminal Hip* activates certain sociocultural contexts within the purview of the spectator. Meaning is not directly apparent, but grasped only in the collision of specific speech genres or discourses: African American; Wall Street market talk, ethnic expressions, street jive, and so on.

Wellman's monologues feature a bombardment of language. This language is refracted by the subjective consciousness of the spectator against the backdrop of the current sociocultural context. Wellman's linguistic enterprise differs from most approaches to playwriting, which happily mirror the current slang and idiomatic usage as a mark of innovation. Wellman's inimitable language is in tension with the current parlance. The "grey look," mass, or density of his writing appears as monologue on the page, yet its effect and purpose is to dialogize both linguistically (on a cultural level) and theatrically (on an aesthetic level). This expansion of monologue's capacity into the linguistic arena alters the traditional concept of what constitutes a play.

An analogy might be to the experiments of Jerzy Grotowski and The Performance Group in the 1960s and '70s that focused on redefining the physical functions and spiritual essences of the actor in performance. Wellman reassesses how language can function in a play, as Grotowski sought to reevaluate prevailing assumptions regarding the actors' potential. Grotowski's paratheatrical experiments eventually isolated the actor in an intensive exploration of the acting process. At times, Wellman's inscrutable experiments isolate linguistic foregrounding to the extent that language momentarily eclipses or suspends the need for dramaturgy. In this sense, Wellman's force of language substitutes immediate moment-to-moment interest as an antistructural device. In fleeting bursts during performance, language achieves a formal essence as images and sounds appear, transfigure, disappear, and reemerge. Wellman has staked out new territory for the playwright, one filled with risk, adventure, and a sense of the unknown.

## TOWARD ANTISTRUCTURE: MAC WELLMAN'S SPATIAL NOUNING

In Wellman's *Whirligig* (1988) the Girl Hun's last speech provides the effect of hurling us through space:

> Plinth . . . Mitake Mura, Dikan'ka, Elmer, Hektor, Doctor Spock, Roswitha, Pia, Wofiana, Erda, Helio, 1935X, McCuskey, Wild, Whipple, Zulu, CrAO, Toro, Hamburga. . . .
>
> (Wellman 1994, *Whirligig*, 173–174)

The linear stacking of word signifiers—Wellman coined the term *nouning*—creates a fission-like reaction, what he describes as the *radioactive effect of language*. This term, *radioactive language*, locates the site of "fission" in the observer: meaning is absorbed contextually in the gaps between words, then through continual deferring until the destination is reached. The playwright's monologic bombardment offers a variety of dialogism. Rather than denying the existence of the "other" or pretending to be the "final word," it is now the "other" as audience who becomes the author of mean-

ture to the audience.

Wellman's interstellar travels through a fictional universe are made strange by juxtaposing "proper" names such as Doctor Spock, Zulu, Hamburga, and others to "space names" such as 1935X and CrAO. Obviously, while this "radioactive effect" is happening any emotional involvement of the spectator with character is precluded. Wellman is inviting the audience to a linguistically theatrical experience. Nouning defers intention to favor sense experience. To an extent nouning also includes a rational response to the ironic juxtaposition of the familiar to the strange. Sonic and semantic relations combine to create moment-to-moment interest. Unlike the work of the traditional playwright/craftsman who attempts to control meaning and structure, Wellman's monologic word barrage obscures not only the character's voice but also overall dramaturgical coherence. By negating coherence and dramatic underpinnings Wellman's nouning creates an antistructure with thrilling effects—but replete with risk. The loss of narrative pull and psychologically rounded characters is offset by the second-to-second unfolding of surprise and the unexpected. The intensity of the moment supplants the traditional build toward climax and resolution. The following, from act 1 of Wellman's *Whirligig*, provides an example of what appears from the playwright's perspective to be free-associational improvisation as Girl inquires about Man's history:

MAN: I am from a place far away, but it is no longer existing.

GIRL: Dad? Sixties' type. Lawyer. Acid Head, hippie, "way out," "cool, man cool." The Beatles, ugh. Law School, tunnel vision, career in venture capital. Suits, hats, coats. Condos. Fuck the poor. Senator Moynihan. The Pope. IRAs.

Hippie yuppie. Huppie Yippie. Yawn . . .

(*pause*)

Mom, the hippie honey. Short skirts, long skirts, short skirts again. Castro, Che Guevera, born again, Jews for Jesus, puke. Moral Majority. Likud. Jogging. Condos for Christ. The West Bank. Summer home somewhere. CDs and Money market. Double yawn . . .

(*pause*)

I ran away from home. Two thousand miles. Home sucks.

(*pause*)

I'm going to the desert.

(Wellman 1994, *Whirligig*, 145)

The conflation of nouns and slogans from the 1960s, 1970s, and 1980s collide meanings and intentions. This "word field" barrage takes us on a journey through time. Phrases such as "Hippie yuppie. Huppie Yippie" foreground a neologism such as *Huppie* and give it connotative value. It suggests possible meanings (a conflation of Hippie and Yuppie?) and spontaneous contexting (a character in the 1980s television drama *Thirty-Something?*). The playwright draws the spectator into the middle of his linguistic "playing field." In its performance, we find that Wellman has evolved a novel form of theatrical interest that substitutes for a more normative structural progression.

The following exercises offer a point of entry into what may be unfamiliar dramaturgical territory. Since the impact of nouning is most noticeable in its sonic aspect, this interactive exercise should prove helpful.

## EXERCISE:
### Nouning

1) In Wellman's *Whirligig*, read the final speech by the Girl Hun for an example of nouning.

2) How does nouning create the sense of travel or movement for the spectator? For the characters?

3) How is Wellman "making strange" by his juxtaposition of proper names to other more or less acceptable space names? How are words affected by their proximity to other words?

4) What effect does this have on meaning within the play?

COMMENT: The nouning exercises are attempts to free playwrights from normative syntactical choices. Daily life is consumed with lists, and nouning activates this impulse. Most rote learning is achieved through the memorization of facts on lists. Beyond that, an associational barrage can release powerful energies in a text or character. Even within traditional playwriting formats the nouning monologue can be a potent tool in your arsenal.

## EXERCISE:
### Freewriting

1) Freely associate names that are associated with given rooms, spaces, or businesses; time periods; or cultural phenomena.

2) Use slogans as well as nouns.

3) Set a timer to four minutes and do not lift pen from paper during this word barrage.

4) Attempt to free the "self-censor"—any tendency to censor your writing.

COMMENT: Language playwrights strive to "do things with words." These exercises demonstrate how words can operate in an exciting, vital way. The playwright should not neglect the spatial effect nouning and proper names have on the sensory imagination of the spectator. Monologue can supply mass in a text, the same way that a large area painted in one color can focus or stabilize a painting. As we will discover in the upcoming exercise on spinning, monologues can become pivot points around which scenes converge—one coming to closure in the monologue as another is born.

## EXERCISE:
### Free Association

This automatic writing exercise is based on the free association of terms and phrases. It uses the *obsessive idea* as a focus point. André Breton, the French father of surrealism, promoted automatic writing as a means to unlock and discover unconscious desires. Breton suggested the writer should obsess on an object, person, or idea as a means to focus the intention.

1) Allow a character in a scene to freely associate on a sexual obsession (for example, a woman or man whom the character observes from a window at given times during the day). The regularity and predictability become habitual, then obsessional.

2) Seek closure. Does the love interest vanish? How does this mark the free association? Or, does the character act on the obsession? How does this choice mark the free association?

3) In what ways does this practice inform your writing?

4) Does it release the character's voice in any way?

### *TERMINAL HIP* AND THE FORCE OF LANGUAGE

Wellman's OBIE-Award winning play *Terminal Hip* (1989), subtitled *The Spiritual History of America through the Medium of Bad Language,* projects a tougher, more intense use of language than does his *Whirligig.* There is neither vestige of plot nor character. A characterless monologue, *Terminal Hip* was performed by Stephen Mellor at Performance Space 122 in New York City in during January 1990. Mellor examined the almost impenetrable script and came to the conclusion that the only way to play it was at close range—phrase by phrase and in a hyperrealistic manner. Mellor established a suitable intention for each moment, and was able to construct a convincing performance. In his guardedly positive review, saying "the work plays better than it reads," Mel Gussow described it as "post-Joycean Jabberwocky," replete with "unidentified flying verbiage" (Gussows 1990, 5). The beginning scene zigzags us into Wellman's idiosyncratic universe:

Strange the Y all bent up and Dented
Blew the who to tragic eightball.
Eightball trumpet earwax and so forth.
Pure chew, loud thump and release pin.
Crabity gotta nail him too sure.
You don't not have no super shoes when as how

you don't need not to never.
Ask for the labernath it's all over sure.
They got music there so bad.
They got music there as do the shame-ball
double up and fall over
three times running while it drills
corrosive z's on that there river bottom.
Technology comes here too am. (1:1)

(Wellman 1994, *Terminal Hip*, 257)

For audiences familiar with the one-person plays of Eric Bogosian or Spalding Gray, Wellman is treading his own turf in an established genre. Unlike the work of Gray or Bogosian, in *Terminal Hip* words and grammatical aberrations become the property of the senses rather than vehicles to purport a character's psychology or the play's exposition. As gestural thrusts and parries they suggest Antonin Artaud's theory that "language cannot be defined except by its possibilities for dynamic expression in space as opposed to the expressive possibilities of spoken dialogue . . . [and] for dissociative and vibratory action upon the sensibility." (Artaud, quoted in Bentley 1968, 55–56).

Wellman's stacked sequential nouning, such as "eightball, trumpet, ear-wax," embodies what Antonin Artaud described in *The Theater and Its Double* as "this solidified, materialized language" (Bentley 1968, 55). While Artaud's essays were highly influential in the creation of the 1960s avant-garde movement in theater, it has been difficult to this point to find an example of what Artaud envisioned regarding stage language. *Terminal Hip* presents, as Artaud suggests, "a language in which an overwhelming stage experience seems to be communicated, in comparison with which our productions depending exclusively upon dialogue seem like so much stuttering" (1988, 56). Artaud's "stutterer," a metaphor for the theater's inability to assert a breakthrough language, may be contrasted to Wellman's master utterer. Wellman's high-octane theatricalized diction is the linguistic corollary to Artaud's overwhelming stage experience. Yet if Wellman is the literary return of Artaud, then he radically illustrates in *Terminal Hip* the novel possibilities of the monologic format as the redemptor of the "stutterer," whereby imitative reality and discourse are syntactically transcended and theatricalized.

Wellman's sheer force of the word horde eliminates recourse to traditional dramaturgical formulae or craft. Stripped of familiar moorings we are hurled into a dream of consciousness, constructed not with plot or character, but by what Gussow called a "crazy quilt of slang and convolutions" (1990, 5). In Artaudian terms, *Terminal Hip* ultimately affects an audience toward a cathartic response brought on neither by pity and fear nor emotional identification, but rather by the intense force (i.e., Artaud's "theater of cruelty") of the language on the sense organs.

*Terminal Hip* provides many examples of what Wellman describes as the beauty of "bad English." Bad English is made up of incorrect syntax, misplaced words, slang, profanity, and so on. The playwright averts acceptable speech norms and conventions of writing dialogue or monologue. Bad English provides an option for multivocal texturing—and takes a high level of craft to effectively accomplish. Nouns and verbs are juxtaposed to create strange or unusual effects.

1) Gather in your scrapbook or journal examples of improper but colorful syntax. Tune your ears to peculiarities of syntax, sentence structure and word choices.

2) Refer to chapter 2 for examples from speech genres. Select from your journal, or seek out, several examples from differing speech genres.

3) Write a five-minute monologue with a multivocal character who is extremely upset about some social wrong (like toxic waste), some societal mistake. Integrate the above into the monologue, focusing on bad English syntactical choices.

## DEMATRIXING TECHNIQUES

New playwrights often dialogize monologue through *dematrixing techniques*. The actor/character can be dematrixed when, or if, they (1) fracture the mold of a specific character; (2) directly acknowledge or address the presence of the audience; or (3) foreground the presence of the actor over character.

Even the audience goes through a kind of matrixing—what Erving Goffman, in *Frame Analysis*, has described as the distinction between onlookers and theatergoers (1974). For example, the stage manager in Thornton Wilder's *Our Town* breaks the matrix through direct address. Nevertheless, a distinction exists between his chiding the incoming audience as theatregoers (cajoling latecomers, for example), and addressing the audience as onlookers during his involvement in the dramatic action. The first instance represents an actor/theatregoer exchange; the second demonstrates the character/onlooker exchange.

In *Careless Love* (a stage version of the radio play *Angel Baby*), Len Jenkin innovates his monologic strategy toward dematrixed dialogism. Jenkin theatricalizes the move between actor and character by requiring microphone-aided speech for Bobby's monologues. The voiceover of the miked Bobby dematrixes Marie's "interior monologue." Bobby's presence on stage heightens the moment's theatricality.

(*In her mind*) You don't need to write poems about us, babe, cause one drop of your sweat when you're on top of me is a coded message that flies out by night, to other worlds. The drop gets translated by intergalactic linguificators into seven thousand hexameters of

immortal, feminine, earth verse . . . [gentle laughing that fades]
(Jenkin 1991, *Careless Love*, 17).

When he uses the microphone, the character Bobby foregrounds the
actor as performer, since the microphone marks the moment as a performance. Later, when he resumes the matrix of unamplified speech and
dramatized event, Bobby is foregrounding the character. The alteration of
speech modes through electronic means such as reverberation affects this
foregrounding. This semantic/sonic variable dialogizes between alternating levels of amplified and unamplified speech. In addition, rather than
Marie recollecting through a past-tense, third-person monologue that
summons the idea of the "absent" lover, Bobby's speech focuses us upon
the palpable presence of their erotic interaction.

A notion from semiotics, *foregrounding* emphasizes the signifier over the
recognizable signified meaning. Linguistically, the sound or look of words
assumes more importance than their meanings as language itself seemingly floats—apart from character. In terms of character, the acting style,
approach, or device is *foregrounded* over the character portrayal (*signified*).
Foregrounding is related to Brechtian alienation effects; in both cases,
there is a heightened awareness of artifice or device.

Jenkin offers a variation of these techniques—juxtaposing voice-overs,
direct address, and songs within Karen's multivocal monologue in his
*American Notes*, produced at New York's Public Theater in February 1988,
under the direction of JoAnne Akalaitis:

> KAREN: (*V.O.* [voice-over]) Where was I? (*LIVE*) Who the hell knows.
> (*Karen notices the candy bar, picks it up. She looks back toward the door.*
> *V.O.*) Oh my God . . . am I that pitiful? (*LIVE*) Snickers. Looks like
> it's been in his pocket in a heat wave. (*She tosses the crushed candy bar
> into a corner. V.O.*) Three days in this hole. Waiting's just like being
> dead, except you still have to pass the time. (*LIVE. Sings.*) "I will sing
> you a song of the New Jerusalem, that far away home of the soul . . ."
> (*V.O.*) That's all I remember. (*LIVE*) Facts. He's late, (*V.O.*) he's very
> late, (*LIVE*) but he's on his way, knowing I'd wait forever, that I'd be
> here . . . (*V.O.*) . . . staring out the window for him till my eyes become
> two tiny swamps where the moss floats, till my lips are food for crows,
> till deep in the grass grown up through this crumbling floor, my
> white bones rot. (*LIVE*) Fuck that. Hell, he'll probably show up any
> minute, with a hard-on and a mouth full of sorry [*a moment's silence*].
> (Jenkin 1993, *American Notes*, 245–246)

The bifurcation of the character into taped and live presences foregrounds the artifice of monologue as it discloses its dialogism. Voice-overs
provide Karen with an interactional "other," whereby the internal taped
dialogue confronts, contradicts, or focuses her live, "quoted" responses
(see Cohn 1978, 58–99). Theatrically, the interactional mode is culminat-

ed as a dialogue between the matrixed live character and her nonmatrixed (nonlive) recording, where the *means* of expression become as significant to the dialogism as what is being said.

## EXERCISE:
### Dialogic Monologue; The Taped or Miked Voice-Over.

1) Have a character pantomime an action (dressing, for example) while her concurrent thoughts are played on tape. She answers each thought back in her character's voice, interacting with the taped speech—the theatrical corollary of talking to herself.

2) For another approach to dialogic monologue, have your character impersonate the voices of other characters. For instance, a character is setting a table for dinner, "conversing" with each guest as she sets up his or her place setting. The running dialogue between herself and the "guest" can vary from the humorous to poignant—an introduction that builds audiences' expectations. (The introduction is a standard expositional device: one, two, or several characters describe a character or characters about to enter.)

3) Interpolate the taped voice of some other character within the speaker's monologue. The quoted monologue is used frequently in novels indicated by "he said," or "she thought to herself," or "she exclaimed," and so on. This application conflates the dialogic "other" within the matrix of the monologue.

## AMPLIFIED SPEECH

Miked speech is a favorite production technique in the new playwriting. Mac Wellman's early years of writing radio plays might have influenced this tendency, although it is Len Jenkin who has really integrated the device, particularly when he is directing his own work. Miked speech can create a disembodied eeriness by foregrounding sound quality in the utterance. The actor doesn't have to push vocally, so this opens up certain resonances in the voice that would not otherwise be heard. Miked speech has its corollary in real-life, theatricalized applications: singing, commenting, radio disc jockeying. In regard to the latter, *Native Speech* by Eric Overmyer actually centers on the character Hungry Mother as disc jockey. In *Fnu Lnu*, Wellman uses miked performers to create a choral sense, an application that has been used in several productions of his *Murder of Crows*. Wellman also uses the device to startle an audience, as, when a character grabs the mike and gives a monologue in *Fnu Lnu*, the effect of the aural texture changes the nature of the event. Perhaps, Samuel Beckett was the first to use taped voice-over techniques in *Krapp's Last Tape*. Krapp, an old man in the play, plays back sections of himself as a younger man, thus dialogizing with an earlier version of self.

With current advances in sound cueing and editing, playwrights can now utilize technological means of speech and sound. These advances will signal more ways of conceptualizing monologue to include multiple voices, dialects, languages, and an array of effect options.

## PROPERTIES OF MONOLOGUE

The "knows where it's going" aspect of monologue comes about through careful composition and editing. Unlike dialogue shared among actors, the monologue is "owned" by the performer. Because it is a "moment" for the actor, he is encouraged to maximize the theatrical potential of the speech. Indeed, the significance of the monologue as the primary audition tool has placed increasing emphasis on signature monologues. Casting agents and directors seek originality, passion, and impressive virtuoso turns by the actor. Critics, on another level, are profoundly affected by the transparency of monologue. During its performance, they receive an unimpeded glimpse of character while qualifying the level of writing talent and dramaturgical skill. Further, for critics, it is monologue that deciphers theme. Reviewers allot more language flexibility to monologue than dialogue, where heightened language may be considered stilted or forced. Playwrights satisfy these expectations by embedding a message in a solo speech, even when the risk is of telegraphing. At its worst, telegraphing force-feeds as it gratuitously serves up information; it may seem that the playwright does not trust the audience to "get it." If telegraphing is a fault, it is certainly one practiced by most playwrights, who defend its authentic "writing on the line"—allowing the character to bare true thoughts, feelings, and intentions. Nevertheless, telegraphing may lack merit because it primarily serves as a playwright's convenience. Eric Overmyer has been successful in transcending this problem through monologues that push the limits of language. His extreme form of writing on the line exalts the virtuosic in performance.

## MONOLOGUE AS ARIA: OVERMYER'S VIRTUOSIC MONOLOGUES

If monologue traditionally focuses a character's credo or belief system at a pivotal point in the play, then its heightened rendering may simulate the aria of opera. Eric Overmyer, who proffers the idea of monologue as the corollary of aria, takes the format to new heights. For Overmyer, monologues should possess showstopping qualities like a big musical number. Overmyer envisions monologue as an opportunity for the playwright to demonstrate virtuosity, for language to be fully explored.

Rather than advance particular themes, causes, or agendas, Overmyer's monologues feature soaring flights of language and rapid turns of character. Some are designed for range, others seemingly for endurance; all are a virtuosic test. Overmyer is to new playwriting what Bob Fosse was to theatrical dance—angular, brassy, gestural, and physical. In *Native Speech* the main character Hungry Mother controls the dynamic of the play. His multivocal monologue in the middle of the play is indicative of Overmyer's penchant for verbal gymnastics:

> HUNGRY MOTHER: So good. I *really* identify. The weather outlook is for unparalleled nausea—followed by protracted internal bleeding. A million dollar weekend. (*Newscaster, like Paul Harvey*) Top headline . . . This . . . or any other . . . hour . . . slavery . . . on the rise . . . once again . . . in most . . . of the civilized . . . world. (Slight pause. Low intense.) Consider if you will , the following felicitous phrases . . . Jones. Slud. Double dog dare. Going down slow. Walking wounded. Hunger artist. Bane. (*Weatherman.*) *Thick as slick out there, you better watch your step.* (Screaming.) Mexican standoff! Yes! Yes! No mother-fuckers can touch me now! I be full! So full of the Night Train! Hear the Midnight Special call my name! I be full, so full of that damn Night Train! Nothin' I ever seen can equal the color of my i-ma-gin-ation! I am the Midnight Prerogative! (Slight pause. Frenzied but quiet, under control, just barely, this is the emotional high of his set.)

> (Overmyer 1993, *Native Speech*, 40)

Note the virtuosic turns in the first one-third of this monologue: the use of ellipses to establish a Paul Harvey–like cadence; the various voices that are impersonated or mimicked; the move from low, intense speech to full-blown screaming; the breakup and repetition of key phrases. Here, monologue dialogizes across multiple strategies. Hungry Mother continues after the "slight pause":

> Speaking of Jones—I got it—for what you've been waiting for—for those with the baddest ones of all—for those with the cold at the core of their soul—*Mother's Junk Report*! Needles are up. Ditto fits and kits. Rubber tubing's down. Likewise brown dreck. Something cleaner cost you more . . . here we go! Black magic go for a dime.

> (Overmyer 1993, *Native Speech*, 40)

Overmyer turns Hungry Mother's dope-market report into a parodic aria of the drug dealing and consuming subculture. A report more relevant to his listeners than the ups and downs of the Dow Jones average, Hungry Mother dishes out the usual caveats:

> The shit is stepped on Jack, stepped on! Worth your life to stick that shit! Cut with fucking Drano, Jack! Drano.

> (Overmyer 1993, *Native Speech*, 40)

Overmyer uses punctuation cues to indicate where the speech crescendos, then cools off—key markers for the actor. The edgy contours and punctuated rhythms give form to the stream-of-consciousness utterances. While freewheeling by design, a close range view illuminates the careful crafting that defines this monologue. We can see this in specific rhyming phrases like "Ditto fits and kits," or in the measured syllable count per phrase.

This technical crafting is also in *Dark Rapture*, in Babcock's first speech. The character is entranced as he watches his California home burn in the near distance:

> BABCOCK: Fuckin A. Nothin' spookier 'n a night fire, man. Makes you feel so all alone. I remember. One time. Big Island. Lava flow. Big orange tongues a molten magma whatever creepin down the hillside like some kinda hellacious glacier. Like some kinda red-hot tectonic taffy. Eerie fuckin' thing to be comin' at ya outa the fuckin' dark, I'm tellin' ya. Fry an egg on that air. That' how hot it was. Softboil one on the palm a your hand. Melt cars. Asphalt like butter, Houses'd just pop. Bang. Like paper bags. Like that. (*He cups his hands and slaps them together, making a popping sound.*) Kablooee. Spontaneous combust. From the sheer fuckin' heat. Kablam. What can you do but grab the cat, count the kids, and say a prayer to St. Jude the lava runs outa geothermal juice 'fore it desiccates you 'n yours like so much delicatessan jerky. Just sit back 'n watch it comin' toward you. Like sheer fuckin' inevitability, Lurchin' outa the dark rapture. . . .
>
> (Overmyer 1993, *Dark Rapture*, 261)

Opening the play, the monologue points entry into a film noir–styled play of intrigue and romantic adventure. The noir speech genre, conflated with cartoonese ("Kablam" and "Kablooee"), provides the formal foundation for Overmyer's dialogic flights. The laconic film noir style is juxtaposed to Overmyer's baroque elocutions with its volcanic force and towering eloquence (see chapter 2). The rapturous rhythm of language simulates the swells and high notes of the operatic aria. The character gets caught up in what he's saying—enjoying the phrasing, relishing the articulation. The force of language energizes a vibrant tension between audience and actor. Babcock's soliloquy is fueled from moment to moment by the raging inferno in the background. This landscape of language oscillates between figure and ground. It transgresses the boundaries of more normative, fixed figure monologues, in which the figure steps forward into the isolating beam of the spotlight.

## EXERCISE:
### Monologue Aria; On Rapture

1) Revise or write a monologue in which a character is describing an event. Put it in the present tense—in the moment the event is occurring.

2) The moment should be an epiphany for the character. Explore range from the ecstatic to the catastrophic: the moment one falls in love or loses everything; a near-death experience; an unexpected victory; or a self-discovery.

3) The character is caught up in the swirl of emotion; use vivid language.

4) Riff with the language and its suggested rhythms—the character takes joy and energy from what is said or described. Notice how Overmyer riffs with word choices and rhythms:

("desiccates/delicatessen"; "grab the cat, count the kids, and say a prayer to St. Jude," etc.)

5) Focus on the *moment* as opposed to the *results*.

COMMENT: For many young playwrights, theater seems too tame or safe. This may account for the success of Blue Man Group and the musical Stomp (particularly with younger audiences), both of which pummel the audience with sound, energy, and musical force. Playwrights can simulate this kind of force in language. This exercise gives you a chance to get extreme, as you try to "top" yourself, giving as much energy to the speech as possible. Rapture can be associated with whipping up frenzy—a move toward the ecstatic.

## WELLMAN AND CONGDON: TRANSFORMATIONAL TECHNIQUES

Dematrixing is pervasive in Wellman's plays, though his techniques differ from Jenkin's or Overmyer's. In *Albanian Softshoe*, characters arbitrarily transform their identities as the scenes in act 1 progress. In scene 4, the setting remains the same while the characters change: Susan becomes Rachel as Harry becomes Fred. Wellman subverts the convention of a consistent character matrix in an ostensibly expositional monologue, utilizing the commonplace phone device to introduce the transformations:

RACHEL: Nell. This is Rachel. Rachel? Your neighbor. Used to be Susan. Right. There's a dead swan in your swimming pool. Oh, it's a nun? Fred it's a nun. I thought I'd tell you because I think Jill has been eating part of it. No, tomorrow is garbage day. Fred is my husband. The same one. Different name. I know it's a little confusing. Done wonders for our sex life. Fred is no longer a homosexual. How about that? So long (Hangs up). (I,14)

(Wellman 1989, *Albanian Softshoe*, 14)

Wellman's monologue focuses on the area between character and actor; accepting the transformation of actors into various characters becomes a source of dialogism among the various roles the same actor plays. In *Albanian Softshoe* Wellman parodies the convention of a unified character by bulking role changes in a manner that confounded audiences' expectations at its world premiere at the San Diego Repertory Theatre. This device theatrically emphasizes the homogeneity of suburban "sitcomia," where character types are interchangeable and lifestyles imitate familiar actions. Neither actor nor syntactical strategies have changed, yet the shifting characterizations bring about dramaturgical estrangement. The estrangement is furthered as Wellman begins act 2 on a distant planet inhabited by space warriors. The shifting characters from act 1 are now seen to have been nothing more than an entertaining, miniaturized "puppet show" for these alien characters.

In the widely produced *Tales of the Lost Formicans*, Constance Congdon splits some characters into humans/aliens. This bifurcation allows the audience to discover the absurdity of human objects as seen through the aliens' fresh eyes. Through this double-identity bifurcation, Congdon focuses our attention on the "strangeness" we take for granted in our everyday lives:

> CATHY/ALIEN: . . . The cushions of the chair are covered in a substance made to mimic the epidermis of the sitter, but treated to hold a sheen which is kept polished by friction of the buttocks against the surface. The significance of the hole in the backrest is unknown to us at this time. It was perhaps, symbolic: a breathing hole for the spirit of the sitter, or even the ever-present eye of God.
>
> (Congdon 1999, *Tales of the Lost Formicans*, 1)

The alien "other" allows us to "see" the chair beyond its limited function. This foregrounding is an example of theater's capacity to transform a mundane object into an object of fascination and wonder. By splitting the characters, Congdon has established this essentially monologic speech in a kind of dialogue with the human half of the character, who is continually present.

The alien's awestruck way of seeing is part of the delight of *Tales of the Lost Formicans*, and trademark of Congdon's distinctive theatrical voice. The following exercise is helpful in opening the semiotic and imaginative possibilities inherent in transformational objects.

## EXERCISE:
### Transforming the Object

1) Write a monologue in which a character describes a common object as if for the first time. The character could be an alien, foreigner, child, one suffering from loss of memory, and so on.
2) Like Overmyer's characters, the character might arrive from another historical period, as a time traveler.
3) Imbue the common object with talismanic qualities.
4) Create an opposite to what is generally recognized as the object's value or function.
5) Describe the negative space created by the shape of the object.
6) Attempt to address the "why-ness" of the design in imaginative and transcendent language.

COMMENT: In a classroom or workshop setting it may be helpful for the playwright to conceal the identity of the "described" object. Only after the monologue is read do other participants attempt to identify the object described.

The student's imaginative resources are focused or stretched. Since the responses are "right-sided" rather than critical, this exercise can work wonders in bringing a positive, relaxed atmosphere to a workshop or classroom situation.

## MONOLOGUE AS STRUCTURAL DETERMINANT

As we have seen, new playwriting tends to parody or make strange accepted monologic conventions. Now let us turn our attention to the structural component of dialogic monologue. Playwrights trained in traditional structure may be unaware of this structural component. Working with these strategies, even if you consider yourself a traditionalist, will allow you more range in making transitions between scenes without resorting to blackouts or abrupt episodic shifts. At their weakest, blackouts exist only for the playwright's convenience, harming rather than aiding the dramaturgy of the script. Scene changes that occur during blackouts are distracting. The following exercises challenge you to achieve better solutions in the dramaturgy of sequence and transition.

The structural nature of Len Jenkin's monologues is evident in the options they afford the director during staging. In order to visualize how the monologue dialogizes in stage terms it is helpful to demonstrate some visual examples. Since Len Jenkin has directed a number of his own plays with great success, it useful to consider his actual staging of a monologue to show how it clarifies the structural matters of temporality and linkage.

In general, Jenkin's plays alternate monologue and dialogue sections to provide the overall structural scheme. Monologue sections supply the scene material for subsequent dialogues among those characters referred to or introduced in the monologue. Sometimes metatheatrical devices like songs or voice-overs are used. For example, *My Uncle Sam* begins with a short song, lip-synched by a duo on one part of the stage. Then the character of Uncle Sam rises from his chair (under the top lighting) as he is described in a monologue by a persona known simply as the Author. The author, who assumes the point of view of Sam's nephew, indicates with his right hand: Young Sam, who represents Uncle Sam in his youth. This use of monologue is structural since it links character and relationships spatially, gesturally, and narratively. A chorus of salesmen lurks in the shadows, faintly silhouetted by the border-lighted backdrop. The Author, who represents the present, appears downstage center under a bright spotlight, his white-shirted figure in sharp contrast to the dark, shadowed ground. Behind the Author is Young Sam, the Author's past childhood memory of Sam. Young Sam is indicated and connected by the Author's righthand gesture (see figure 11.1), and his middle-seated position and sideward, side-lighted pose reinforce a separate past. Notice how the monologue dialogizes across several spatial/temporal fields. Old Sam is situated at a *farther* distance from the Author than Young Sam, suggesting

**Fig. 11.1** *My Uncle Sam*
New York Shakespeare Festival, Public Theater. Director: Len Jenkin          PHOTO BY GEORGE JOSEPH

the later time in his life, and a period of remoteness when he had lost contact with his nephew and the outside world. Jenkin's opening monologue establishes the network of time relativity crucial to an understanding of the play. Several time periods are juxtaposed simultaneously. From a directorial perspective they can be delineated through the use of lighting, the use of spatial depth, and contiguous spatial fields. Thus, the playwright has opened up possibilities in the mise-en-scène.

Jenkin's narrative dramaturgy then segues to dramatic sequences that offer some compelling possibilities. Figure 11.1 demonstrates how lighting in *My Uncle Sam* provides a linking device from the narrator to the characters, who lurk in shadowy silhouette. As characters in the past they are positioned on the upstage platform until the call directs the scene downstage. Stage space is "relativized," or *dialogized,* as the planes from upstage to downstage indicate different periods and times.

## EXERCISE:
### The Monologue and Spatial Fields

1) Select a monologue for revision. It should contain references to other characters, either present or in the character's mind. Consider the space theatrically, rather than a realistic reconstruction of place and time.

2) Have the character referred to in the monologue seen at a distance or in a spatial relation indicated by the speaker—in other words, nearer or farther away depending upon the context and relation in time.

3) Give the character referred to a definitive action that is suggested in the monologue.

4) Use gestures and bodily movements to suggest relations or shifting relationships.

COMMENT: Theater is the recaptured memory of a nonevent. Through this exercise the playwright is effectively juggling time and place in a manner that is theatrically sound, while visually reinforcing sets of relations. There is, in effect, a more sophisticated kind of dramaturgy at work here.

## ESTABLISHING THE DOMINANT: THE STRUCTURAL KEY

In *My Uncle Sam*, the Author's monologue addresses both audience and the figure of Sam—in the deadpan style of a narrator from a 1940s crime movie:

> I saw my Uncle Sam once a year. He was my grandfather's brother, my great-Uncle Sam actually. He was exotic. Points of exoticism: ONE: He lived in Pittsburgh. . . .
>
> (Jenkin 1993, *My Uncle Sam*, 124)

The listing of points in the monologue continues through point 6 when the Author's description "He smoked cigars" coincides with the playwright's stage direction (*The figure lights a cigar*).

Past-tense narration and present action coexist in Jenkin's strategy. The speaker concludes (in upper case in the script), "UNCLE SAM SOLD NOVELTIES!!," at which point enter a cadre of 1940ish novelty salesmen comparing the accouterments of their trade: rubber masks, luminous crucifixes, imitation platinum French rings with views, goozeleum goggles, poop cushions, and the novelty salesmen's joy buzzer. The penultimate line "UNCLE SAM SOLD NOVELTIES!!" is crucial to the monologue since it describes the sequential turn—a command, or a dialogic call for the next scene to begin. The call is a prime component of Jenkin's dramaturgy. It operates as a form of dialogism within the text, allowing the narrative and dramatic elements to fully interact. The call provides the dominant textual "motivation" that indicates the transition to dramatized sections. A crucial component of this structural scheme is that it allows theatrical space and time to exist in a state of continual evanescence.

## DEFINING THE DOMINANT: THE CALL

The dominant may be defined as the focusing component of a work of art: it rules, determines, and transforms the remaining components. It is the dominant that guarantees the integrity of the structure (see Matejka and Poworoska, 1978, 82). In this case, the impetus for a change in scene is provided by a literary or theatrical device rather than by a character's psychological motivation or need.

The *call* is the focusing structural component of *My Uncle Sam*, and it is also at work in Jenkin's *Kid Twist*, in which the eponymous main character is confined to a hotel room awaiting trial as a federally protected witness.

Fig. 11.2 *My Uncle Sam*
New York Shakespeare Festival,
Public Theater.
Director: Len Jenkin

PHOTO BY GEORGE JOSEPH

The calls here are framed as the Kid's dreams; they transport the action to various worlds outside the motel room. Another example of the call is the monologue that begins Jenkin's *American Notes*. The Mayor's opening monologue is delivered to the mentally slow, Chuckles. After telling Chuckles he might be able "to place a man of his talents," the Mayor tells him to look around, at which point he makes reference to the desk clerk of the motel. Lights go up on her area, segueing us into the next scene of dialogue. In the journey play, monologue invariably contains a marker that leads us forward, thus giving the play direction, focus, and progression.

### MULTIPLE NARRATORS AND RELATIVITY

Returning to the point in *My Uncle Sam* where the dramatized salesmen scene begins, the Author participates in the action, but now as the character Man. Jenkin's technique "brackets" the scene as the others listen attentively (see figure 11.2). As a playwright, you can see that the use of past tense, and narrative literary style, simulate a kind of reader's theater:

> MAN: After a certain period in his life, he contrived, or rather he . . . happened . . . to sever himself from the world—to vanish—
>
> ALL: Aaaah!
>
> MAN: —to give up his place and privileges with living men without being admitted among the dead (*They slowly back away, staring at Old Sam. Young Sam is the last to leave. They're gone. Three secretaries remain, in a row, pencils poised.*)
>
> (Jenkin 1993, *My Uncle Sam*, 128)

The shifting of mode from dramatic to narrative is an attempt by the Author character to regain control of the story from Old Sam. The actions of Jenkin's characters tend to deconstruct any attempt at a single authorial speaker. At one point, Old Sam's ruminations cause the Author to shriek, "That's enough. Got it!" Here Jenkin, through the voice of the

Author, dialogizes the struggle of narrative—whose story is it?—by thwarting Old Sam's attempt at historical recreation and self-aggrandizement. In his wily attempt to control the narrative and maintain "face," Old Sam closes with a vivid reference to his ex-girlfriend, Lila, the nightclub singer. This transports us to scene 2, and a call for the MC (another narrator) to enter and introduce us to the Club des Morts, where Lila has performed. Jenkin's strategy of intertwining narrative and dramatic elements relativizes the play's meaning. It contradicts our earlier definition of monologue as "pretending to have the last word" or not acknowledging the "other." As in *American Notes*, Jenkin situates the monologic voice(s) between dialogues, blurring the traditional dramaturgical distinctions between dramatic and narrative.

Jenkin's use of narrators differs from Peter Shaffer's, since multiple, rather than single narrators continually vie for "authorship" of the story. From a playwriting standpoint, this dialogism among the narrator/characters provides one level of interest. The call provides structural links to the disparate voices. Otherwise, the play would be haphazard and incoherent. For playwrights, the call can have applications along a broad continuum or spectrum: from single narrators and shifting scenes to multiple narrators and shifting worlds. The best example of this phenomenon in action is Jenkin's *Dark Ride*.

## THE CALL AND THE JOURNEY PLAY: MONOLOGUE AS STRUCTURE IN *DARK RIDE*

In scene 3 of Len Jenkin's *Dark Ride*, the character Margo picks up a postcard referring us to her lover, a character Jenkin has simply named the Thief. While the postcard suggests the casual regard of the Thief for Margo, it establishes structural links to the next scene. The postcard device exploits one way of dealing with the absent "other," although Jenkin takes the dramaturgical move one step further. The last three phrases read by Margo: "outskirts of some city, for miles alongside highways, feeding out into suburban streets," become the opening lines of the Thief's monologue. More importantly, Jenkin's dramaturgical move is indicative of how structure is created in a journey play. Jenkin's repetition posits a dialogism that is temporal, A to A in terms of the repetitive sequence whereby A reflects itself, but also spatial, A to B, as the shift in character and stage space initiates a new scene:

> Outskirts of some city, for miles alongside highways, feeding out into suburban streets, and I'm walking, and I keep looking back over my shoulder to see if anyone's behind me. I have the damn thing in a leather bag around my neck and I'm heading south and I figured I better . . . after three days on the road I figured I better . . . I figured I better get inside somewhere, I figured I better eat something. I'm in America, coming into town. There's these long stretches of seedy

apartment houses. Some people on the steps of them with a baby, and they're drinking beer, and they say hello in the dark, and they don't even know who they're talkin' to, you know but I say hello back anyway, and that seems to be it cause I just keep walkin' and they don't say anything else. O.K. Now I'm really hungry but it's a long way between neon, and then I see one coming, a red blur in the distance, and I squint at it, wanting it to say Cafe or Eat Here or something but it ends up saying Tri-City Furniture or Red Robin Autos— Used but not Abused—and finally I see another one, and it's a revolve, turning and turning, and it says THE EMBERS. We Never Close, so I go in. I'm here. Jukebox.

(Jenkin 1993, *Dark Ride*, 69–70)

At this point, a waitress appears, seats the Thief, and a dramatized scene follows in a restaurant.

Spatially, Jenkin's on-the-road drifter is set against the shifting ground of a highway landscape. The monologue is evocative in unraveling a closely observed pastiche of roadside Americana. This down-on-his-luck drifter with a point of view is a staple of American lore. This character is drenched in fear, but driven by the desire to satisfy his appetite. The syntax is present tense, yet thrusts us into future events. The transitory narrative casts the Thief in unfolding interactions with his environment. A destination is found, but not in the linear or unified sense. Note the digressionary passage through the seedy apartment buildings, and the inner dialogue between hoped for "Eat here" and actual "Tri-City Furniture." Strong visual images, such as "Red Robin Autos," the revolving neon sign, "Embers," and "jukebox" delineate name associations for the spectators' imagination, and a path for the spectator to follow in the journey through language space. The monologic spatial field becomes interactive as each utterance shifts both the spectator and the actor to a defined "other." Words serve a spatial and temporal function, as language imbues the stage with protean characteristics. Chameleon-like, the stage changes colors and location with fluidity and ease. Jenkin's syntactical techniques in the monologue underscore the scene's action. The length of the Thief's phrases corresponds to his distance from his eventual destination. As he approaches the restaurant, his utterances truncate. Phrasing choices reflect the actual space.

Jenkin's proper name labeling is a part of a predilection he shares with Mac Wellman for lists, specific names, and their combinatory powers. Within monologue, proper names create vivid images, suggest a mood, or provide concrete detail. Jenkin eliminates past tense explorations of character psychology as necessary links to present behavior. By doing so, Jenkin voids the creation of subtext. Mood states replace subtext in the subjective realm of the new playwriting. Mood emerges as an external condition in which the character operates, rather than as a manifestation of inner psychology. The symbolic nature of the language, and the reliance on transitory mood states, recall certain tenets of symbolist theater, although the new playwriting is rarely static or minimalist.

## FASCINATION WITH FORM

Form devices like the call motivate the narrative shifts and concomitant divulgence of content. Form is foregrounded in *Dark Ride* and *My Uncle Sam* as the audience is readily aware of the device. Jenkin notes to the director in the Dramatists Play Service edition, "The director and performers should be aware that *Dark Ride* is a weave of tales, of scenes within scenes, like the facets of the diamond. That a scene is within a book, or a picture, or in someone's mind makes it no less 'real' in terms of staging. The 'real' point of view is a shifting one" (Jenkin 1982, 47–48). In departing from the unity provided by a central character, Jenkin's statement echoes one of his literary heroes, Franz Kafka. Jenkin opposes causal linearity, favoring the restlessness of a shifting form featuring an array of characters. Although steeped in the lore of American types and literary conventions, Jenkin rejects the notion of a dominant narrative or story line. Jenkin's polyvocal narratives pull the audience away from empathic identification by creating a field of diverse plots, multiple ironies, and shifts of mood. These dramaturgical techniques link him to Brechtian alienation, but without didactic ends.

## SUMMARIZING THE CALL

Jenkin provides multiple narrators whose dramaturgical functions are to call scenes forth into being or intervene within active dramatic sections in order to disrupt the action and transit the sequence elsewhere. After characters finish role-playing as narrators, they return to the action, move to another area, or disappear altogether. Thus, each sequence of the action is literally wrapped within a given narrative, formal device. This may appear complex and intricate, yet in practice it is really quite straightforward. The exercise below explores the most prevalent of Jenkin's narrative techniques—the call, or invocation—essential to understanding the concept of sequence in his playwriting. In the *call* the narrator's function is twofold; he must (1) establish the basic story or subject matter of the play (usually from memory, dreams, or fantasy) and (2) call forth the dramatized scene. The call occurs near the end of the narrated story or passage, and is generally positioned in the penultimate sentence or phrase of the speech. This placement allows the other characters to enter and assume actions as the narrator finishes the speech. At that point, the narrator enters into the dramatic action, assumes another area of the stage, or exits the scene.

The call is a fundamental technique to effect sequence and transition without cumbersome blackouts. By using the narrator(s), the playwright can finesse an otherwise awkward stage shift. A narrator can mediate between simultaneous scenes, bridge gaps in time, or move time forward or backward. I usually assign this next exercise as a ten-minute play, whereby the playwrights are required to limit blackouts to one—at the end.

## EXERCISE:
### The Call

1) Have one character pick up a letter, a postcard, a photograph, or painting of someone she is in a relationship with, or has been in close emotional involvement with.

2) At the point where reference is made to the other character, the other should appear at another place on the stage.

3) The character from step 1 reads a direct quote from the other character, the last lines of which this other repeats, and the transition is made to the next sequence.

4) The first character disappears as the other enters a building, the house of a lover, a church or any other place depicted in the monologue. This narration represents the call for a new dramatized scene to begin.

### NARRATIVE CAPTIONING

In Jenkin's *My Uncle Sam* various narrators appear sporadically throughout the play, recounting what has already happened. In several scenes, narrators relate back story or provide reportage, servicing the need of the audience for instant exposition and explication:

NARRATOR: AT THE UNIVERSITY, scene 14.

YOUNG SAM: Before I get there . . .

ANOTHER NARRATOR: Stella! (*As Stella enters*) Her furnished room wasn't very far from the university. Now she stands gazing out over the college town, smiling a triumphant smile.

STELLA: Fundamentals of Botany. That's one course I won't have to worry about anymore.

NARRATOR: Stella opens the closet, unhooks a slinky black cocktail dress from the rack . . .

STELLA: It's time to roll out the big guns.

MITZI: (coming in) Stella! Say, where are you going?

NARRATOR: It was Mitzi, Stella's roommate.

(Jenkin 1993, My Uncle Sam, 156)

The multiple narrators stand beside or occupy the middle ground between spectator and performer. Jenkin's treatment of the narrative "voice" allows the director flexibility in the casting of narrators. The nar-

**Fig. 11.3 "The Miked Narrator" in *My Uncle Sam***
New York Shakespeare Festival, Public Theater.
Director: Len Jenkin

PHOTO BY GEORGE JOSEPH

rators need not be consistent throughout the play, nor are they necessarily the same actor in performance. Thus, actors can double or triple parts, moving back and forth between dramatic and narrative functions.

In the world premiere production of *My Uncle Sam,* director Jenkin favored one of the devices he later utilized in stage directions to his plays (see his *American Notes* and *Careless Love*)—the technique of the "miked" narrator (see figure 11.3). These brief narrative sequences simulate dialogue, but actually serve as captions or "titles" that frame each set of onstage actions (see chapter 9). The term *title* here refers to its use in radio drama, where it establishes place or situation and sets the scene. This form of internal dialogism helps to establish the heterogeneous dramaturgical system in which narrative and dramatic elements are in a continual state of interruption and interaction.

Slippage sometimes occurs between a narrator's commentary and the action onstage. The ironic technique can be quite humorous in performance. In *My Uncle Sam,* the first Narrator informs us that this is "scene 14," when it is actually scene 7 in Jenkin's scheme (the published text). Immediately following, Young Sam "appears" to tell us that this scene takes place before he arrives. This slippage toward relativity is overtly ironic and estranges this theatrical experience from an "imitative" world.

The movement between narrative and dramatic voices offers several options. For example, if you want to abbreviate a dramatic action in a script or short-circuit it, the move to narrative voicings can alter not only the linear track, but create counterrhythms to the dramatic dialogue. This creates a kind of patterning that is most appropriate for certain kinds of plays: historical subjects, those based on journalistic sources, recounts of personal narrative, and so on.

# THE BASIS OF JENKIN'S NARRATIVE DRAMATURGY

Jenkin regards his mixing of the narrative and dramatic element as natural. It derives from his fascination with the hard-boiled private detective novels of the 1940s, in which the laconic reportage as narrative stands side by side with the action. Dialogue sections in these novels consist of quoted quips, usually accompanied by the narrator's take on the circumstances. In a sense, these takes resemble captioning, or titling, of various sections. The technique may seem to have a comic-book flavor whereby individual frames are captioned, dialogue is present in the boxes, and the images (characters) are two-dimensional types.

## EXERCISE:
### Captioning

1) Captions or titles resemble the metatheatrical aside, in which a character breaks frame to provide commentary directly to the audience. This technique functions to telegraph a particular moment or aspect of a scene. The caption is a frame. In a three- or four-character scene utilize one or two characters to caption a moment in the scene. Captioning works best if there are subsequent actions that are framed.

2) Caption phrases or sentences disguised as dialogue but which are actually a species of narrative: use the third person rather than second, past tense rather than present in the character/narrator's response. An ironic take is preferred between the caption and the actual event, creating a sense of slippage between comment and occurrence.

3) The in-and-out nature of captioning allows narrators/characters to enter into or stand beside the action. It may provide a character with omniscience in knowing the future or outcome of events, for example. Play with these functions of the captioning character as it suits your scene.

## DIGRESSIONARY MONOLOGUE (THE HIRAM BIRDSEED EFFECT)

The digressionary monologue is often formatted as a direct address to the audience. Since it does little or nothing to further the plot, the digressionary monologue works as a kind of verbal *lazzi*. Lazzi were physical and rhetorical "shticks" utilized by the commedia dell'arte. These moments were plugged in at various points in the performance text, providing comic relief. The digressionary monologue may function to provide humor or amplification of theme. There is a caveat for the playwright who overuses the digressionary monologue: dramaturgs or play developers may assert that since the material serves no crucial dramatic function it should be cut. On the other hand, what would the work of Anton Chekhov be without the occasional digression? Indeed, the digressions seem woven into the fabric of his dramaturgy. In the new playwriting, Jenkin is a master of the digressionary monologue. An example from the Young Man's speech in *My Uncle Sam* is typical:

Tell you what I'm gonna do. Special price for you and the missus on any of the selection of exciting book I have to offer. Here's one called *Confessions of a Nun* . . . this one's written in the kind of plain language anyone can understand. I can see you're a man of the world. Here's a copy of *From Ballroom to Hell* by an ex-dance teacher . . . awful dangers to young girls in the dancing academy. How about *HIRAM BIRDSEED AT THE WORLD'S FAIR?*

[*Aside to audience*] This *Hiram Birdseed at the World's Fair* is my biggest seller published by the same company in Philadelphia. For men only. You know the kind—*Sam Savage in the South Seas* . . . "the naked maidens surrounded him . . ." and so on. It's like the same guy wrote them all, though they got different names on 'em. But Hiram Birdseed is different. It's like this writer of all of them was hit by fantasy exhaustion one day and he hadda stay in bed, so for one time he hired another guy . . . a little guy with a dirty green cardigan sweater and glasses, and he was given this title, *Hiram Birdseed at the World's Fair,* and the farm boy gets involved in international sex in New York City and this little guy goes back to his furnished room, and he writes. He stays up all night, his mind at white heat, and as the dawn filters through the Venetian blinds he finishes the first half. He falls into a fitful doze. The pages on the desk flutter in an early morning breeze . . .

(Jenkin 1993, *My Uncle Sam*, 159–60)

Jenkin's Young Sam continues to discuss the contents of the book, including in detail a chapter called "Hiram Birdseed's Dream." The entire content of the monologue is framed at the beginning and end to characters in the play; yet in the middle, it is framed to the audience. Thus, the story exists as a digression for the audience, but one in which there is a shared intimacy with the performer, and by extension, the playwright. Hiram Birdseed is Jenkin's world in a nutshell: playful, strange, funny, intelligent, marginalized, and wildly imaginative. For playwrights, the key to the success of the digressionary monologue is best described by the French term *disponbilité*, which describes an openness or "availability" to the moment at hand. The great artist must remain open to the moment of disponbilité, and audience and dramaturgs must understand its value—not so ready to cut the digressionary thread that somehow informs, and most definitely, delights.

## SPINNING

The digressionary monologue is related to the concept of riffing that I discussed earlier. Award-winning playwright Matthew Maguire describes the effect, as used in his plays *Throwin' Bones* and *Phaedra*, as *spinning*. Spinning occurs when dialogue scenes are born in and then transpire into monologues. As the pace of a dialogue between two characters quickens, there is a spinning effect of wordplay that creates an oblique, vertiginous effect in the dramaturgy. At some point in the dialogue a character spins into a monologue that digresses from the topic of the dialogue. In other words, an interactional scene between characters closes in a monologue that is only tangentially related to the scene. The subject matter of the monologue relates to an area of interest of the character speaking (in *Throwin' Bones* it's strange hobbies: collecting brass knuckles, chastity belts, Tiepolo's illustrations). When the monologue concludes the characters are at a different horizon level and a new dialogue ensues. These monologues are forceful dramaturgic components and keys to the thematic structure of the piece, although they do not advance the plot in the traditional sense.

## MONOLOGUE: FUTURE EXPLORATIONS

What does the future hold for explorations in monologue? Do these methods posit a new mode of dramaturgy in which distinctions between narrative and dramatic elements have become problematic, or possibly moot? To the former question, one answer may be considered in opening the spatial/temporal field on the stage. Craig Lucas's play *Prelude to a Kiss* uses a kind of monologic "hot-wiring" as the character Peter transports us from scene to scene. In this sense, Lucas readdresses the annoying passage-of-time contrivances of realism, such as those during scene changes or through exposition, by directly addressing the audience in the *call* technique—while set changes occur upstage, Peter fills us in and moves us forward. We find a similar use of monologue in Margaret Edson's *Wit*— monologues provide segues between scenes, as they explore character interiority. The playwright dematrixes monologue in the beginning scene when the actor, playing the lead character, asserts that this is a play, not a representation of real life. This dramaturgy posits a strategic theatrical ontology in which past, present, and future merge (and dialogize) as consciousness and material life are given palpable form and language reemerges as the "dominant" arbitrator of the mise-en-scène.

# Works Consulted

Aristotle. *Poetics*. 1954. Trans. Ingram Bywater. New York: Random House.

Artaud, Antonin. 1958. *The Theater and Its Double*. Trans. Mary Caroline Richards. New York: Grove Press, Inc.

Bakhtin, M. M. 1986. *Speech Genres and Other Late Essays*. Trans. Vern McGee, ed. Caryl Emerson and M. Holquist. Austin: University of Texas Press.

———. 1981. *The Dialogic Imagination: Four Essays*. Ed. Michael Holquist, trans. C. Emerson and M. Holquist. Austin: University of Texas Press.

———. 1968. *Rabelais and His World*. Trans. Helen Islowsky. Cambridge: MIT Press.

Beber, Neena. 1990. "Dramatis Instructus." *American Theatre*, January, 22–26.

———. Plays from author: *Hard Feelings* (1999); *Thirst* (1998); *Common Vision* (1998); *The Goddess* (1992); *Tomorrowland* (1997).

Benjamin, Walter. 1977. *Understanding Brecht*. Trans. by Anna Bostock. London: NLB.

Bentley, Eric. 1968. *The Theory of the Modern Stage*. Harmodsworth, UK: Penguin.

Bossler, Gregory. 2000. "Between East Coast and West End." *The Dramatist*. (May/June: 24–31).

Castagno, Paul. C. 1997. "The New Dramaturg and The New Playwright: An Approach to the First Draft." *Dramaturgy in American Theater: A Sourcebook*. New York: Harcourt Brace.

———. March 1993. "Informing the New Dramaturgy: Critical Theory to Creative Process." *Theatre Topics* 3:1, 29–44.

———. May 1993. "Varieties of Monologic Strategy: The Dramaturgy of Len Jenkin and Mac Wellman. *New Theater Quarterly*. 10:34, 134–46.

Cohn, Dorrit. 1978. *Transparent Minds: Narrative Modes for Presenting Consciousness in Fiction*. Princeton: Princeton University Press.

Congdon, Costance. 1994. *Tales of the Lost Formicans and other plays*. New York: Theatre Communications Group.

Culler, Nathan D. 1997. *Literary Theory: A Very Short Introduction*. Oxford: Oxford University Press.

Debré, Olivier. 1999. *Espace pensé, espace créé: la signe progressi*. Paris: Cherche midi.

Edson, Margaret. 1999. *Wit*. New York: Dramatists Play Service.

Fornes, Maria Irene. 1986. *Maria Irene Fornes: Plays*. New York: Performing Arts Journal Publications.

Fuchs, Elinor. 1985. "Presence and the Revenge of Writing." *Performing Arts Journal* IX:2: IX:3, 163–172.

Goffman, Erving. 1974. *Frame Analysis: An Essay on the Organization of Experience*. New York: Harper and Row.

———. 1959. *The Presentation of Self in Everyday Life*. New York: Doubleday.

Gomez-Peña, Guillermo. 1996. *The New World Border*. San Francisco: City Lights.

Gould, Christopher. 1989. *Anti-Naturalism*. New York: Broadway Play Publishing.

Gumperz, John J. 1982. *Discourse Strategies*. Cambridge: Cambridge University Press.

Gussow, Mel. 1998. "Playwrights Who Put Words at Center Stage." February 11. (4:5, 44). *New York Times*.

Hare, David. 1989. *The Secret Rapture*. London: Faber and Faber.

Hirschkop, Ken, and David Shepherd. 1989. *Bakhtin and Cultural Theory*. Manchester: Manchester University Press.

Holquist, Michael. 1990. *Dialogism: Bakhtin and His World*. London: Routledge.

Jenkin, Len. 1993. *Dark Ride and Other Plays*. Los Angeles: Sun and Moon Press (*Limbo Tales, American Notes, My Uncle Sam, Poor Folk's Pleasure*).

———. 1999. Unpublished plays from author. *Careless Love* (1991); *Candide* (adapted from Voltaire) (1989); *Dream Express* (1992); *Tallahassee* (written with Mac Wellman), 1991.

———. 1988. *Kid Twist* in *7 Different Plays*, edited by Mac Wellman. New York: Broadway Play Publishing.

Jennings, Michael W. 1987. *Dialectical Images: Walter Benjamin's Theory of Literary Criticism*. Ithaca: Cornell University Press.

Jones, Jeffrey. Play from author. *Der Inka von Peru* (1992); *Seventy Scenes of Halloween in Theatre of Wonders: Six Contemporary Plays* (1985). Los Angeles: Sun and Moon Press.

Kramer, Sherry. 1987. *The Wall of Water*. New York: Broadway Play Publishing.

Lodge, David. 1990. *After Bakhtin: Essays on Fiction and Criticism*. New York: Routledge.

Maguire, Matthew. 1995. *Phédra*. Los Angeles: Sun and Moon Press.

——— . Play from author. *Throwin' Bones* (1998).

Mahon, Sydné. 1994. *Moon Marked and Touched by Sun: Plays by African-American Women*. New York: Theatre Communications Group.

Mamet, David. 1990. *Theater Week*. March 6.

———. 1985. *Speed the Plow*. New York: Grove Press.

Mann, Thomas. 1960. "Versuch über das Theater." *Gesammelte Werke* (Frankfurt), 10, 29.

Marranca, Bonnie. 1996. *Ecologies of Theater*. Baltimore: Johns Hopkins University Press.

———. 1996. *Plays for the End of the Century*. Baltimore: Johns Hopkins University Press.

Matejka, Ladislav, and Krystyna Pomoroska. 1978. *Readings in Russian Poetics*. Ann Arbor: University of Michigan Press.

Medvedev, P. N., and M. Bakhtin. 1978. *The Formal Method in Literary Scholarship*. Baltimore: Johns Hopkins University Press.

Messerli, Douglas. 1998. *From the Other Side of the Century II: A New American Drama (1960–1995)*. Los Angeles: Sun and Moon Press.

Mukarovsky, Jan. 1977. *The Word and Verbal Art*. Trans. John Burbank and Peter Steiner. New Haven: Yale University Press.

Overmyer, Eric. March 1996, Spring 1997. Personal Interviews with author, Tuscaloosa, AL.

———. 1995. *Eric Overmyer: Collected Plays*. New Hampshire: Smith and Krause. (*Dark Rapture Collection*. See *In a Pig's Valise, In Perpetuity throughout the Universe, On the Verge, The Heliotrope Bouquet, Native Speech*).

———. 1987. *Native Speech*. New York: Broadway Play Publishing.

———. 1986. *On the Verge, or the Geography of Learning*. New York: Broadway Play Publishing.

———. Plays from author. *Alki* (Peer Gynt adaptation); 1997.

Parks, Suzan-Lori. 1995. *Imperceptible Mutabilities in the Third Kingdom*. Los Angeles: Sun and Moon Press.

Patterson, David. 1988. *Literature and Spirit: Essays on Bakhtin and His Contemporaries*. Lexington: University of Kentucky Press.

Petrey, Sandy. 1990. *Speech Acts and Literary Theory*. New York: Routledge.

Quinn, Michael. 1988. "Svejk's Stage Figure." *Comparative Drama*. XXXI:3. September, 330–341.

Robinson, Marc. 1989. "Don't Fence Them In," *American Theatre*, November, 28–34.

Schoen, Walter. 1990. Personal interview with author, Washington, D.C.

Smiley, Sam. 1971. *Playwriting: The Structure of Action*. Englewood Cliffs, N.J.: Prentice-Hall Publications.

Steiner, Peter. 1984. *Russian Formalism: A Metapoetics*. Ithaca: Cornell University Press.

Tessari, Roberto. 1981. *Commedia dell'arte: la maschera e l'ombra*. Milano: Mursia.

Todorov, Tsvetan. 1984. *Mikhail Bakhtin: The Dialogical Principle*. Trans. Wlad Godzich. Minneapolis: University of Minnesota Press.

Turner, Victor. 1982. *From Ritual to Theatre: The Human Seriousness of Play*. New York: Performing Arts Journal Publications.

Weeks, Jerome. 1995. "Erik Ehn: Bowling for Transcendence." *American Theatre*, January, 35–36.

Wellek, Rene. 1980. "Bakhtin's View of Dostoevsky: 'Polyphony' and 'Carnivalesque.'" *Dostoevsky Studies*, 1, 31–39.

Wellman, Mac. 1995. *The Bad Infinity*. Anthology. Baltimore: Johns Hopkins University Press. (*Harm's Way, The Bad Infinity, Whirligig, Terminal Hip, Crowbar, Professional Frenchman, Energumen*).

———. 1992. "Figures of Speech." *Performing Arts Journal*, Spring, vol. 14, no. 1, 43–51.

———. 1991. *Murder of Crows*. TCG *Plays in Process*. 13:3.

———. 1985. *Theatre of Wonders: Six Contemporary Plays*. Los Angeles: Sun and Moon Press.

———. 1984. "Theatre of Good Intentions." Symposium on New Writing for the Theatre. Minneapolis, February.

———. Unpublished plays from New Dramatists and author. *Albanian Softshoe* (1989); *Bodacious Flapdoodle* (1984); *Cleveland* (1986); *Dracula* (1990); *Fnu Lnu* (1997); *Hyacinth Macaw* (1994); *Second Hand Smoke* (1996); *Sincerity Forever* (1990); *Three Americanisms* (1994).

# Index

Absent "other"
  defined, 7
  monologue and, 145–147
Acts, 130–131
Akalaitis, JoAnne, 156
*Albanian Softshoe* (Wellman), 23, 65,
  68, 69, 89, 122, 125, 161–162
Albee, Edward, 1, 123
*Alki* (Overmyer), 46, 54
*Amadeus* (Shaffer), 77
American College Theater Festival, 141
*American Notes* (Jenkin), 27, 32, 34,
  64, 72, 73, 74, 75–76, 122, 125,
  156, 166
*Angels in America* (Kushner), 30, 57,
  122, 129, 130
*Anti-Naturalism* (Gould), 54
Antistructure, 150–152
*Arcadia* (Stoppard), 49, 58
Archetype versus stereotype, 74
Aristotle, 1, 54–55
Artaud, Antonin, 154
Asterisk, 109–110
*Aunt Dan and Lemon* (Shawn), 58–59

Back channels, 7
*Bad Infinity* (Wellman), 32, 89, 112,
  123, 125
*Bad Penny* (Wellman), 124
Bailey, Sheri, 141
Baitz, Jon Robin, 68
Bakhtin, Mikhail, 2–3, 8, 22, 31, 41,
  55, 149
*Bal* (Nelson), 54, 113, 122
Baroque style, multivocality
  compared to, 20–22
Beat(s)

asterisk and slash, 109–110
  defined, 7
  dictionary stop, 102–103
  as gesture, 105–106
  parole versus langue, 97–98
  riffing, 98–102
  shifting, 95–97
  spacer, 106–109
  speech acts or performatives,
    103–105
  tag lines, 106
Beat segment
  contour, 114–115
  defined, 7, 8, 110–112
  exercise on, 113
  marker, 115–118
Beber, Neena, 56
Beckett, Samuel, 157
Belief-driven scene, 125
Benjamin, Walter, 105
*Betrayal* (Pinter), 149
*Betty's Summer Vacation* (Durang), 125
*Birthday Party, The* (Pinter), 104
Blue Man Group, 37
*Blue Room* (Hare), 57
Boccaccio, Giovanni, 36
*Bodacious Flapdoodle* (Wellman), 62,
  105
Bogosian, Eric, 37, 154
Brecht, Bertolt, 6, 12, 57, 59, 97, 105,
  116
  *Caucasian Chalk Circle*, 37, 46
Brenton, Howard, 49, 57
Brontë novels, 4
Burroughs, William, 42

Call, 165–166, 167–170

Captioning
  *See also* Framing
  defined, 7
  narrative, 170–171
  scene, 126–129
*Careless Love* (Jenkin), 76, 155–156
Carnivalesque, 7–8, 17, 55
*Caucasian Chalk Circle* (Brecht), 37, 46
*Cellophane* (Wellman), 88
Character/characterization
  archetype versus stereotype, 74
  Aristotelian model, 54–55
  beyond protagonist, 53–54
  carnivalesque, 7–8, 17, 55
  clash, 8, 68–71
  commedia dell'arte, 63–66
  continuums of, 55–56
  dialogic versus dialectic, 57–58
  dominant, 75–76
  doubling, 84–86
  Euclidean, 9, 87–91
  equivocal, 80–84
  Jenkin's, 66, 72–79
  language and the creation of,
    90–91
  language-based, 87–91
  markers, 116
  mask, 66–67
  new approaches to, 52–53
  Overmyer, 80–86
  performative, 79
  satirical approaches, 58–59
  stage figures, 72–79
  storyteller, 76–78
  tenets of theatrical, 59–63
  thematic-based, 56–57
  Wellman's, 87–91
Character specific, 8, 90
  language, 18
Chekhov, Anton, 114, 137, 140
*Cherry Orchard, The* (Chekhov), 114
Chops, 8, 132
Churchill, Caryl, 110
Circumstance-driven scene, 124–125
Cirque du Soleil, 6, 37
*CIVIL WarS* (Wilson), 50
Classical style, 121, 123–124
Cohn, Dorrit, 139
Cohn, Roy, 30

*Colored Museum, The* (Wolfe), 123
Command, 104
Commedia dell'arte, 8, 36, 63–66
Conceptualization, 124–125
Congdon, Constance, 3
  *Tales of the Lost Formicans*, 8, 12, 49,
    65, 68, 69, 85–86, 95, 122, 162
Conflict-driven scene, 124
Contexting, 8
Contour, 8, 114–115
*Country Doctor* (Jenkin), 46, 54, 73–74,
  75
*Crowbar* (Wellman), 124
Culler, Jonathan, 2
*Cure, The* (Foreman), 107
*Curse of the Starving Class* (Shepard),
  129

*Dark Rapture* (Overmyer), 13, 18, 21,
  40, 54, 85, 122, 124, 125, 160
*Dark Ride* (Jenkin), 10, 12, 33, 47, 62,
  73, 74, 77, 78, 96, 108,
  120–121, 122, 125, 127–128,
  167–168
*Death of the Last Black Man in the
  Whole Entire World, The* (Parks),
  23, 24
Debré, Olivier, 87–88
Deictic language, 9, 125
Dematrixing, 9, 62–63, 155–157
*Der Inka von Peru* (Jones), 41–42, 96,
  122, 131
Dialects, 23–25
Dialogic clash, 3–5, 9
*Dialogic Imagination, The* (Bakhtin),
  149
Dialogic plays, monologic versus, 11
Dialogism
  defined, 2, 9
  examples of, 3–5
  intertextual, 66
Dialogue
  conceptualization, 124–125
  monologue versus, 148–149
  revising, 135–136
Dickinson, Emily, 137
Dictionary stop, 102–103
Difference, 9
Digressionary monologue, 172–173

Discourse
exercise on developing, 28
from, to slang, 26–27
Disponbilité, 9
Dominant
characters, 75–76
defining, 9, 165–166
establishing, 165
Doubling, character, 84–86
*Dream Express* (Jenkin), 63, 73
Dryden, John, 137
Durang, Christopher, 125

*Eastern Standard* (Greenberg), 129
*Ecologies of Theater* (Marranca), 49
Edgar, David, 57
*Pentecost*, 58, 69
Edson, Margaret, 1, 148
*Einstein on the Beach* (Wilson), 50
Ellipses, 106, 108–109
*Energumen* (Wellman), 63
Episodic style, 121–122
Equivocal character, 9
interruption and, 80–84
Euclidean character, 9, 87–91
Exploratory monologue, 145
Exposition, riffing and, 99

Fables, 46–47
Faceting, 33–34
Finley, Karen, 37, 122
*Fires in the Mirror* (Smith), 6, 138–139
*5 of Us* (Jenkin), 56, 73
*Fnu Lnu* (Wellman), 63, 157
*Fool for Love* (Shepard), 129, 149
Foregrounding, 9, 156
Foreignisms, 23–25
Foreman, Richard, 107
*Forest, The* (Wilson), 50
Formalism, 9
Fornes, Maria Irene, 113, 141
Found texts, 9, 10
*Frame Analysis* (Goffman), 155
Framing, 7, 9–10
reframing, 44
storyteller and, 77–78
ten-minute, 78–79
Free radical, 10
see beats, 95–98

French scene, 10, 111
Fronts and façades, 44–46

Gestural beats, 105–106
*Glengarry Glen Ross* (Mamet), 22
Goffman, Erving, 44, 155
*Gogol* (Jenkin), 23, 60, 61, 62, 65, 73
Gomez-Peña, Guillermo, 37
*New World Border*, 25, 122, 138
Gould, C., 54
Grafting, 10, 41–44
Gray, Spalding, 37, 137, 154
Greenberg, Richard, 129
Grotowski, Jerzy, 150
Guare, John, 129, 141
Gurney, A. R., 140
Gussow, Mel, 153

*Hamlet* (Shakespeare), 139
*Hamletmachine* (Müller), 57–58
Hansberry, Lorraine, 68
Hare, David, 57
*Secret Rapture*, 141, 143–144
*Harm's Way* (Wellman), 7–8, 13, 18,
45, 64, 89, 122, 124
*Heliotrope Bouquet, The* (Overmyer),
24, 61, 80–83, 98–99
Heteroglossia, 8, 41
*Homecoming, The* (Pinter), 104
Honzl, Jindrich, 79
*Hot L Baltimore* (Wilson), 129
Howe, Tina, 140
*How I Learned to Drive* (Vogel), 1,
48–49, 77
*Hyacinth Macaw, The* (Wellman), 19
Hybridization/hybrid play
conceptualizing spatial/temporal,
49–51
defined, 10, 35–37
exercise on, 40–41
future for, 51
grafting context, 41–44
new playwriting and, 37–39
sources, 39–40
variations, 48–49

Ibsen, Henrik, 46, 54
*Iceman Cometh, The* (O'Neill), 129

*Imperceptible Mutabilities in the Third Kingdom* (Parks), 18
*In a Pig's Valise* (Overmyer), 127
*In Perpetuity throughout the Universe* (Overmyer), 8, 10, 23, 24–25, 49, 66, 84, 116–117
Interruption, 10
   ellipsis and, 108–109
   equivocal character and, 80–84
   shifting beats and, 95–97
Intonation, 118

Jenkin, Len
   *American Notes*, 27, 32, 34, 64, 72, 73, 74, 75–76, 122, 125, 156, 166
   *Careless Love*, 76, 155–156
   characters, 66, 72–79
   *Country Doctor*, 46, 54, 73–74, 75
   *Dark Ride*, 10, 12, 33, 47, 62, 73, 74, 77, 78, 96, 108, 120–121, 122, 125, 127–128, 167–168
   *Dream Express*, 63, 73
   *5 of Us*, 56, 73
   *Gogol*, 23, 60, 61, 62, 65, 73
   hybrid sources, 39–40
   *Kid Twist*, 13, 23, 38, 54, 62, 68, 73, 74, 77, 124, 125, 149, 165
   *Kitty Hawk*, 3–4, 8, 62, 69
   journal, keeping a, 42
   *Like I Say*, 38, 56
   *Limbo Tales*, 19, 26, 38, 39, 64, 73, 76, 108, 122, 126, 148
   monologues, 163–172
   *My Uncle Sam*, 12, 23, 24, 27–28, 47, 60, 63, 69, 73, 74, 75, 76, 111–112, 114, 115, 124, 128, 149, 163–167, 170–173
   *Pilgrims of the Night*, 45, 73, 76, 77
   *Poor Folk's Pleasure*, 8, 10, 22, 38–39, 45, 56, 64, 65, 74, 122–123, 124
Jones, Jeffrey, 3
   *Der Inka von Peru*, 41–42, 96, 122, 131
   grafting context, 41–42
   *Seventy Scenes of Halloween*, 30–31, 64–65, 131
Journals/scrapbooks

   exercise on, 43–44
   keeping, 42–43
Journey play, 10

Kafka, Franz, 46, 54, 169
*Ka Mountain* (Wilson), 50
Kennedy, Adrienne, 8, 68–69
*Kid Twist* (Jenkin), 13, 23, 38, 54, 62, 68, 73, 74, 77, 124, 125, 149, 165
*Kitty Hawk* (Jenkin), 3–4, 8, 62, 69
Kramer, Sherry, 141
*Krapp's Last Tape* (Beckett), 157
Kushner, Tony, 3, 137
   *Angels in America*, 30, 57, 122, 129, 130

*Landscape* (Pinter), 149
Language-based characters, 87–91
Language markers, 116
Language playwriting, 3
Langue, 97–98
LeComte, Elizabeth, 7
*Le Ronde* (Schnitzler), 57
*Like I Say* (Jenkin), 38, 56
*Limbo Tales* (Jenkin), 19, 26, 38, 39, 64, 73, 76, 108, 122, 126, 148
Linney, Romulus, 49, 140
*Literary Theory: A Very Short Introduction* (Culler), 2
*Long Day's Journey into Night* (O'Neill), 129
Lucas, Craig, 1, 3
   *Prelude to a Kiss*, 85, 86, 122, 129, 174
   *Reckless*, 54, 122, 129

Maguire, Matthew, 3, 56
   *Phédra*, 91, 173
   *Throwin' Bones*, 91, 96, 173–174
Mamet, David, 30, 55
   *Glengarry Glen Ross*, 22
   *Speed the Plow*, 22, 100–101
Mann, Emily, 139
Mann, Thomas, 139–140
Markers, 10, 115–118
Marranca, Bonnie, 49, 50, 58
Masks
   of commedia dell'arte, 63–66
   creating, 66–67

Mattei, Peter, 96
Mellor, Stephen, 153
*Menopausal Gentleman* (Shaw), 86, 96, 137
Metadrama, 11
Metamorphosis, 135
Metatheater, 11
Miller, Arthur, 56, 68, 123
Molière, 114
Moment, 121
Monologic versus dialogic
    continuum, 11
Monologism, 11
Monologue
    absent "other" and, 145–147
    Congdon's, 162
    dialogue versus, 148–149
    exercises on, 142–143, 160–161
    exploratory, 145
    digressionary, 172–173
    function of, 138–139
    future of, 174
    growth in popularity of, 137–138
    Hare's use of integrated, 143–145
    interpolation in new play
        development, 141
    Jenkin's, 163–172
    Overmyers's, 158–169
    properties of, 158
    as structural determinant, 163–165
    traditional functions in plays,
        139–141
    Wellman's, 161–162
*Mud* (Fornes), 113, 141
Mukarovsky, Jan, 124, 144
Müller, Heiner, 57–58
Multivocal character, 11, 17
Multivocality
    compared to the baroque style,
        20–22
    defined, 2, 17–19
    exercise on, 20
    faceting, 33–34
    menu, 19–20
    profanity, 30–32
*Murder of Crows* (Wellman), 56, 59,
    62, 64, 89, 123, 125, 157
Music and sound, use of, 63
*My Uncle Sam* (Jenkin), 12, 23, 24,
    27–28, 47, 60, 63, 69, 73, 74,
    75, 76, 111–112, 114, 115, 124,
    128, 149, 163–167, 170–173

*Native Speech* (Overmyer), 21, 22–23,
    61, 109, 114, 157, 158–159
Negative space, 11
Nelson, Richard, 3, 103
    *Bal*, 54, 113, 122
    *Some Americans Abroad*, 129
New Playwrights' Program, 141
*New World Border* (Gomez-Peña), 25,
    122, 138
Nonserial juxtaposition, 122–123
Nouning, 11–12, 152

*Old Times* (Pinter), 22, 149
O'Neill, Eugene, 56, 68, 123, 129
*On the Verge: The Geography of Learning*
    (Overmyer), 4–5, 12, 48, 95–96,
    107, 120, 122, 126–127
Ostranenie, 12
*Our Town* (Wilder), 155
Overmyer, Eric, 3
    *Alki*, 46, 54
    characters, 80–86
    *Dark Rapture*, 13, 18, 21, 40, 54, 85,
        122, 124, 125, 160
    *Heliotrope Bouquet, The* 24, 61,
        80–83, 98–99
    *In a Pig's Valise*, 127
    *In Perpetuity throughout the Universe*,
        8, 10, 23, 24–25, 49, 66, 84,
        116–117
    monologues, 158–160
    *Native Speech*, 21, 22–23, 61, 109,
        114, 157, 158–159
    *On the Verge*, 4–5, 12, 48, 95–96,
        107, 120, 122, 126–127
*Owl Answers, The* (Kennedy), 8, 68–69

Papp, Joseph, 4
Parallel episodic approach, 122
Parks, Suzan-Lori, 3, 61, 149
    *Death of the Last Black Man in the
        Whole Entire World, The*, 23, 24
    *Imperceptible Mutabilities in the Third
        Kingdom*, 18
Parole, 98

Pauses, 106–109
*Peer Gynt* (Ibsen), 46, 54
*Pentecost* (Edgar), 58, 69
Performance Group, The, 150
Performance Space 122, 153
*Phaedra* (Maguire), 91, 173
*Pilgrims of the Night* (Jenkin), 45, 73, 76, 77
Pinter, Harold, 22, 104, 106, 145
Plot markers, 116
*Poetics* (Aristotle), 1, 54–55
Point of attack, 135–136
Points, 12, 120–121
Polish, 135, 136
Polyvocality
    *See also* Hybridization/hybrid play
    defined, 2, 12, 17
    fable and story forms, 46–47
    role-playing, 12, 44–46
*Poor Folk's Pleasure* (Jenkin), 8, 10, 22, 38–39, 45, 56, 64, 65, 74, 122–123, 124
*Prelude to a Kiss* (Lucas), 85, 86, 122, 129, 174
Profanity, 30–32
*Professional Frenchman, The* (Wellman), 32–33, 89, 123, 125
Promise, 103–104

Quest, 47–48
Quotables, 105–106

Rabe, David, 30
Racine, Jean, 114
*Reckless* (Lucas), 54, 122, 129
Revisions
    exercise on, 27, 133–134
    process, 131–136
Rhetorical levels, extreme, 32–33
Riffing, 12, 98–102
Role-playing, 12, 44–46
*Romans in Britain* (Brenton), 49
*Rumstick Road* (Gray), 37

Satire, 58–59
Saussure, Ferdinand de, 97–98
Scenario, 12
Scenes
    into acts, 130–131

captioning, 126–129
conceptualization, 124–125
defined, 120–121
numbering, 129–130
revisions, 131–136
sequence, 121–123
space, 126
Schnitzler, Arthur, 57
*Secret Rapture* (Hare), 141, 143–144
Semiotization, 146
Serial episodic approach, 122
*Serious Money* (Churchill), 110
*7 Blowjobs* (Wellman), 59, 62, 89, 107, 117–118, 123, 125
*Seventy Scenes of Halloween* (Jones), 30–31, 64–65, 131
Shadow riffs, 100–102
Shaffer, Peter, 77, 137
Shakespeare, William, 36, 37, 114, 122, 137, 139
Shaw, Peggy, 37, 122
    *Menopausal Gentleman*, 86, 96, 137
Shawn, Wallace, 58–59
Shepard, Sam, 68
    *Curse of the Starving Class*, 129
    *Fool for Love*, 129, 149
Shifting beats, 95–97
*Sincerity Forever* (Wellman), 40, 59, 89, 116, 125
*Six Degrees of Separation* (Guare), 129, 141
Slang
    from discourse to, 26–27
    exercise on, 29–30
    as speech genre, 28–30
Slash, 109–110
Smith, Anna Deavere, 37
    *Fires in the Mirror*, 6, 138–139
Solo riffs, 99–100
*Some Americans Abroad* (Nelson), 129
*Southern Girls* (Temple and Bailey), 141
Space, 126
Spacer beats, 106–109
Spatial/temporal hybrid, conceptualizing, 49–51
Speech, miked, 157–158
Speech acts
    defined, 12, 103

exercise on, 104–105
forms of, 103–104
Speech genres
defined, 22–23
exercise on, 23
slang as, 28–30
*Speed the Plow* (Mamet), 22, 100–101
Spinning, 12, 173–174
Split Britches, 137
Stage figures
defined, 12, 72
Jenkin's, 72–79
Stereotype characters, archetype
versus, 74
*Stomp*, 37
Stoppard, Tom, 49, 58
Story forms, 12–13
fable, 46–47
quest, 47–48
Story markers, 116
Storyteller, 76–78
Strategy, 104
Style, 121–123
Super marker, 120

Tag lines, 106
*Tales of the Lost Formicans* (Congdon),
8, 12, 49, 65, 68, 69, 85–86, 95,
162
Telegraphing, 13
Temple, Dura, 141
*Terminal Hip* (Wellman), 34, 61, 88,
105, 123, 124, 153–155
Tessari, Roberto, 66–67
"Theatre of Good Intentions"
(Wellman), 24, 87
Theatrical characters, tenets of,
59–63
Thematic-based characterization,
56–57
Threat, 103
*Three Americanisms* (Wellman), 26, 54,
61, 88, 105, 123, 124
*Three Sisters* (Chekhov), 114
*Three Tall Women* (Albee), 1
*Throwin' Bones* (Maguire), 91, 96,
173–174
*Tiny Dimes* (Mattei), 96
Tracking, 13

Turns
defined, 13
shadow riffs and, 100–102
Twain, Mark, 137

Virtuosity, 5
Vogel, Paula, 3
*How I Learned to Drive*, 1, 48–49, 77
Vow, 104

*Wall of Water* (Kramer), 141
Wasserstein, Wendy, 140
Webster, John, 137
Wellman, Mac, 3, 12
*Albanian Softshoe*, 23, 65, 68, 69,
89, 122, 125, 161–162
*Bad Infinity*, 32, 89, 112, 123, 125
*Bad Penny*, 124
*Bodacious Flapdoodle*, 62, 105
*Cellophane*, 88
characters, 87–91
*Crowbar*, 124
Dictionary Stop, 102–103
*Energumen*, 63
*Fnu Lnu*, 63, 157
*Harm's Way*, 7–8, 13, 18, 45, 64, 89,
122, 124
*Hyacinth Macaw, The*, 19
hybrid sources, 40
journal, keeping a, 42
monologues, 161–612
*Murder of Crows*, 56, 59, 62, 64, 89,
123, 125, 157
*Professional Frenchman, The*, 32–33,
89, 123, 125
*7 Blowjobs*, 59, 62, 89, 107,
117–118, 123, 125
*Sincerity Forever*, 40, 59, 89, 116,
125
*Terminal Hip*, 34, 61, 88, 105, 123,
124, 153–155
"Theatre of Good Intentions," 24,
87
*Three Americanisms*, 26, 54, 61, 88,
105, 123, 124
*Whirligig*, 8, 23, 53, 65, 99–100,
109–110, 149–152
*Whirligig* (Wellman), 8, 23, 53, 65,
99–100, 109–110, 149–152

Wilder, Thornton, 155
Williams, Tennessee, 56, 68, 123, 137,
    140
Wilson, August, 68, 140
Wilson, Lanford, 129
Wilson, Robert, 7, 49, 50
*Wit* (Edson), 1, 148
*Witness for the Prosecution* (Mann), 139

Wittgenstein, Ludwig, 90
Wolfe, George, 123
Wooster Group, 7, 37
*Word and Verbal Art, The*
    (Mukarovsky), 144
Writing "off the line," 13
Writing "on the line," 13